SEA TURTLES

For Dawn

First published in Great Britain in 2006 by
Colin Baxter Photography Ltd, Grantown-on-Spey, PH26 3NA Scotland

www.worldlifelibrary.co.uk

Text © Blair Witherington 2006.   Illustrations © 2006 Dawn Witherington.
Maps © 2006 Colin Baxter Photography based on mapping supplied by Map Resources.
All rights reserved

A CIP Catalogue record for this book is available from the British Library

ISBN 1-84107-331-8   978-1-84107-331-6

Photography © 2006 by:

Front cover © Masa Ushioda/SeaPics.com
Back cover © François Gohier
Page 1 © NHPA/Kevin Schafer
Page 3 © NHPA/Linda Pitkin
Page 4 © Masa Ushioda/SeaPics.com
Page 6 © Colin Baxter
Page 7 © Reinhard Dirscherl/SeaPics.com
Page 8 © James D Watt/SeaPics.com
Page 9 © Masa Ushioda/SeaPics.com
Page 10 © Kelly Spranger/V&W/SeaPics.com
Page 11 © SA Team/Foto Natura/Minden Pictures
Page 12 © Doug Perrine/SeaPics.com
Page 13 © Doug Perrine/SeaPics.com
Page 14 © Masa Ushioda/SeaPics.com
Page 16 © Colin Baxter
Page 17 © Douglas David Seifert/ardea.com
Page 18 © Reinhard Dirscherl/SeaPics.com
Page 19 © Colin Baxter
Page 21 © Doug Perrine/naturepl.com
Page 22 © Andre Seale/SeaPics.com
Page 23 © Jeff Rotman/naturepl.com
Page 25 © Colin Baxter
Page 26 © David B Fleetham/SeaPics.com
Page 28 top © Doug Perrine/SeaPics.com
Page 28 bottom © Doug Perrine/SeaPics.com
Page 30 left © Tom Walmsley/Splashdown Direct
Page 30 right © Ben Osborne/naturepl.com
Page 31 © Mike Parry/Minden Pictures
Page 33 © Mark Conlin/SeaPics.com
Page 34 © Ben Osborne/naturepl.com
Page 37 © NHPA/Jany Sauvanet

Page 38 © NHPA/Kevin Schafer
Page 39 © Steve Winter/National Geographic Image Collection
Page 40 © NHPA/Kevin Schafer
Page 41 © Pat de La Harpe/naturepl.com
Page 42 © Gerry Ellis/Minden Pictures
Page 44 © Valerie Taylor/ardea.com
Page 45 left © Doug Perrine/SeaPics.com
Page 45 right © Doug Perrine/SeaPics.com
Page 47 © Doug Perrine/SeaPics.com
Page 49 © Lisa Steiner/SeaPics.com
Page 50 © Doug Perrine/SeaPics.com
Page 52 © Tom & Pat Leeson
Page 55 © Jez Tryner/SeaPics.com
Page 56 © Doug Perrine/SeaPics.com
Page 59 © Jurgen Freund/naturepl.com
Page 60 © Colin Baxter
Page 61 © Gavin Parsons/ardea.com
Page 63 © Michael Patrick O'Neill/SeaPics.com
Page 64 © Mark Strickland/SeaPics.com
Page 65 © Walt Stearns/SeaPics.com
Page 66 © Amar Guillen/SeaPics.com
Page 67 © Jez Tryner/SeaPics.com
Page 71 © Norbert Wu/Minden Pictures
Page 73 © Valerie Taylor/ardea.com
Page 74 © Doug Perrine/SeaPics.com
Page 76 © Valerie Taylor/ardea.com
Page 77 © Valerie Taylor/ardea.com
Page 80 © Peter Steyn/ardea.com
Page 82 © Doug Perrine/SeaPics.com
Page 84 © Norbert Wu/Minden Pictures
Page 85 © Flip Nicklin/Minden Pictures

Page 88 © Robert van Dam
Page 90 © Colin Baxter
Page 91 © Norbert Wu/Minden Pictures
Page 92 © Robert van Dam
Page 93 © Colin Baxter
Page 97 © Doug Perrine/SeaPics.com
Page 98 © Frans Lanting/Minden Pictures
Page 100 © Tim Martin/naturepl.com
Page 101 © François Gohier
Page 105 © Doug Perrine/SeaPics.com
Page 106 © Pieter Pritchard/SeaPics.com
Page 107 © Doug Perrine/SeaPics.com
Page 108 © Anne Heimann
Page 109 © Doug Perrine/SeaPics.com
Page 113 © Ben Osborne/naturepl.com
Page 114 © Ben Osborne/naturepl.com
Page 115 © Jean-Paul Ferrero/Auscape/Minden Pictures
Page 119 © Rowan Byrne/SeaPics.com
Page 120 © Karik Shanker
Page 122 © Doug Perrine/SeaPics.com
Page 123 © Doug Perrine/naturepl.com
Page 124 © Patricio Robles Gil/Sierra Madre/Minden Pictures
Page 126 © Gavin Parsons/ardea.com
Page 127 top © Colin Baxter
Page 127 bottom © Colin Baxter
Page 128 top © M.Watson/ardea.com
Page 128 bottom © M.Watson/ardea.com
Page 129 © Anne Heimann
Page 130 © Ben Osborne/naturepl.com
Page 131 © Jurgen Freund/naturepl.com

Front Cover: *A green turtle near Kona, Hawaii.*   Back Cover: *A basking green turtle.*
Page 1: *A green turtle hatchling departs Ascension Island.*   Page 3: *A green turtle off Maui, Hawaii.*

Printed in China

SEA TURTLES

Blair Witherington

Colin Baxter Photography Ltd, Grantown-on-Spey, Scotland

Contents

A Caribbean hawksbill turtle glides by a colorful tapestry of sponges lining Bloody Bay Wall, Cayman Islands.

Sea Turtles

Some may find it difficult to imagine a turtle with the elegance of a bird. It is a conception that seems to surpass the broadly accepted turtle quintessence – that of a plodding reptilian beast, hardened by millennia into a rigidly built, sluggish, almost rock-like form. But this description overlooks many turtles, and it is perhaps least representative of the group of creatures I introduce here – the sea turtles. They are indeed ancient. But throughout those millions of years of life on Earth, epochs before birds ever flew, sea turtles have glided with fluid form through their gossamer world, leaving the stereotypical turtle far behind. As a group, the sea turtles have acquired the shapes of animals inspired by the oceans challenges. They are dynamic, graceful, and capable of astounding athletic feats. Sea turtles are animals consummately at home in the sea, and they are truly elegant.

Before I first encountered sea turtles in their element, I had my own preconceived notions about how they should behave. I was a college student visiting a friend in the Virgin Islands, an archipelago dotting the northeastern rim of the Caribbean Sea. At the time I was developing an interest in herps, that is, reptiles and amphibians, a related grouping of scaly or moist-skinned animals that tend to crawl on their bellies.

As a budding herpetologist, my sea turtle preconception came mostly from general accounts of their nesting. Sea turtles, I learned from limited descriptions, were marine reptiles inextricably tied to the land for their reproduction. Thus, a female sea turtle gravid with eggs is driven to leave her familiar element, drag herself above the tide, and struggle through a series of critical steps associated with burying and hiding her eggs. There on land, an intimate process is

acted out where any uninitiated observer can sit closely by, watch, and take notes. In popular accounts especially, there is often an emphasis on the apparent tribulation of the turtle's task. The female's bulk, gravity, and human empathy being what they are, many observers convince the reader that sea turtles

A green turtle glides downward within the clear Celebes Sea off Borneo.

suffer the fate of most large reptiles – a life of stalwart, slow-paced responses to adversity.

I had hoped to see the turtles that grazed the seagrass pastures off St. John. So, slipping with mask and snorkel into the vividly clear Caribbean, I kicked out from one of the island's rocky cove beaches, beyond the bare coralline sand and toward broader waters. After only a few minutes I was hovering over the lush seagrass beds common in the

Sea turtles 'fly' using their wing-like flippers and are surprisingly swift at sea.

shallows surrounding the Virgin Islands. It was a serene place where slowly waving green ribbons of turtle grass (*Thalassia*) pointed out the gentle flow toward a bright teal backdrop. There in the filtered distance, creatures faded into view that would substantially alter my impression of the reptilian lot in life.

The sunburst shell coloration of a green turtle contrasts with the silvery reflections of swimming jacks.

They were green turtles... three of them. Each of their shells was a brilliant teardrop as broad as my own torso and patterned with seabottom sunbursts. Their forelimbs were tapered wings that paused with graceful hesitation between beats, punctuating an underwater flight that seemed effortless. I had drifted into their path, and in formation, the three turtles glided around me, making a complete circle with a cautious radius and presenting me the greatest breadth of their shells. Each streamlined head was turned

so that I could be closely examined. In excitement, I found myself kicking toward them, but the distance between us held constant, no matter how vigorously I struggled to close the gap. Gliding through their wide orbit, the turtles angled their backs and eyes to me while they calmly, cautiously, surveyed the gawking alien. Then, each turtle banked away, and with a few rapid flaps, they dissolved into their world.

My first swim with sea turtles changed my notions about them and presented me with a view of these animals that persists still. To me, sea turtles are beautiful and intriguing creatures that tease us with a contrast of both accessibility and mystery. It is a view shared by a tightly knit group of people who are committed to learning ever more about sea turtles and their world. Biologists find their study of sea turtles benefiting from the way that these fascinating animals present themselves to us, and recently, our understanding about the lives of sea turtles has broadened greatly. Yet, many deep and provocative secrets seem to remain just out of reach.

I hope that this book will provide an appropriate portrait of our seven species of living sea turtles. It has neither the depth nor the detail of a complete description of their biology. Rather, it is an introduction. The overture seems fitting for the familiarity needed to begin a healthy relationship. The book begins with descriptions of how sea turtles go about their lives, and ends with a look at the connections between sea turtles and humans. For, as enigmatic and distant from us as sea turtles seem to be, clues continually arise describing how our lives are intertwined.

Blair Witherington

*Hawaiian green turtles at a 'cleaning station' submit to the
attentions of tangs. This symbiotic reciprocity, exchanging food for cleanliness,
is but one of many ecological links between sea turtles and their world.*

Ancient Origins

Sea turtles were shaped on a planet that we would barely recognize as our own. The splendid peak of experimentalism in sea turtle species was a time when more than 30 forms plied Earth's oceans. It was a time when a proto-Atlantic was just broadening with volcanic fits and starts between a splitting Gondwana super-continent. It was roughly 75 million years before human beings walked upright, the island India was still separated from Eurasia by a vast ocean, most of Europe was under water, flowering plants were a novel introduction to the world, and a diverse radiation of dinosaurs enjoyed their dominance on land. The Atlantic Ocean of this Cretaceous-period world was a thin seaway that snaked between the Americas and Africa, and at its northern extent, a rich, shallow Niobrara Sea covered the center of North America east of the Rocky Mountains. In this sea swam *Archelon ischyros*, an immense sea turtle named with Greek roots for primitive turtle and strength.

Archelon was indeed robust: 15 ft (4.5 m) in length, flippers spanning well over 16 ft (5 m), a 3 ft (1m) long head more than 2 ft (0.5 m) wide, and a weight of roughly 4850 lb (2200 kg). It was a turtle more massive than many modern automobiles, and its home included the sunlit sea that once covered South Dakota. There, the enormous turtle pursued equally monstrous Cretaceous squid, seizing them with its powerful curved beak. This great turtle bore the stiff, wing-like fore-flippers and smooth hydrodynamic form of modern sea turtles, but differed enough to be categorized in a separate family from what may be the closest living *Archelon* relative, the leatherback turtle (*Dermochelys coriacea*).

Both *Archelon* and the leatherback share characters that include an incompletely boned shell and relatively rapid growth, the latter trait indicated by the vascular, blood-rich growing ends of their long bones. *Archelon* may well have been a highly specialized turtle with narrow food tastes and parochial habits. As a specialist, *Archelon* would have had trouble coping with the cataclysmic world changes that took place during the late Cretaceous, changes that obliterated the once wildly

The leatherback turtle, a survivor of many cataclysmic world events occurring over millions of years, is now facing extinction.

successful dinosaurs, many other large vertebrates, and every other marine reptile except for our present-day sea turtles and one marine crocodile.

As old as *Archelon* seems, the origins of sea turtles lie much deeper. As a group, turtles have persisted with their distinctive shelled form since the Triassic Period, 210 million years before present. Their appearance predates the dinosaurs by just a few million years. The earliest known turtle, *Proganochelys* (new Latin

Sea turtles similar to this hawksbill have been around for about 100 million years.

for brilliant turtle-predecessor) lived in marshy areas but was not specialized for purely aquatic life. The truest marine-adapted turtles would not appear for another 10 to 50 million years or so, during the Jurassic Period, when members of two distinct turtle families (Pleurosternidae and Thalassemyidae) began to live in the shallow seas covering Europe. But these turtles did not leave the sea turtle descendants we know today. These earliest sea turtles

Ancient Hawaiian petroglyphs (rock carvings) depict honu, the green turtle, symbol of creation, longevity, prosperity, and wisdom.

had only partially modified limbs for stroking in shallow waters and disappeared before the most recent trials with ocean living took place in the Cretaceous.

The Cretaceous was the heyday for sea turtles, and all of the sea turtle species we know today have their roots in this period. Between 110 and 65 million years ago there were dozens of species varying among four (or by some opinions, three) families:

Toxochelyidae: Sea turtles in this family had circular or broad, heart-shaped shells. They last swam 30-50 million years ago, but these turtles may belong with the hard-shelled sea turtles alive today, the cheloniids.

Protostegidae: This family of *Archelon* included other large turtles. Each had a partially boned shell with distinct keels. Protostegid sea turtles last swam roughly 60 million years ago and may have been snuffed out by the same asteroid that led to the demise of the dinosaurs.

Dermochelyidae: Turtles of this family are not well represented by fossils and some species are known only from bits and pieces. There is a single species living today, the leatherback. Members of this family have shells that are a mosaic of bony elements rather than a solid covering of interconnected bone. In the leatherback we see that this carapace of composite bone and connective tissue is covered with thick skin. The leatherback's family is linked to the family of *Archelon*, the protostegids.

Cheloniidae: These are the thecate or hard-shelled sea turtles. Six species survive today and each has a bony carapace covered with thin skin protected by broad plates of keratin. Our living cheloniid sea turtles are probably more generalized and more coastal than many of the specialized oceanic forms that are no longer with us.

The sea turtles of today probably had a single common Cretaceous ancestor, but the evidence of this forebear has yet to be uncovered. At one time, the sea turtles were not considered a 'natural' grouping because of the highly variant form seen in the leatherback. However, ancestral trees developed from both DNA similarities and from the appearance of unique physical structures affirm that leatherbacks are more closely related to other sea turtles than to other turtles in general.

Six of the seven species of modern sea turtles have a hard shell and are grouped together in the same family.
Sea turtles were formerly more diverse, having four families and dozens of species.

Form and Function

The Essence of Being Turtle

We are at least a little bit like turtles. Both turtles and we have four limbs, bound by bony girdles to a column of vertebrae ending in a neck that bears a prominent skull and movable jaws. We both are vertebrate animals. But among the vertebrates, turtles deserve awards for some of the most creative and bizarre uses of a skeleton.

The bizarre creativity of turtles is to be able to hide within their own bony, thoracic framework (their ribcage). In chelonians, thoracic bones and skin coverings have evolved into turtle armor – a tough shell that protects most or all of the indispensable parts of a turtle. In some species, everything that could be chewed on by a predator can be withdrawn into the shell, but in sea turtles, head, limbs, and tail remain outside. The basic elements of a turtle's shell are the bony carapace (upper shell), sheathed in skin that is completely covered by tough keratinized plates or scutes in most turtles, and the slightly less bony plastron (lower shell), which is also generally covered in scutes. Roughly 50 sutured bones make up the carapace of most turtles and nine bones form the plastron. In the shell of most adult turtles, spine, ribs and carapace bones are fused, and connect to the plastron to form a rigid box.

To know a turtle's shell is to know their life strategy – their method of survival that has persisted through millions of years of predator evolution. The difficulty in cracking that tough shell has protected turtles from most predators, lengthened their lives as individuals, and has allowed a lifestyle that is the very model of conservatism. In many ways, the turtle's shell has allowed many of the other traits thought of as being 'typically turtle.' Turtles are generally described as being persistent in form, deliberate in behavior, late maturing, and long lived.

A turtle's shell is as unlikely as it has been influential. The development of a turtle's shell from garden-variety vertebrate parts involved some profound and innovative steps in evolution. For one, the girdles that support limb movement have been drawn into the ribcage. In this trick of utmost contortion, it is as if a broad thoracic 'umbrella' swallowed up the shoulders and hips, which are outside the ribs in a typical vertebrate. The ribs themselves can hardly be considered a cage, given that the spaces between the bars have filled in with thick dermal bone (different in origin from the ribs themselves). The dermal bone of the carapace begins in young turtles as a fusion that binds spine and ribs together into a rigid shield. Toward adulthood, this dermal bone grows outward between the ribs and out to their ends to meet a chain of marginal carapace bones at the edges of the shell. Beneath the carapace, dermal bones in the turtle's plastron grow outward and in some species join with the carapace.

Part of the uniqueness of sea turtles is in their modification of the archetypal turtle shell. The rigid box of fused bone has become too confining for sea turtles, and they have evolved a more flexible shell in which carapace and plastron are joined by a bridge of supple cartilage. In the hard-shelled sea turtles, the cheloniids, the adult carapace is mostly rigid and is covered with broad scutes that vary in thickness. Hawksbills are protected by tough, partially overlapping carapace plates as thick as a fiberglass boat hull, whereas flatbacks are so thinly covered that a human fingernail can scratch the shell down to bleeding skin. In the leatherback, bone in the shell has been reduced most of all, with the ribs broadened but separate, and dermal bone limited to hundreds of coin-like bony plates embedded beneath thick skin and connective tissue that covers the carapace.

Nearly all of a sea turtle's flipper is its hand: a wrist and long fingers within a wing-like web.

Sea turtles rise to the surface
to breathe every 20 minutes
or so, but a relaxed turtle may
remain submerged for hours.
Just before they reach the surface
they blow a cloud of bubbles.
At the surface, the turtle's head
tilts upward as it draws air into
its mouth.

Another hallmark of turtle form is their beak. Turtles have long ago abandoned the use of teeth for biting. Their toothless jaws accomplish the everyday tasks of seizing, snipping, or crushing thanks to horny beak-like sheaths lining both their upper and lower jaws. These jaw coverings, called rhamphothecae (plural of rhamphotheca) vary among turtle species and their eating habits. In vegetarian turtles like the green turtle, cutting edges of the beak are serrated into 'pseudo teeth'.

Life at Sea

Although the marine environment has allowed sea turtles to keep many of their ancestral turtle traits, some highly specialized changes to this fundamental form have been required to live a life at sea. Movement through a fluid medium demands tradeoffs. To move efficiently through water, sea turtles have had to give up some of the protections offered by their ancestral shell in return for hydrodynamic efficiency. For instance, streamlining their bodies has meant forgoing the shell-space for their head and forelimbs. Pockets beneath an overhanging shell that would accommodate these extremities would create expensive drag and reduce swimming speed. So, what would have been hollows at the neck and shoulders of sea turtles are instead bulging with the powerful muscles that drive their swimming strokes. Their shoulders are a rounded prow covered by tight but supple, almost scaleless skin that blunts the turtle's leading edge between carapace and plastron. Sea turtles can withdraw their necks into their shells, but their heads remain exposed. As a remedy to this potential vulnerability to large-jawed predators, the sea turtles have evolved robust skulls that are completely roofed over with dense bone to form a cranium every bit as tough as the turtle's shell.

In comparison to their helmet-shaped relatives, sea turtles have shells that are far more resistant to aquatic drag. The shells of marine turtles are generally a flattened teardrop shape,

with roundness and posterior tapering that vary between species. In the hard-shelled sea turtles, the shell is covered with scutes that are smooth, except in juveniles of some species. In leatherbacks, the demand for a smooth hydrodynamic form has been met with a highly tapered shell covered by tight, scaleless, rubbery skin.

Certainly, the most conspicuous characters separating the sea

This hawksbill shows its tapered hydrodynamic shape.

turtles from their kin are their flippers. Sea turtle flippers are highly modified limbs used for a number of tasks, but the principal force that has driven their form is clearly the need for undersea flight. Like flight in air, fluid propulsion and control in water requires both power and steerage. For power, sea turtles use their front flippers. These are decidedly wing-like, although narrower than a bird's wing (except the penguin's wing, which they greatly resemble), and are tapered toward the tip. The front flippers are stroking hydrofoils, with leading edges blunt and trailing edges sharp, especially near the tip, where sharp scales can easily slice through human skin. Although there is a chance that razor-edged fore-flippers may have deterred a predator or two interested in eating some subsequently successful sea turtle ancestor, the greatest advantage to come from this trait is probably sheer high-performance hydrodynamics.

Inside a sea turtle's front flipper lie the standard limb bones that most vertebrates share, but with important modifications. The upper arm bone (humerus) is stubby and short, and only

When chased, a green turtle can swim at 15 mph (24 kph)

about twice as long as it is wide. About midway down the bone, a lumpy process multiplies the area of bone that the strong pectoral muscles can cling to, which allows more swimming muscle to deliver more powerful strokes. At the end of the stocky upper arm extends an even shorter set of forearm bones – the radius and ulna. These bones are fused together by fibrous connective tissue. This same tough connective tissue binds the wrist and hand bones (carpals, metacarpals, and phalanges). The widest part of the flipper blade bears the wrist and palm, with the fingers (five of them, just like us) extending outward within the

tough webbing. In the hard-shelled sea turtles, the turtle's thumb ends in a claw that pokes out at the flipper's leading edge.

As well as being wing-like in form, a sea turtle's fore-flippers are wing-like in their use. Flippers and wings trace the same motion to drive their user's flight. When viewed from the side, the tip of a sea turtle's fore-flipper can be seen to travel through an elongate figure-eight pattern. Because a turtle brings its flippers both forward and upward before stroking back and down, the figure the tip traces actually leans forward halfway between an eight and an infinity. Just as in birds, most of the power is on the down stroke.

The rear flippers of a sea turtle are just as broad and flat as the front flippers but are about half the length and are rounded at the end. The broadest part of a turtle's rear flipper is almost at the end, suggesting a shape that is less like a wing and more like the rudder of a sailing vessel. As this rudder-like form suggests, steering is exactly what a sea turtle's rear flippers do best. Following a swimming sea turtle, one can see the rear flippers perform their guiding movements. Along a straight course, hind-flippers trail "soles" down, but during turns, the inside flipper reaches out to catch the water and force the turn in its direction. In rapidly swimming turtles, the rear flippers are constantly making subtle movements to fine-tune the course.

Similar to the fore-flippers, the hind flippers are a webbed, hand-like extremity bound within a flat blade. But by comparison, the rear flippers have phalanges (toes) that are far more dexterous. The critical nature of this toe movement becomes evident as a nesting female turtle digs the neatly shaped hole for her eggs. There will be more on this amazing feat (and these amazing feet) later.

There is more to ocean life than swimming. To survive in an ocean world, sea turtles have had to adapt to many physiological challenges, not the least of which is breathing. Sea turtles take their oxygen from the atmosphere just as land animals do. Although this ties them to the ocean's surface, sea turtles do their best to push the limits of these ties during their dives. Adult turtles commonly spend 20 minutes to an hour underwater during relaxed dives, and a calm turtle in cool water may spend as much as five hours submerged. In more active dives, depths reached by turtles extend to 330 ft (100 m) or more, and in the case of the leatherback, a dive may be well over 3300 ft (1000 m) deep.

Given that sea turtles spend only about 3 per cent of their time at the surface, they are almost always holding their breath. Thus, taking along enough oxygen to survive underwater is an everyday challenge for sea turtles. But it is not enough to merely survive each dive. To survive a lifetime, sea turtles must perform underwater as they find their food and escape from their predators. Sea turtles meet these underwater challenges by having a specialized strategy for breathing, an adjustable metabolism, a tolerance for low oxygen, and an uncanny ability to squeeze more oxygen from every breath than almost any other animal.

The study of sea turtle diving behavior and physiology has benefited greatly from the design of instruments that turtles take with them into the depths and that act as vicarious observers for us. As a researcher at Hubbs Sea World Research Institute, Scott Eckert has made many vicarious observations of turtles by attaching and recovering time-depth recorders. To link the resulting dive profiles to a turtle's physiological state requires additional detective work, such as the careful descriptions of anatomy and blood chemistry from researchers at the New England Aquarium and Florida Atlantic University. From such a variety of sources, sea turtle diving is beginning to be understood in pieces so that an entire portrait of a dive can be

imagined. What could it possibly be like to meet the ocean challenges that sea turtles face? What might it be like to accompany a sea turtle, such as the prodigious leatherback, during its dive? Try and imagine the following description.

Our companion leatherback is just approaching the surface on return from a modest dive of 330 ft (100 m) or so. As her head

Sea turtles are nearly always holding their breath.

breaks through the surface she is surrounded by rolling billows of exhaled air. Immediately following the forceful exhale, her head is raised to draw her next breath. Air rushes in through jaws cracked so slightly that her mouth might not even be considered open, yet the breath is made conspicuous by her bulging muscular throat. As her throat contracts, it forces a final volume of atmosphere into her lungs, and our leatherback lowers her head into a dive.

With slow strokes from her broad flippers, she glides downward toward indigo, and eventually, beyond the dimmest flicker of penetrating sunbeams. Already, her metabolism and heart rate have descended as well. With a surface resting heart rate that is already low, perhaps 20 beats per minute, our turtle's heart slows to less than one beat per minute, a rate that corresponds to a miserly use of her stored oxygen.

Continuing down beneath twilight depths, the surrounding water pressure compresses our turtle's air-filled lungs. At the surface, an average leatherback has the lung volume of a 2-liter beverage bottle, but at 1600 ft (500 m) down this volume is reduced to less than a squash ball. Rather than battle against the many tons of hydraulic force, sea turtles submit to it by allowing their lungs to collapse. With this lung collapse comes a controlled crushing of their bodies that is aided by the flexible cartilage interconnecting their bony undershell. In leatherbacks, these plastral bones are merely a girdle-like ring. Instead of the thick carapace bones seen in other sea turtles, a leatherback's shell is surrounded by a flexible mosaic of tiny bones. As the turtle continues downward, her plastron sinks in as her shell accommodates to the intense sea pressure.

Now of course, something draws the turtle to dive so deep, and this goal is food; perhaps a smack (group) of mesopelagic jellyfish, ready to be slurped down. So as if just reaching this depth were not challenging enough, our leatherback has work to do upon her arrival. It may be that we will never know how calmly a leatherback cruises at depth, searches for the faintest glimmer of potential food, and seizes its sluggishly undulating and slippery prey from the stunningly cold darkness; but we can speculate that our turtle would do all of this with a bare minimum of spent energy. She has to. After all, with a heart beat and metabolic rate only slightly higher than death, and with minimal blood flow shunted from her extremities to her brain and vital organs, vigorous activity is not only imprudent, it's impossible.

Near the end of our turtle's dive, little oxygen remains in her lungs and more of this precious gas is drawn from dissolved stores in the turtle's blood and other tissues. Leatherbacks' capacity to store oxygen in tissues outside their lungs exceeds that of the other sea turtles, and they are similar in this regard to the deepest-diving marine mammals. With diminishing oxygen also come increasing levels of toxic carbon dioxide and lactic acid, a dilemma that sea turtles seem to address with sheer tolerance. Some sea turtles have remarkable abilities to withstand high lactic acid and lack of oxygen (anoxia). It is a talent that apparently allows hibernating sea turtles in cool water to remain submerged for days, weeks, or even months.

Sensing it's time to revisit the atmosphere, our leatherback serenely directs herself toward the surface with slow, deliberate front-flipper strokes. After several minutes, the blue surrounding her lightens. As bubbles and head emerge together, a restoring breath is taken, perhaps several of them. At the end of the most strenuous dives, a turtle might need multiple, spaced breaths to purge her lungs of carbon dioxide and re-saturate her tissues with oxygen. In terms used by submariners, this surface time is equivalent to charging her batteries for the next deep dive.

Aside from breathing, one of the greatest challenges to sea turtles and other marine animals is procuring usable water. As Coleridge's Ancient Mariner observed ('...Water, water, everywhere, nor any drop to drink'), the sea does not easily relinquish its water. With about 3.5 per cent of seawater being salt (of which 80 per cent, or four fifths, is table salt, sodium chloride), extracting enough water to live on becomes a tricky and somewhat expensive endeavor.

Sea turtles are in general no saltier on the inside than most other vertebrates. To stay this way, they must actively deal with a constant invasion of toxic salts from the sea they swim in. Their method to acquire water and cope with salt is to become their own desalinization plant. As such, sea turtles incessantly purge their bodies of salt with specialized lachrymal (tear) glands behind each

Like fish, sea turtles must extract usable water from the salty sea.
Sea turtles do this by excreting excess salts within a super-saline fluid produced
by glands near their eyes. They cry themselves free of salt.

This green turtle's nose is used to smell both underwater and in the air.

of their eyes. The critical function and difficult job that these salt glands must perform is indicated by their size, which is several times the size of the turtle's brain (only the size of a plump grape in adults of most species). Although the salt glands are continually excreting a viscous fluid twice as salty as seawater, their action is most readily apparent when nesting sea turtles come to land. On nesting beaches, the thick streams of mucous from a turtle's eyes are made conspicuous by their dangling collection of sand. Of course, the tears have nothing to do with the turtle's emotional state, yet the apparent 'crying' of mother turtles has always generated great empathy from their human observers.

In feeding, sea turtles make attempts to limit the amount of seawater they take in — not an easy task when swallowing large, irregularly shaped, or slippery critters. To cope, sea turtles have a muscular esophagus that is almost entirely lined with backward-pointing spikes. These cone-like papillae are stiff with keratin. They seize hold of any item in the turtle's throat while strong throat muscles squeeze out inadvertently swallowed seawater. The papillae are especially helpful to leatherbacks who make a living packing in and keeping down bushels of slippery pulsating jellyfish.

Sea Turtle Senses

No doubt, sea turtles see, hear, smell, taste, and feel a world that is different from ours. This is largely because of the sensory filter they live in — the ocean. But a sea turtle's ability to detect and process its world is shaped not only by the challenges that the sea presents but also by its opportunities. For instance, the opportunity for extensive migrations across boundless oceans seems to have brought about an uncommon ability in sea turtles to sense where they are and where they are going. Although it is unclear which senses are most important for a sea turtle's heightened sense of place, it is likely that they use many of the senses that also serve them well in the more mundane tasks of finding food and avoiding danger.

Vision is probably one of the most important senses a sea turtle has. Just as we do, sea turtles coordinate a wide variety of important tasks based on what they see. Judging from the nature of their eye, sea turtles see well underwater but are myopic in air. More than likely, they can discriminate between colors well, although the colors they see are a bit different from the rainbow familiar to us. All of the species studied have shown an ability to

Vision is one of the most important senses for a sea turtle.

see well in the ultraviolet region of the spectrum but poorly in the red end of the spectrum. Their shift in spectral sensitivity is toward the shorter wavelengths (violets, blues, and greens) in our own visible spectrum. Not surprisingly, it is this short-wavelength light that penetrates seawater the deepest, coloring the blue world that sea turtles see for most of their lives.

To a casual observer sea turtles do not have ears and they might not be expected to hear very well. But a closer study of their anatomy reveals an auditory sense that is not only adapted to ocean life but also capable of remarkable detection. Although a sea turtle's ear is inside its head, it employs the same system for sound collection, conduction, and analysis performed by the outer, middle, and inner ears of many other vertebrates.

The part of a sea turtle's ear that collects sound is a trumpet-shaped structure made of fatty tissue. These fatty trumpets lie with their bells pointing outward just beneath the scaly skin on each side of the turtle's head. Because the density of the fatty tissue is the same as seawater, sounds from the ocean become funneled to the narrow end of the trumpet bell. The narrow end of the bell connects to a long, thin, middle ear bone called the columella (also known as the stapes). The narrow bone, which is about a third of the width of the turtle's head, conducts vibration to the cochlea of the inner ear. This inner ear also determines a turtle's sense of balance, just as it does for humans and other land vertebrates. Although hearing is probably sensitive in sea turtles, it is restricted to a range of low bass at the bottom of our own hearing scale and below – the infrasound. These are the sounds that dominate the symphony of the seas – sounds of waves pounding shorelines, of whale bellows, and of the drumming of fishes. Thus far, any sound a sea turtle might make to contribute to this orchestration has not been found.

Being covered by keratinized skin and a protective shell, one would not expect that a sensitive touch would be important to sea turtles. Perhaps it is the least developed of their senses, but sea turtles do respond to tactile feel. I have seen turtles show both exaggerated flinches at the slightest touch, and no response at all to the cutting of a skin biopsy (an experience I know to be at least a little painful). Although it is likely that the softer exposed areas of sea turtle's skin are the most sensitive to touch, they have at least some ability to detect contact even through their carapace.

It is a neat trick for an air-breathing animal like a turtle to use its nose underwater, but they do. Sea turtles have senses of both taste and smell, although of these, their ability to smell is most extensively developed. Openings to a turtle's nose are both external, above the apex of its beak, and internal, in the palate at the roof of its mouth. This allows a turtle to run either water or air through its nose in either direction. Behavioral experiments have shown that sea turtles can readily detect smells underwater. Whereas it certainly makes sense that such ability would help a turtle locate its food, the ability to detect faint odors also has long been hypothesized to allow sea turtles to orient and navigate by chemical cues.

A mysterious nasal offshoot called the Jacobson's organ adds to speculation about the nose's role in a sea turtle finding its way. This structure's wiring of nerves is different from the connections made by the main nasal membranes thought to detect smells. But both kinds of structures are connected to an olfactory bulb (the part of the brain important for smelling) that is quite large compared to other vertebrates. Some have proposed that the Jacobson's organ may involve the most intriguing of sea turtle senses, their feel for the Earth's magnetic field.

Although many animals have been shown to have a magnetic sense, sea turtles are one of few animal groups for which a highly developed geomagnetic skill has been so thoroughly described. It is a skill that involves more than a simple compass sense. But, like a compass, this ability allows a constant orientation relative to the Earth's magnetic field. Suspect players in a turtle's magnetic sense are tiny particles of an iron oxide known as magnetite. These particles, which are suspected to lie near a sea turtle's nose, might act as miniature compass needles whose orientations stimulate the turtle's brain with a sense of magnetic location. The amazing magnetic sense of sea turtles is explored further in the chapter on World Voyagers describing sea turtle migrations.

A sea turtle's awareness of magnetic fields is the sense least familiar to humans. Waters that to us appear featureless, are posted with a wealth of magnetic information for a traveling sea turtle.

Life Cycle and Life History

A convenient place to begin contemplating the life cycle of sea turtles is at the nest. All sea turtles leave the ocean to lay their eggs in nests made on sandy ocean beaches. In these nests, turtles leave behind a lot of eggs, more eggs than other reptiles or birds normally lay. In a single installment of eggs (a clutch), a female flatback may average 50 eggs in her nest, whereas a nesting hawksbill of about the same size will commonly lay 140. But a sea turtle's egg-laying work for the season is not finished with a single nest. Ridley sea turtles generally leave two to three 100-egg clutches in installments separated by roughly three weeks. By comparison, leatherbacks may lay ten or more clutches, with about 80 eggs each, separated by 10-day intervals.

All those eggs in each of those nests incubate on their own, with no attention or protection from their mother. She is occupied with the job of adding yolk and shells to her next clutch of eggs, or she might already be on her way back to her home foraging waters. For a mass of sea turtle eggs, their world during the next several weeks of incubation is a hole in the sand. They lie under 2 ft (0.5m) or so, and are hopefully above the reach of wave-wash erosion.

Each egg begins as a ping-pong-ball-sized packet of nutriment sealed within a white, parchment-like carbonate eggshell. As the female lays them, eggs are anointed with glistening, clear, lubricating fluid exuded from the cloaca. The flexible eggs leave their mother with a small dimple, like miniature semi-flat soccer balls. As such, they greet their nest and nest mates with a cushioned bounce. After a few days, the dimple in each egg is pushed out with the absorption of water from the humid nest and the eggs become turgid spheres.

The tiny developing turtles have almost everything they need within their papery eggshell. A rich yolk and watery albumen supply energy and moisture for growth, and a membranous sac (the allantios) serves as a repository for waste. The membranes and eggshell surrounding the embryonic turtle are porous, allowing the egg to breathe. Although sea turtle eggs can be momentarily inundated by the tide without harm, extended periods underwater can drown them.

A couple of weeks into incubation, an embryonic sea turtle reaches a period during which a critical determination is made — whether it will be male or female. In sea turtles, eggs incubating under cool conditions (less than 29° C or so) become male hatchlings and eggs experiencing warmer conditions become females. It remains an exasperating mystery to us just why sea turtles (and some other turtles and crocodiles) would trust their progeny's gender to environmental fate this way. In almost all other vertebrates, sex is determined by a genetically orchestrated cascade of developmental events that start the moment of fertilization. With this typical draw of the genetic cards determining gender, sex ratios of most animals tend to be roughly one male for every female. But for sea turtles, the cards determining either male or female hatchlings are arranged by nest temperature. Commonly, this results in having an entire clutch produce only one sex.

Near the end of incubation, sea turtle embryos within the egg are in a fetal curl, hunched over their remaining yolk sac. In this posture, hatchlings are bent forward on a creased plastron with their front flippers pressed to their backs. By this point, their eggshells have thinned to the point of being a chalk-flaked balloon.

This juvenile hawksbill bears no external clue revealing its sex, which was determined by the temperature it experienced within a nest of eggs incubating on a sandy beach. Warm sands make sea turtles into females, and cooler sands produce males.

Like this Kemp's ridley hatchling (left), newly hatched sea turtles escape their papery eggshell by cutting through it with a triangular point at the tip of their beak. This hatchling was left behind by its dozens of siblings and dug up from the bottom of a nest. Eggshells are normally left below the sand by emerging hatchlings.

These green turtle hatchlings (right) sense the world outside their nest for the first time as they struggle from the sand. The group emergence of hatchlings from a nest usually occurs during the cool of the evening.

Turgid with fluid, the eggshells mildly erupt as they are pierced and torn by each hatchling's egg-tooth. This caruncle (not a real tooth) is a triangular extension below the turtle's nose that slices through the eggshell as the turtle swings its head in a circle.

Over a day or two, nearly all of the successful eggs will pip, producing walnut-sized hatchlings. With the loss of fluid from the pipped eggs, an airspace is created within the nest that allows the little turtles working room for the task ahead of them. Within this pocket, hatchlings gradually envelop their remaining yolk sacs, straighten their shells, and begin to organize in convulsive group bouts of thrashing. The unified spasms of dozens of sets of tiny flippers eventually whittle away at the sandy ceiling and elevate the mass of hatchlings to just below the surface of the beach. There they wait in quiescence for the surface sand temperature to lower, a cue they rely on to indicate nightfall. After dusk, the uppermost hatchlings begin to stir. This motion creates a top-down transfer of excitement, and in a matter of minutes a boiling mass of squirming turtles begins bursting from their nest.

At this point, all sea turtles are confronted with the first of many challenges in finding their way. Having never experienced the ocean, hatchlings must identify it, scramble toward it, and enter the relative safety of its waves as quickly as they can. Failing in this challenge means feeding a predator, exhausting limited energy, or dehydrating in the morning sun. How hatchlings make this important orientation decision is discussed in the chapter on World Voyagers.

In their sprightly run down the beach, sea turtle hatchlings begin a period of frantic activity called the hatchling frenzy. The duration of the frenzy varies between species but it commonly lasts about 24 hours. In this time hatchlings scamper from the nest, enter the wave wash, dive beneath the tumbling breakers, and beat their flippers out to sea. The incessant activity of swimming hatchlings ensures that they move quickly through the shallow waters off the beach, waters that are commonly dense with predatory fishes that could easily suck down a little turtle.

Away from land most young sea turtles disperse into ocean currents that carry them along watery circuits that cross entire sea basins. This begins the oceanic stage of a sea turtle's life and it can vary in length from a year to a decade or more, depending on the species. In the flatback, this period in the open ocean is very short, or perhaps even nonexistent. Conversely, leatherback turtles never really end their deep-water, open-ocean phase and are likely to spend the majority of their lives far from land.

The life of young turtles in the open sea seems to be one of floating and waiting. Although a turtle may actively swim and dive on occasion, too much of this activity wastes energy that could be put into growth. It could be that a young turtle seldom really needs to exert itself to find its food. Young oceanic sea turtles live at the surface within convergence zones that collect both turtles and floating turtle habitat. Within these swirls of currents that young turtles ride, wind and water can be expected to eventually drag a variety of bite-sized, surface organisms by the nose of a quietly floating patient spectator.

For sea turtles, growth leads to safety. Risk of death decreases dramatically as developing turtles graduate from a hatchling, to stages of small juvenile, large juvenile, and adult. Population biologists estimate that only about 1 in 1000 eggs eventually matures into an adult sea turtle, and it is mostly the eggs and smallest turtles that fail in this progression. Eggs are vulnerable to land predators and erosion, and small turtles are a snack-sized swallow for many fish predators. But by the time young oceanic turtles have grown into the size of rugby balls, few predators but the largest sharks could likely make a meal of them. Up to this size, juveniles employ a number of strategies to avoid being eaten, which range from active diving to mimicking inanimate floating objects. In addition to having a shell that hardens with growth, the

Gulls are quick to snack on little turtles that misinterpret temperature cues and emerge from nests during daylight.

Sea turtle hatchlings run frantically to the sea to avoid predators and exposure to the sun. Night and early morning emergence from the nest helps them slip by predators and avoid overheating.

smallest open-sea juveniles of loggerheads, ridleys, and hawksbills add some structural defenses to deter predation. As they grow out of the hatchling stage, they develop thick shell scutes that form ridged keels of rear-pointing, spine-like projections.

For Kemp's ridleys, hawksbills, and green turtles, achieving rugby-ball size is the milestone for abandoning the open ocean and settling into shallower coastal waters. Similar-sized flatbacks have probably never left this coastal habitat. In olive ridleys and loggerheads, even large juveniles and adults may forage in the open ocean, although most loggerheads are found over shallow seabottom by the time they are half grown. All sea turtles may shift between development habitats and are unlikely to reach adulthood in the same waters they foraged as a juvenile.

The span to sea turtle adulthood rivals almost any animal, including us. Although the ridleys may reach maturity in just a little over a decade, loggerheads and green turtles do not begin to reproduce as adults for three to five decades. Longevity beyond first reproduction is a mystery, especially because sea turtles stop growing beyond adulthood. In this aspect sea turtles are like we are, with any given group of adults containing many sizes of individuals, and each size group containing a full spread of ages. Thus, in turtles and in people, the largest adult and the smallest may be no different in age.

With a cessation of sea turtle growth, there are no known marks — like the annual rings within tree trunks — that would record the passage of time in an adult turtle. Although biologists have observed the same individual loggerheads, hawksbills and green turtles on nesting beaches for 20 years or more, the limited persistence of identification tags may make this a vast underestimate of reproductive lifespan. By the same token, the loggerheads known from aquaria have been limited in longevity by the age of the buildings that house them; some of these turtles are at least 80 years old. When it comes to observations of sea turtle lifespan, it seems clear that we haven't been watching long enough. With persistence, we are likely to find that sea turtles are among the longest-living animals on Earth.

The fortunate few turtles that reach maturity are of great value to their population. In order to make their arduous developmental journey and patience count, they will need to produce thousands of fit offspring over decades of reproductive life. For a female sea turtle, this challenge begins with a voyage over hundreds or

As this leatherback swims away from its natal beach, it may be memorizing features that will guide it back to nest as an adult.

thousands of miles to a beach she experienced only once, as a hatchling, decades ago and at one ten-thousandth her size. This return of a sea turtle to her natal beach has been long speculated but it has been demonstrated only recently. Early on in our studies of sea turtles we reasoned that it is a difficult task for a female to find a beach where her offspring will survive. Any randomly chosen coast might be too hot, too cold, too wet, too dry, too rocky, plagued with predators, or away from ocean currents that would disperse her hatchlings. So then, what better testament to a beach's suitability than one's own survival?

An empirical demonstration of returning to their natal beach existed only in the example of Kemp's ridley. For the most part, this is a turtle that nests on only one beach, a sandy stretch of Mexican coast on the westernmost Gulf of Mexico. So it was clear that at least these turtles returned to nest on their natal beach. But for other species, biologists waited for advances in genetic identification to provide definitive evidence. In 1990, this evidence came from studies in which beach-by-beach comparisons were made of green turtle DNA inherited only from the turtle's mother. These found that female green turtles sharing a nesting beach also shared the same maternal inheritance. It was clear that their mothers, their mothers' mothers, and their vast maternal lineage, had remained faithful to the same stretch of coastline for thousands of years. How sea turtles go about locating and recognizing the beach they left as a hatchling is a mystery which is discussed later.

A female sea turtle encounters her potential mates in courtship areas directly off the nesting beach, or on the long migration to her natal beach from distant foraging waters. Male sea turtles are not as choosy as females. In fact, male sea turtles have shown many notable examples of their rash mate choices, ranging from mounts of plywood models to amorous attachment to hapless scuba divers. Although females do seem to have some options for refusal, in courtship areas with high numbers of males, females may seek refuge in shallow water to avoid unwanted advances.

When coupling occurs, males are not likely to soon let go. To help them hang on, they develop a soft lower shell that snugly fits above the rear half of the female's carapace. Their thumb claws have become larger and more recurved with adulthood, allowing them to attach at points above the female's shoulders. The male's tail is long, muscular, and prehensile, which allows it to latch onto the female from behind. Males are along for the ride at the whim of the female, which includes opportunities for breathing at the surface. The attachment of a male to his mate may last several hours. This male obstinacy is not a requirement for insemination itself, but it does allow a male to guard a female that might otherwise encounter another mate. Such a subsequent encounter would dilute the original male's contribution to his offspring. This mate-guarding does not always work completely; multiple paternity does occur and clutches of eggs may have several fathers.

Males come and go during the earliest part of the nesting season, leaving females to their task of nesting. Because females store the sperm that will fertilize all their successive clutches for the season, males may find it fruitless to continue hounding already mated females later into the season. Around the world and between the species, nesting seasons vary. Outside the tropics, nesting takes place predominantly during the late spring and summer. Closer to the equator, nesting seasons expand so that almost any month may see nesting, although wet seasons seem to be favored over dry seasons, and warm-humid monsoons are favored over cooler dryer monsoons.

Throughout a four-month or greater nesting season, female sea turtles exhaust and deplete themselves for the next generation. Having crossed seas without feeding to arrive at her home beach, a female will drag herself onto land to make repeated nests into which she'll bury hundreds of eggs. In most species, the eggs left to incubate in multiple nests spend more than 15 per cent of an individual female's body mass. Only rarely are there opportunities to feed near the nesting beach. Many females may not restock their energy stores until the end of the long migration back to their foraging waters. Not surprisingly, few sea turtles are able to make this reproductive commitment every year. In most species, females replenish themselves for one to several years between these intense reproductive efforts.

A male green turtle clings to his mate using his thumb claws, rear flippers, and strong, prehensile tail.

From Sea to Land to Sea

Sea turtles do not attend to their developing young but they do what they can to ensure the most favorable conditions for their progeny's survival on land. In this effort, sea turtles rely on the positioning and construction of a sand nest made most often under cover of darkness. How a turtle leaves the ocean, creates a nest, and returns to the surf has become the most well-known part of sea turtle biology.

Nesting beaches chosen by sea turtles are almost always sandy shores exposed to the pounding of ocean waves. Gravel or cobble beaches won't do, nor will silted or muddy flats lining sheltered waters. Many sea turtles nest on oceanic island beaches or barrier strands as well as on continental shores. To know the world's sea turtle nesting beaches is to tour some of Earth's most remarkable places.

Tortuguero, Caribbean Costa Rica: Green turtles, leatherbacks, and hawksbills all share a long, western Caribbean beach made of coarse, dark, volcanic sands backed by a low dune covered with palms, cocoplum, and invading lowland rainforest.

Ostional, Costa Rica's Pacific coast: Olive ridleys nest en masse in synchronized arribadas (arrivals) that occur on a short, coarse-grained beach spanning rock outcroppings and a river that flows into crashing breakers.

Archie Carr Refuge, Florida, USA: Loggerheads nest with green turtles and leatherbacks on a barrier island beach of broken shell and quartz sand, backed by scarped dunes tufted with sea oats.

Rancho Nuevo, Tamaulipas, northeastern Mexico: On a long, dry, powder-sand beach, Kemp's ridleys emerge in synchronized daylight arribadas on blustery days that erase all but faint signs that the beach had been visited.

Ascension Island, isolated in the central Atlantic Ocean: Diverse cove beaches tucked between rocky ledges and promontories, so different that no two are alike, host nesting green turtles that come ashore amidst the great rolling breakers of the mid-Atlantic.

The island of Zakynthos, Greece: Cocoa-brown sand beaches within the wide mouth of Laganas Bay beckon loggerhead sea turtles that nest above waves rolling in from the deep central Mediterranean.

Ras Al Hadd, Oman: Where the morning sun first shines onto the Arabian Peninsula, green turtles crowd onto sets of soft, coarse-grained beaches isolated by sheer cliff faces that were once the bottom of the ancient Tethys Ocean.

Cousin Island, the Seychelles granitic archipelago: Isolated far into the Indian Ocean, a haven for seabirds also attracts hawksbills, which nest in coarse sands of crushed, bleached coral.

Crab Island, Queensland, Australia: In the Torres Strait south of New Guinea, flatback turtles emerge with the high tide, mist tawny sands over their nests, return to the surf, and dart to evade the jaws of 16 ft (5-meter) saltwater crocodiles.

Just as sea turtle nesting beaches vary upon a common theme, so do the ways that sea turtles make their nests. After a gravid female has located the stretch of beach she left as a hatchling, her next challenge is to haul herself up onto that beach. Her mobility on land is as hampered as one might expect for a marine animal. Range in limb movement, application of muscle strength, and flipper design are all tailored for frisking through fluid. Thus, to most who witness a sea turtle's emergence and nesting, the event seems to be a struggle.

The nesting struggle begins as a female approaches near-shore waters shallow enough to trip waves into breakers. On some

The first of thousands of olive ridleys emerges at sunset to participate in a mass-nesting event on a Pacific beach in Costa Rica.

beaches, the turbulent energy from crashing waves must certainly be enough to tumble a turtle onto its back. But somehow, these events are rare. Beyond the tumbling breakers and into the uprush of spent waves, the mass of the Earth tugs ever harder on the egg-laden female. Her crawl up the beach is an impeded shuffle against gravity. Her belly shell bears much of her bulk. As the wrists and forearms of her rear-pointing front flippers gouge the sand, and as her rear-flipper webbing pushes the beach behind her, the turtle moves incrementally forward.

Among the sea turtles there are two basic styles of beach-crawling. The first is the typical alternating gait that many crawling animals use – left-rear combined with right-front, then right-rear combined with left-front. This is the crawling gait of most of the smaller and medium-sized sea turtles – hawksbills, loggerheads, and the two ridleys. Green turtles, being slightly larger, and leatherbacks, being largest of all, trudge through sand with a simultaneous butterfly-stroke gait. In this, green turtles and leatherbacks dig all four flippers into the sand and heave themselves forward with a synchronous push. Flatbacks crawl with a butterfly style as well but may revert to an alternating gait when climbing or descending slopes. Turtle shape, size, and gait result in a broad tractor-like track that is different enough to readily identify most species the morning after they've visited a beach.

Most nesting turtles crawl beyond the wet sand, above the reach of typical spring tides (the highest monthly tides), and even into the dune or vegetation line facing the sea. There the nesting female prepares a nest site by sweeping sand from in front of her with exaggerated fore-flipper strokes. With her hind flippers also making wide strokes and pushing sand behind her, she slides slowly forward into the pit that her strokes have formed, nestling in so that the rear of her shell tilts down within the deepest end of a slanting depression. Here again, there are subtle differences in style between the species. In both ridley turtles, the flatback, and

the hawksbill, the body pit is a shallow, quickly dug depression made as the turtle swivels with alternating flipper sweeps. In loggerheads, synchronous fore-flipper and alternating hind-flipper strokes make a pit almost as deep as the turtle's body, with prominent spoil mounds to the pit's sides and rear. Leatherbacks make short work of their body-pit digging, but because of powerful simultaneous front flipper strokes, the resulting pit often accommodates half the depth of her enormous body. The body pit made by green turtles is the most extensive of all. Green turtles use synchronous front-flipper strokes to blast out sand three to five turtle-lengths away from a pit deep enough to completely contain the nesting female. This preparatory body pit in all species probably allows turtles to judge the suitability of the site. But in addition, the pit also creates a working space where dryer surface sand is unlikely to slide into the egg chamber she'll dig and where the depth of her eggs can be more than the length of her rear flippers (her tools for the next excavation in the nesting sequence).

At the bottom of her body pit, a nesting sea turtle digs an egg chamber with her rear flippers. Here, in contrast to her occasionally awkward use of aquatic tools for terrestrial applications, the turtle's webbed limbs seem elegantly suited. The hole for her eggs begins with careful strokes alternated between flippers. In a stroke, each rear flipper performs like a hand in a webbed glove – probing downward into soft moist grains, twisting and cupping to isolate a loose ball of sand in its palm, elevating it from the hole with scarcely a crumble reentering, and quickly rotating to the side to dump and compress the extracted sand. Then, instantaneous with the halt in one flipper's work, the other snaps forward to flick its own previously dug sand over the head and sides of the turtle. The flipper then curls almost to a fist and gracefully opens upon entering the hole to dig. After several minutes and dozens of traded digging strokes, the egg chamber deepens into a vase-shaped receptacle. It is slightly wider at the

A leatherback turtle on a beach in French Guiana sweeps sand over her nest site to camouflage her eggs.

Green turtles excavate deep pits as they dig their nest and cover their eggs.
In the dry sands of Ascension Island it is especially important for female turtles to dig down
into sand moist enough to hold the shape of their egg chamber without collapsing.

bottom than at its throat, a shape that becomes honed as each rear flipper begins contouring rotations before withdrawing its scoop of sand. This digging sequence is remarkably similar among species. But the sizes of rear flippers involved can vary from 10 in (25 cm) length in ridleys to 30 in (75 cm) or more in leatherbacks.

During any of the preceding stages leading up to egg laying, a turtle may abandon her nesting attempt and return to the sea. Difficult digging conditions, wet sand, and the presence of predators (especially humans) often prompts such a retreat. But on occasion, the reasons for withdrawal seem known only to the turtle herself.

Toward the end of digging the egg chamber, several flipper strokes often fail to reach the cavity's complete depth, even as the turtle strains with her fore-flippers to tilt her hind flippers deeper into the hole. With the last stroke comes a brief relaxation. In ridleys, loggerheads, and hawksbills, the rear flippers rest astride the egg chamber, and with flatbacks, green turtles, and leatherbacks, the flippers cover the egg chamber. In leatherbacks, one flipper is left to dangle into the hole. Then the turtle's cloaca (the vent that opens halfway down her short tail) also relaxes and partially distends into the top of the egg chamber.

The first egg falls farthest, but is resilient enough not to break. In the voluminous hole of the leatherback, the first eggs dribble down the turtle's dangled flipper for a slightly softer entry into the world. Eggs continue to come from the cloaca in ones, twos, threes, and fours, with just a few releases each minute. In most species, visible contractions accompany each egg release. These spasms in loggerhead females cause the turtles' resting rear flippers to curl upward so that her arches point momentarily skyward.

At the end of egg-laying the widest part of the egg chamber is filled with glistening white eggs. To cover her eggs, the female makes slow rear-flipper sweeps that push sand within reach into the hole. Then, compression of sand above the eggs begins with kneading motions that apply either the flat web

(in green turtles, flatbacks, and leatherbacks) or the leading edge (in other species) of each rear flipper. In Kemp's and olive ridley turtles, packing sand atop the eggs also involves several bouts of rapid side-to-side dances in which the edges of the female's plastron thump the beach sand near the clutch. During a mass *arribada*, the dull thumps from nearby turtles pounding their plastrons can sound like dueling drums.

The eggs of this olive ridley have overflowed the chamber she dug for them and may be scrambled as she attempts to cover them.

With the eggs mostly buried and packed in, the nesting female begins to obliterate the evidence that might lead a predator directly to her eggs. She reaches forward with her front flippers to dig a purchase into the beach and sharply flings the gathered sand broadly behind her. In bouts of multiple, decisive, swimming strokes, she casts dual arcing pulses of sand spray over her nest site, often slapping the sides of her shell with the conviction of each flap. Following front-flipper strokes, her rear flippers sweep side to side to spread the excavated sand. A raised head and the rush of a great breath often precede a rest between each bout of sand throwing. The intermission seems forced by exhaustion but ends abruptly with the repeat of more vigorous flipper strokes heaving sand. The casting of sand by a female takes up about one third of her time on the beach. The effort generally leaves a mound of sand a bit larger than the turtle that made it. Green turtles leave deep pits and extensive mounds resulting from

A green turtle returns to the Atlantic from Ascension Island after a two-hour nesting process.

energetic strokes made while slowly creeping forward. Leatherbacks leave even larger nests owing to the great span of their flippers and to their tendency to turn and crawl several steps between periods of sand tossing.

With a short pause after her last weary stroke of sand, the nesting female lifts her head, and in a wide-eyed, myopic, over-the-shoulder scan, she searches for the ocean behind her. It is a task whose accuracy determines whether a turtle ever reaches

the sea at all. In the leatherback, to crawl is to haul the equivalent of a small car through the sand. This effort magnifies the risk of her entrapment by obstructions landward of her nest. Thus, in what may be a response to the consequences of failure, leatherbacks commonly turn a complete orientation circle before selecting the most likely seaward direction. For Ridleys and hawksbills, the crawl to the sea ends a nesting sequence lasting less than an hour. Loggerheads and flatbacks nest for a little more than an hour, green turtles take about an hour and a half, and leatherbacks are commonly on a nesting beach for more than two hours.

After crawling from her first nest of the season and into the surf, a female sea turtle will soon ovulate her next clutch of eggs. They will be fertilized with sperm stored from her previous encounters with one to several males. The time to her next nesting attempt will be 9 to 10 days if she is a leatherback, or roughly two weeks if she is one of the hard-shelled sea turtles. However, ridleys waiting for just the right conditions to signal an arribada may forestall nesting again for three or four weeks. The nesting season for most sea turtles is spent preparing for and making from one to seven nests. Exhausted by all that is required for such a reproductive effort, most turtles will not return to their nesting beach for two to four years.

In seven to ten weeks the nest site is again a center of activity as hatchlings surge upward out of the sand. For male turtles, this frenzied dash to the sea will probably be the last time they will ever experience gravity's tug on land. For the females, at least those favored by fortune and fitness, decades may pass before they again find themselves without the familiar support of buoyancy. Again at their natal beach, these females will have come full circle.

Sea turtles, like this loggerhead, orient seaward after nesting by directing themselves toward the bright open sky over water.

World Voyagers

Every good epic journey requires a return home. For sea turtles, home is a nesting beach. It is an origin that becomes the focal point for a lifetime of travels. But throughout their long lives, most sea turtles will form and dissolve allegiances to other areas as well. These patches of habitat within widely separated ranges become transitory stops on a great life voyage.

The First Big Swim

Immediately upon their entry into the world, sea turtle hatchlings must accurately locate an ocean they've never seen and begin a swim for their lives. At its beginning, a hatchling is one of dozens of siblings erupting from a nest and out from the sandy depression above their buried empty eggshells. Amidst hundreds of tiny thrashing flippers, a hatchling scrambles to a vantage point atop the weathered mound left by its mother and stops to clumsily wipe a soft fore flipper across an eye crusted with sand. Head up in a glistening stare, rotund orbs blink, and reveal to the hatchling its first scene – a starry night sky over two opposite horizons. Choosing between the two horizons is a decision that will either lead a hatchling from nest to sea or condemn the little turtle to death within a tangled dune.

Hatchlings orient to the sea by locating the center of a bright, broad, unobstructed horizon. These characters typically match the open view of the night sky over a glittering ocean. But on coastlines modified by humans where electric lighting is visible from the nesting beach, hatchlings strive to reach an artificial brightness that overpowers the subtle cues from nocturnal celestial light. So deceived, a hatchling is unlikely to ever reach the sea. On beaches lighted only by the twinkle of stars, hatchlings crawl on precise bearings toward the brightness of an ocean, acting on a biological hunch that has proven correct for ages. But on beaches lit by the glare of electric lights, an innate movement toward brightness is likely to lead entire nests of hatchlings ever further from the sea.

As a frenzied hatchling reaches the hard wet sand of the swash zone, it nears the rush of frothy water from the exhausted breakers. To a walnut-sized little turtle, the waves are mountains. Entering the rushing sheets of water often takes several attempts as each foamy collision tumbles the tiny turtles back up the beach. Hatchlings so spit forth by the ocean right themselves with wide rotations of their head, blink to reacquire their target, and continue seaward undaunted. Crawling hatchlings with the luck to enter the rush of water at the apex of its upward movement are enveloped, and shoot down the beach with the seaward slide of the returning flow.

Suspended by water, hatchlings immediately swim. A two-second head-up breath precedes a dive into rapid front-flipper powerstroking. Still among breaking waves, a hatchling will dive just before the arrival of each looming boil of turbulence. The dive takes the hatchling beneath the crash of the wave and is elegantly performed to place the little turtle in position to be pulled out with the withdrawing undertow. Dive by dive and breaker by breaker, hatchlings make their way out beyond the surf.

Most of what is known about swimming orientation in sea turtle hatchlings comes from studies of loggerheads, but it seems likely that all species share their tactics in this challenge. The challenge is to continue seaward orientation where the visual differences between landward and seaward directions become indistinguishable to a turtle poking a bean-sized head above the surface. Within and just outside the turmoil of the surf, hatchlings begin to ignore brightness cues and instead direct themselves into

Green turtle hatchlings scramble toward the brightest horizon after a nocturnal emergence from their nest.

oncoming swells. Faith in this tactic is reaffirmed by the physics of wave motion. As swells generated anywhere out to sea approach land, part of the wave is slowed by the shallows off the beach. Thus, waves approaching the beach pivot on the end first reaching the shallow water. This refracts the wave, bending it, so that its travel is steered directly toward the shore.

A hatchling's use of wave motion for orientation is a subject that

A newly hatched green turtle pauses for a breath during its furious swim out to sea.

has been studied by researchers at Florida Atlantic University and the University of North Carolina. They have found that a hatchling bobbing and stroking through the waves senses its orientation by the orbit it makes with each wave's passage. As a wave rolls by, hatchlings swimming in the seaward direction feel movement backward, then downward, then forward, then upward, within the motion of circular movement inside the wave. Thus, a hatchling surging first to one side turns on the opposite flipper until its swimming is in line with the orbits of waves marching to shore.

As they leave the waters off their natal beach, hatchlings are

but specks on a wide-open sea. Their frenzy of activity on the beach has carried over to the vigor with which they swim. About 2 ft (0.5 m) under water, hatchlings stroke fore-flippers to a constant beat for 20 seconds or so, rise to the surface for a momentary head-up breath during a four-flipper dogpaddle, and dive again to cruising depth. In these incessant cycles of powerstroking and breaths, hatchlings of most species cover the length of a football field about every five minutes.

In only an hour of swimming, a hatchling is likely to find itself more than half a mile from the beach and beyond the point where the shallows turn the waves to shore. Here the swells cannot be trusted to lead a traveler out to sea. Yet, hatchlings persist in seaward movement, having calibrated a skill in navigating they may rely on for a lifetime of journeys. This remarkable skill lies in sensing the character of the Earth's magnetic field. In sea turtles, this geomagnetic aptitude rises to levels beyond simply determining a compass direction. Already in its incipient sensations of the world, a hatchling at this milestone has not only learned the magnetic feel of movement out to sea, but it has also acquired a magnetic awareness of location applicable to any of their travels from that point forward. Much of what we know today about this remarkable skill in sea turtles comes from the work of researchers at UNC Chapel Hill led by Ken Lohmann.

Only with instruments can we sense, as sea turtles do, the variety in the magnetic envelope surrounding our planet — our magnetosphere. In this field are lines curving from magnetic pole to pole, lines that are horizontal near the equator, and inclining to vertical at the southern (off the coast of Antarctica due south of Tasmania) and northern (the Canadian Arctic) ends of the planet. In a reading of the tilt of these magnetic field lines, a hatchling assesses not only which way a pole is, but also how distant it is. In addition to this sensation of direction and latitude, hatchlings also show the ability to detect varying strengths of the local magnetic field. These strengths vary over the earth along distorted

Kemp's ridley sea turtle hatchlings
released into the Gulf of Mexico
by conservation workers.

A hatchling loggerhead swims at
a frenzied pace through a calm
surf out to deep blue waters.

gradients. Although field strength is greatest at the poles, many areas of the globe have lines of equal field strength that cross the lines of equal field-line tilt. Thus, with a reference for constant direction, with an ability to sense position on a magnetic grid equivalent to latitude and longitude, and with a magnetic memory for the places they've been, a hatchling has the essential tools of a navigator at hand: a compass, a sextant (perhaps even a Global Positioning System – GPS), and a map.

Young Turtles: Pilots or Passengers?

After a day or so of constant oriented swimming, a neonate sea turtle begins to pace itself, marking the gradual end of the hatchling frenzy. Although levels of activity during and after the frenzy vary among the species studied, all settle into a period of reduced activity before their second day at sea. Of the seven species, the flatback stands out as having a frenzy only hours in duration, which does not serve to disperse their hatchlings very far. The flatback is the only sea turtle thought to forgo an open-ocean life stage. As hatchlings of the other species end their frenzied swimming, they may be well offshore and within major ocean currents.

The progression from a dispersing propagule into a developing oceanic sea turtle is best understood for the loggerhead, whose behavior may be representative of the other species, except for the flatback. Following a successful escape from land, a loggerhead hatchling's only fuel for continued swimming is the residual yolk sac it has internalized from its egg. With active swimming, this source could last only a few days, but by resting for extended periods it could last much longer. Typically at the beginning of a little loggerhead's second day at sea, the cycle of diving and powerstroking ends and the turtle continues seaward with a more relaxed surface-swimming style. In this more relaxed pattern, a turtle holds its front flippers back with their undersides pressed against the sides of the upper shell and the only movement comes from a simultaneous frog-like kick of the rear flippers. A few times

each minute, this slow steady stroking is broken by a brief head-up four-flipper dogpaddle and breath. As if slowing from a run to a walk, this conservation of energy will be essential to a little turtle who may not chance upon food for days.

Three or more days after first entering the sea, a loggerhead hatchling has reduced its activity to only a few hours of daylight rear-flipper kicking. When inactive, the little turtles bob about in a position known as a tuck. Tucked loggerheads hold their front flippers flat against their backs and overlap their tiny rear flippers to conceal their tail. Motionless, with a lump-like profile and no exposed appendages to be nibbled at, the young loggerhead does its best to avoid confrontations with curious predators. Many of the fishes likely to take a snack-sized little turtle, such as the dorado or dolphinfish (*Coryphaena hippurus*), are perpetual swimmers that are likely to overlook an unexciting bit of inanimate flotsam.

Little loggerheads insert themselves into a dynamic ocean world where opportunities for feeding are patchy. It contains a vast emptiness where rare resources are both dispersed and concentrated by winds and currents. Where and when the sea's forces move surface waters together and press flotsam into lines, there are ephemeral oceanic oases. These are briefly assembled habitats where little floating turtles and their food can meet. The small animals on which young loggerheads feed are, like the young turtles, cast adrift. Thus, in a world where too much effort could actually take a turtle farther from its prey, the only sensible way to pursue a meal is to stop and wait for it.

The good things that come to a waiting loggerhead are often wrapped within patches of a floating golden plant called *Sargassum*. One of the brown algae with berry-like floats for buoyancy, this plant circles the Atlantic and forms the basis of a diverse community of organisms, including little loggerheads. In the western Atlantic, hatchling loggerheads that have dispersed from the beaches of the southeast U.S. end up in lines of assembled *Sargassum* where the Gulf Stream current sheers by continental shelf waters. On, in, and around the leafy amber tangles of *Sargassum*, young loggerheads feed on clinging hydroids, worms, snails, tiny crustaceans, and dozens of other creatures small enough to fit into a pint-sized turtle's mouth. On a calm sea, the subtle surface effects of one current slipping beneath another keep a bountiful *Sargassum* salad bar together. But when winds chop the sea into whitecaps, a turtle's bounty can quickly disperse away into nothingness. Seemingly capitalizing on the good fortune of finding themselves amongst food, neonate loggerheads bite at any floating shred or fleck that contrasts against the backdrop of *Sargassum* and deep blue sea. It is an indiscriminate feeding style common to all young sea turtles, perhaps in anticipation of the lengthy fast that may precede their next access to the sea's abundance. But with modern consequences that are gravely unfortunate for the turtles, this haphazard feeding commonly results in small turtles acquiring deadly loads of indigestible plastic bits and tar balls. Unfortunately, bite-sized elements of human discards are ubiquitous and are concentrated with turtles as they are swept along the ocean currents.

Poking about patches of flotsam in the wide-open sea, a young sea turtle may cross an entire ocean. For a young Kemp's ridley, green turtle, or hawksbill, this ride on the currents may last one to five years. But for a juvenile loggerhead growing up on the high seas, this travel may last well over a decade. It is astounding to imagine that a loggerhead hatched on a beach in southern Japan will circle the entire north Pacific, perhaps even multiple times, long before it reaches half the age of adulthood. It is a prodigious migration spanning tens of thousands of miles during which the turtle is largely a passenger. Yet, at the appointed time when a young turtle must leave the open ocean, a pilot's skills and abilities rise to meet the challenge.

Maturing Turtles: Homebodies or Gadabouts?

How and where a young sea turtle decides to make a living in shallow coastal waters is one of the greatest mysteries to those who study sea turtle biology. It is a decision that marks a dramatic shift in lifestyle. For a small turtle bobbing at the surface of a heaving sea thousands of feet above the cold dark seabottom,

This juvenile loggerhead, near the Azores in the eastern Atlantic, is likely to have hatched on a beach in the southeastern USA.

finding food anywhere but near the surface is not an option. Yet, for most sea turtles to complete their development into adults, they must shift their feeding to organisms that thrive on the bottom of sunlit seas.

The first juvenile green turtles to arrive in shallow coastal waters are the size of dinner plates (about 12 in or 30 cm in shell length) and have just begun to feed on algal patches and seagrass. Hawksbills and ridleys also enter coastal waters as plate-sized turtles but seek a different type of food. Juvenile hawksbills settle from the open ocean onto tropical reefs where they browse on sponges tucked into vibrantly ornamented rocks and corals. Kemp's ridleys of the same stage begin their pursuit of sprightly crabs in turbid gulf and estuarine waters.

Loggerheads and olive ridleys postpone their entry into the shallows until they are roughly the size of a serving platter (20 in or 50 cm in shell length), a size that is likely to be about one third of their weight as an adult. Of these two species, loggerheads become the most closely tied to shallow waters where they search for large, slow-moving, hard-shelled animals inhabiting seabottom types ranging from mud to reef. Olive ridleys may feed on slightly smaller bottom-dwelling invertebrates but they also spend a great deal of time in deep waters far from land where they eat a wide variety of pelagic animals.

Of all the sea turtle species, the leatherback is most reluctant to forage in coastal waters. Perhaps by specializing on large gelatinous invertebrates that are frequently concentrated in the open ocean, and perhaps because they are able to descend to tremendous depths in order to access this abundance, leatherbacks can attain adult size without ever giving up their oceanic lifestyle.

Movements of foraging sea turtles seem to be linked to their dependence upon localized food resources. For instance, green turtles grazing on seagrasses spread over underwater pastures are known to maintain closely cropped plots that they return to time and again. Their fidelity to these manicured seagrass plots ensures them access to the nutritious new growth of the lengthening grass blades. So it is not surprising that green turtles may spend years within the same patch of seabottom. In experiments where juvenile green turtles were captured from their home range and released many miles away, the turtles almost invariably swam directly back to their familiar foraging plots.

The carnivorous sea turtles like hawksbills and loggerheads also seem faithful to particular areas. Occasionally, these turtles are observed repeatedly within a small corner of hard-bottom or reef that is indistinguishable from the wide spread of adjacent similar habitat occupied by its own resident turtles. These patches of familiar habitat often contain a resting area, such as a nook beneath a rocky ledge, where turtles wedge themselves to sleep at the end of each day.

In a sea turtle's tendencies for neighborhood fidelity we again find an impressive skill made possible by extraordinary senses. One important sense in neighborhood recognition is the feel for geomagnetism that turtles first used as hatchlings. In an attempt to understand the feel that a maturing turtle has for its shallow-water home, researchers took green turtles from a Florida lagoon and placed them in tanks beneath the large wire lattice of a magnetic field coil. From the coil, they could replicate magnetic fields from locations that were hundreds of miles away from the turtles' home lagoon. It was a test to determine whether the turtles have a magnetic map in their heads that would allow them to orient homeward. And apparently, they do have just such a map. The green turtles within a field mimicking the conditions of a site north of home directed their swimming southward, and vice versa. Although it is difficult to imagine such a radical displacement from home occurring in the real world, sea turtles are seemingly able to understand their magnetic surroundings enough to deal with such an abrupt relocation.

With the sort of fixation that sea turtles have for their familiar foraging grounds, one might think that most sea turtles settle into a parochial existence as reclusive homebodies, but this is not the case. One generality among most sea turtles is that their development is spanned by many migrations between successive habitats. For example, in the loggerhead sea turtles of the western Atlantic, as young 55 lb (25 kg) turtles arrive in shallow waters,

Loggerheads like this juvenile may circle entire ocean basins before growing large enough to feed in coastal waters.

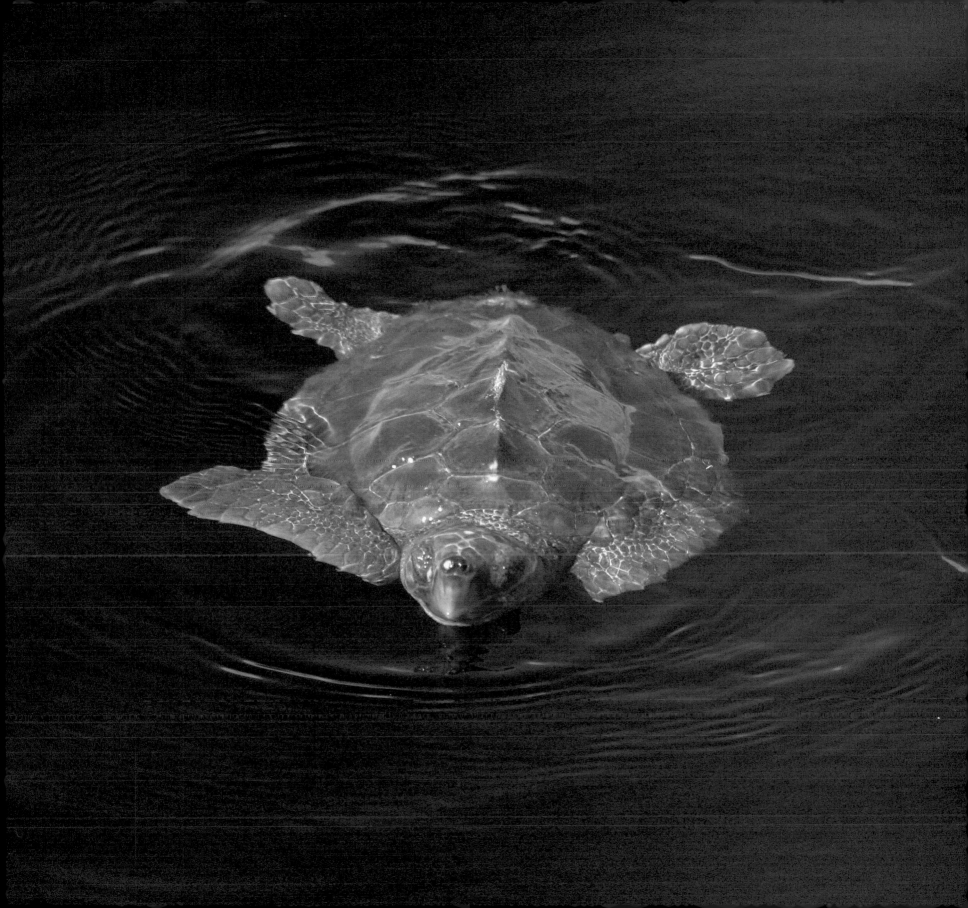

they may be found throughout the shores of North America south of New England. But as the loggerheads grow, they tend to inhabit coastal waters farther south. Upon reaching pubescence and adulthood, most loggerheads of this western Atlantic assemblage find themselves in the warm waters between the southernmost Florida peninsula, the Greater Antilles, and the Bahamas.

This gradual shift in range may be superimposed upon many seasonal migrations. Along the southeast Atlantic United States, loggerheads foraging in Chesapeake Bay and the sounds of North Carolina depart in the fall. The turtles spend colder winter months in Florida or out on the continental shelf where the warm waters of the Gulf Stream edge by. However, just as some assemblages of birds are made up of some that migrate and some that stay put, many sea turtles in tolerably warm waters find no need to swim hundreds of miles between seasons.

Among the wanderings of sea turtles, the summer-winter commutes of leatherbacks are truly global in extent. In what is the first complete glimpse of where these turtles spend their seasons, Canadian and US researchers have tracked leatherbacks with satellite-monitored transmitters. The satellite broadcasts of the turtles scatter points from their positions that trace a path from their summer range off Newfoundland to their winter range in the central Atlantic just north of the Equator. It is a yearly round trip of over 6000 miles (10,000 km). In less direct routes north to south and back again, leatherbacks from Florida nesting beaches tracked by researchers have traveled the western Gulf Stream from Florida to Nova Scotia, occasionally making extensive looping sojourns across the North Atlantic. These great loops have spanned an entire ocean basin in a season of wandering, from the Carolina's Outer Banks, to Portugal's Azores Islands, to the waters off West Africa, and to the windward fringe of the Caribbean.

Reproductive Journeys

The most impressive of grand voyages are not only extensive; they are also precise. As our own species began to set out on ocean passages, it was the precision part of the exercise that proved to be the greatest challenge. Traveling across a vast and featureless sea from point A to a distant point B required considerable problem-solving skills and technology. Most people find it astounding that a sea turtle with none of these advantages can accomplish such a challenging navigational task. It is a bewilderment that underscores how little we know about the intimate connections between sea turtles and their world.

Archie Carr, considered to be the most influential pioneer in understanding and interpreting the lives of sea turtles, continually marveled at their navigational precision. In what is still one of the most compelling descriptions of this ability, Carr traced the voyages of female green turtles that had been marked with flipper tags on the nesting beaches of the mid Atlantic island of Ascension. Over years, a picture of the voyages of Ascension green turtles slowly developed. Returns of the tags came from fishermen who had caught the turtles far to the west, 1200 miles (2000 km) or more away, in the waters off Brazil.

Ascension is easily overlooked. It is but a speck of land – a single exposed seamount in the center of the equatorial Atlantic so neatly between Africa and South America, so isolated, and so inconspicuous that the place often goes unrepresented on maps. Yet, Ascension Island serves as one of the most important nesting aggregations for green turtles in the world. Before the arrival of British sailing ships and an island garrison, a human occupancy that consumed about 1500 nesting turtles per year during a large part of the 19th century, the number of green turtles visiting the island was even greater than the 2000 to 3000 annual visits seen today.

This young green turtle in the shallow waters surrounding Borneo is small enough to have just graduated from the open-ocean stage of its life. Most sea turtle species disperse from beaches as hatchlings and remain within oceanic surface currents for one to several years.

The circuit between Ascension and Brazil involves a round trip approaching 3000 miles (5000 km) over a deep ocean basin with no opportunity for green turtles to feed. Thus, a green turtle must store in the fat reserves and developing egg follicles she takes with her, every calorie of energy required to make the arduous trip. This means surviving for three or more months, producing more than

Place memories that persist for decades help guide the lives of green turtles.

44 lb (20 kg) of eggs, burying and hiding them in four installments or so, and swimming the long return to Brazil. With this task at hand, green turtles heavy with eggs set out from their seagrass meadows and algal patches throughout Brazil's long tropical Atlantic coast to cross an ocean and locate a seemingly impossible target.

It is a job that would be difficult enough for turtles that made a regular commute to Ascension. But consider the task of a female approaching her first reproductive season. There, on her familiar pastures off the northern shelf of South America, fattened and restless, she draws upon a memory registered 30 years or more

ago when a tiny, frantic hatchling was swimming for its very life. And with whatever clarity has remained in that recollection, an experience first imbedded in a brain the size of a sesame seed, a green turtle is guided on her journey.

Through the work on sea turtle genetics done by Brian Bowen, then at the University of Florida, in conjunction with colleagues from all over the world, it now seems clear that this persistence of natal memory is key to a female green turtle returning to her home beach. Evidence for this comes from a close examination of the relatedness of green turtles that share foraging areas but migrate to different nesting beaches. The rich coastal waters at the eastern bulge of Brazil serve as foraging grounds for green turtles that nest either at Ascension, or westward on the northern coast of South America in Surinam. Although the overlap on their feeding grounds is broad, individual tagged turtles have never been seen to have more than a single nesting area. This faithfulness to a beach is also revealed in the turtle's DNA that is passed on only from mother to daughter (mitochondrial DNA). With extensive sampling of mitochondrial DNA, green turtles nesting in Surinam and those from Ascension were found by Bowen and others to have distinctly different genetic markers. The results showed that green turtles have a high degree of faithfulness to their natal beach, a trait called philopatry. It is a trait that has been shown for all the species of sea turtles examined and would seem to add eidetic memory to a sea turtle's list of useful navigational skills.

Lately, Ascension Island has become a laboratory in the study of how sea turtles can accomplish such pinpoint navigation. University of Wales researchers Brendan Godley and Graeme Hays along with Floriano Papi and Paolo Luschi at the University of Pisa have worked to challenge the senses of green turtles desiring to nest at Ascension. Challenges to turtles have included being displaced over 60 miles (100 km), either upwind or downwind from the island, and in some trials, turtles bore magnets strapped to their heads. Remarkably, even without the opportunity for an upwind sniff of their goal, and with their detection of the geomagnetic field presumably overwhelmed by the bar magnet they carried, green turtles driven to nest consistently found their way back to Ascension.

The results from this mid-ocean laboratory suggest the depth of what we don't know about the ability of sea turtles to sense and move in their world. At present, there are many sensory modalities that have been proposed as ways that sea turtles navigate. But the rigorous experiments required to demonstrate how a turtle uses its skills are difficult, and few hypotheses have been discarded. The magnetic map hypothesis is still a valid explanation of some of the biological instrumentation in the sea turtle navigator's toolbox, along with abilities to smell and measure wind waves. It seems likely that the toolbox of Ascension green turtles is well stocked. By a number of senses and types of landmarks, perhaps used within a system for both recognizing reliability and reverting to contingencies, green turtles know well their way to Ascension.

The Ascension Island example is but one of many lengthy crossings between sea turtle feeding areas and nesting beaches that biologists have observed. For instance, leatherbacks foraging in the North Atlantic off Nova Scotia voyage to nest just a few degrees from the equator in Surinam and French Guiana, a one-way trip approaching 3100 miles (5000 km). Why sea turtles travel so far to lay their eggs has been a vexing puzzle to biologists, although we do have our ideas.

One idea is that the best feeding areas and the best nesting spots seldom occur together. For instance, the Ascension Island green turtle beaches seem perfect for producing young. There are no mammalian predators to dig up eggs (at least there were none before humans arrived), and a short swim out from the island puts hatchlings directly into their oceanic habitat and away from the coastal fishes that would make a meal of them. The trouble is, Ascension is surrounded by nothing that would interest a hungry adult green turtle. Beneath the waters around the island there is a barren slide down to more than 2 miles (3km) deep, allowing little growth of the vegetation that green turtles need to grow up and make little turtles. However, the same limitations on foraging opportunities do not exist for the island nesting beaches just off Brazil's easternmost coast where hundreds of green turtles choose to nest. Intermingled off Brazil's coastal foraging grounds are not only the green turtles faithful to Brazilian beaches, but also the thousands of equally faithful green turtles whose beaches range as far west as Costa Rica and as far east as Ascension. So it seems that the perfect nesting beach may be as elusive a concept for sea turtles as it is for us.

Just as there are differences of opinion on the adequacy of nesting beaches, so are there differences concerning where the best feeding places are. On the black sand beaches of Tortuguero on Costa Rica's Caribbean coast, tens of thousands of green turtles have had the trailing edge of their front flippers tagged with numbered stainless steel clasps meant to identify the turtle should it be seen again. Hundreds have been, most often by someone who has captured the turtle to eat it. The annual tagging effort was a study of green turtle dispersal begun by Archie Carr in the late 1950s. Carr hoped that anyone who saw the turtle and noticed the tag would read the terse reward statement and return address printed on it and post a letter describing where they saw it. They did. In terms of numbers of verified connections between a nesting beach and its turtles' foraging grounds, the Tortuguero tagging project has been the most successful study of sea turtle dispersal ever conducted.

My opportunities to discuss the subject of sea turtles with Professor Carr came only in the final years of his life. I recall him as active and vibrant, and although he was not taking on graduate students, he offered a tour of his office at the University of Florida and introductions to faculty who might accept a student interested in questions about sea turtles. There in his office I first saw the map — a chart of the Caribbean studded with hundreds of green pins designating the tag-recovery locations from well over a thousand green turtles tagged at Tortuguero and seen again elsewhere. There was a dense cluster of green north of Costa Rica off the eastern tip of Nicaragua — the Miskito Cays. And there were pins farther to the north off Yucatan, Jamaica, Cuba, Hispaniola, and the Bahamas. To the south, green pins poked from waters off Panama and Colombia, and eastward to Venezuela. In one sense, the map was a grim statement of how broadly the taste for green turtle affected the population whose reproduction centered on Tortuguero. In another sense, it showed how widespread the population was, even though their breeding focused on only a tiny strip of Costa Rica shoreline. It may be that maps like this also represent the diasporas and pilgrimages of lesser-known sea turtle populations as well.

Of all the sea turtles, hawksbills may make some of the shortest commutes between feeding areas and nesting beaches. But many of these trips are likely to take turtles over open waters between islands, and from one country's waters to another. Rare is the sea turtle of any species that lives out its life in the seas of a single nation. Thus, the migrations of sea turtles make them both multinational and international travelers, linking them as a resource to human communities spread throughout the globe.

Navigational Talents of Animal Savants

Most of us would never strike out on our own to travel the world without the technological trappings designed and built by legions of brilliant scientists and engineers. Without technology, we are lost. It makes us realize what a tricky business navigation is. Without our satellite receivers, maps, compasses, and clocks, we are naked and, when it comes to navigating, a bit stupid.

The ability of sea turtles to travel the globe and return precisely to specific locations astounds us. This is partly because we admire the talent, much in the way that we admire the geniuses of our own species. But the special talents of sea turtles astonish us further by the humble package that contains them. After all, sea turtles are but simple reptiles, without the traits of sapience we reserve largely for ourselves. Yet, they are creatures that accomplish remarkable feats of intelligence. They seem to know where they are, and almost wherever they are taken, they are able to direct themselves to where they would like to be. They do this by using senses, memory, and calculations of direction that seem to show absolute brilliance. But in the simple intelligence tests that are often applied to animals — for instance, quickness to learn where food is by trial and error — reptiles as a group do poorly compared to larger-brained creatures.

Sea turtles are animal savants. By comparison to other animals, they may be either simple or clever. As such, they accompany a host of other brilliant simpletons, from birds to insects, which have also shown their navigational talents. However, sea turtles remain unique in their aptitude for the specific tasks that allow them to survive in their own world. Pinpoint navigation across an ocean to a dot of land may have had its origins within the simplest animals, but the expression of this skill by sea turtles seems singularly appropriate for their unique lives. At some time when we are able to fully understand the awareness that sea turtles have of their world, we will have taken great strides towards better understanding our own.

This hawksbill, at home on its neighborhood reef in the South China Sea, knows its world in a way we can only imagine.

*The sun sets on a Pacific beach in Costa Rica as an 'arribada'
begins. Before the night is over, thousands of female olive ridleys will
crowd onto this small stretch of beach to lay their eggs.*

The Role of Sea Turtles

The role that sea turtles play in running the world – their ecology – is difficult for us to comprehend. After all, sea turtles live on a grand geographic scale, which greatly limits our ability to observe and measure their effect on the equally vast ecosystems they occupy. These systems are generally more poorly known than terrestrial systems. As in most animals, the ecological place of sea turtles is determined not only by their presence but also by their abundance. So in a world where we have only shadows of historical numbers, the influence of sea turtles must be subdued. With the decline of sea turtles, many aspects of their world, and of our world, have changed.

One conspicuous example of an important remaining influence between sea turtles and their environment can be seen in profound events that occur where we terrestrial beings can easily watch, the *arribadas* of ridley turtles. In some populations of the olive ridley, these events are still prominent enough to deserve a description as grand ecological phenomena. In Spanish, the word *arribada* simply translates as 'arrival', an English term that seems to fall short in describing the event's significance.

One stage for this remarkable gathering of organisms is a short stretch of dark volcanic sand on Costa Rica's Pacific shore. Most nights out of the year, this beach near the tiny village of Ostional may see one to several olive ridleys, locally called tortuga golfina, emerging from the sea to put their eggs in the sand. But once each month during the last half of the rainy season, a ridley convention builds. Responding in unison to cues that are not well understood, olive ridley females converge by multitudes into the waters out from the line of breakers tumbling onto Ostional Beach. Some lunar influence seems present because of the monthly separation of events, although many phases of the moon may light these gatherings. Similarly, a strong wind out to sea seems to correlate with ridley arrivals, but not always. Whatever

the synergy of weather, tide, and moon convincing ridleys they should nest, the argument must be compelling, for only a small fraction of ridleys choose to nest without the company of this massive building crowd.

Just before nightfall on the first night of an *arribada*, the gathered turtles begin their invasion of the beach. Like landing craft they emerge from the wave-wash and trudge up the beach. Some crawl shoulder to shoulder, some advance on others, and some rest momentarily and are nudged aside by the more anxious among the building throngs. By midnight, advancing waves of domed silhouettes completely fill the lower beach, and sights and sounds of tens of thousands of digging, huffing, sand-scattering turtles consume the upper beach. With a beach length of only 800 linear meters, every meter of Ostional's shore will be visited by more than a hundred nesting ridleys over the next two or three nights.

To a naive witness of this event, the invasion is a disaster. Turtle after turtle thrusting her hind flippers into the sand withdraws the sticky yolk from pierced eggs that were buried by the turtle she had just pushed aside. Turtles covering their nests unearth more eggs, flinging shells, and dripping egg contents upon themselves and their dozen or so diligently nesting neighbors. And to this carnage come silhouettes of cautiously curious animals drawn by the thick smell of fat-rich yolks. In the darkness, feral dogs and raccoons tunnel into partially exposed nests amidst the vastly spread pile of turtles pursuing their single-minded task.

At the lightening of the hazy sky over the jungle behind the beach, only a thousand or so ridleys remain from the tens of thousands that had visited. As they crawl down the beach to the sea, they scuff through drifts of gleaming eggshells that cover the breadth of the beach like a dusting of snow. In the creeping daylight, raccoons and dogs hustle with distended bellies through flocks of black vultures hopping and skipping as the skimmed golden riches drip from their beaks.

This visible scene of devastation overlies a less evident one. Infused in the sand are the turtle-deposited nutrients that have turned the beach from antiseptic wave-washed sand into an enormous petri dish rife with pathogens. Developing eggs that have not been penetrated by insect larvae frequently succumb to infections from the soup of bacteria and fungi in which they incubate. Of the immense load thrust upon the beach, only a small fraction of the eggs will produce hatchlings. Although the fraction of hatched eggs may be small, the great number of original eggs laid makes for a profoundly important mass departure of hatchings some two moons after the tumult of the *arribada*.

Hatchlings seem to be everywhere. Over only a few nights, one million or more tiny dark gray ridleys bubble from nests and flow down the beach to the sea. It is the event that brings fruition to the preceding *arribada*, and it is every bit as popular with the local predators. Although the nocturnal timing and surprise of this potential bounty allows most hatchlings passage by overwhelmed beach crabs and night herons, tardy hatchlings still on the beach at break of day become helpless tidbits for vultures, cara caras, coatis, and dogs.

Taking stock of effects on the slice of the world where olive ridleys have chosen to nest, we see an animal with many important relationships. On the short Ostional beach alone, nesting ridleys bring nearly 4.5 million pounds of eggs each season, much of which is converted into other organisms, including human beings. The few hundred people who live in the Ostional village gather roughly 10 per cent of the eggs laid, for consumption throughout Costa Rica. This predation is managed by the government to occur mostly at the beginning stages of each *arribada*, a strategy that is thought to ensure that mostly 'doomed' eggs are taken. Of course, also in the line of benefiting predators and scavengers are the multitudes of other mammals, birds,

reptiles, fishes, crustaceans, insects, fungi, and bacteria that eat turtle eggs, or that eat the things that eat turtle eggs.

In all, the *arribada* phenomenon is a grand ecological event. Yet, the richness brought to a tiny area of sand and its adjacent waters does not explain the reason for an *arribada*. Selection for this intense reproductive gathering lies with its success in making little turtles, not with feeding the neighborhood. So, is it successful? With its persistence, we assume so. Although the mortality of eggs is high, the hatchlings that emerge do so in a massive, largely unanticipated pulse that probably overwhelms and surprises potential predators. But it is also clear that the *arribada* is not the single correct answer to the problem of maximizing reproductive success. Apparently, the solitary ridleys that nest on the beaches fringing the main *arribada* beach and during periods between mass nestings benefit from a strategy of inconspicuous 'flight beneath the radar' that rivals the bold confrontation of *arribada* turtles.

The unintentional contribution made by sea turtles to the coastal ecosystems they breed in is significant for many major nesting beaches. In their calculation of the nutrients contributed by Florida loggerheads to their nesting beaches, researchers at the University of Florida found these turtles to be major sources of nitrogen and phosphorous. In the 660,000 lb (300,000 kg) or so of eggs that loggerheads bury on Florida beaches every year, much remains as the organic residue of reproductive failure. This lingering nitrogen and phosphorous, which amounts to thousands of pounds of fertilizer each year, greatly benefits the plants that struggle to grow on the nutrient-poor dunes. In this transportation of nutrients between sea and land, sea turtles glean energy and compounds critical to life over hundreds of thousands of square miles and intensely focus their ecological delivery onto single stretches of sandy coastline.

Although the effects of sea turtles on land are easiest for us to see, their effects on marine ecosystems are certainly the most

The unhatched eggs left behind in the nests of these green turtle hatchlings are an important nutrient source for beach plants.

Hawksbills eat a particular array of sponges and fulfil a unique ecological role on coral reefs.

important. In what may be a parallel between grassy ecosystems on land and in the sea, a single species of grazing animal can be instrumental to the basic function of an ecosystem on which thousands of species depend. Green turtles certainly were, and to a lesser extent are now, influential grazers of seagrass and algal pastures.

Sea turtle ecologist Karen Bjorndal has estimated that the Caribbean basin once supported over 30 million adult green turtles. This figure is comparable to the abundance of American bison that once grazed the great tall-grass prairies of North America. Like the great herds of bison, Caribbean green turtles must have been integral to the functioning of the marine meadows they foraged in. Dr. Bjorndal and Alan Bolten have speculated that the Caribbean seagrass pastures of today, grazed by green turtles at only about 5 per cent of their historical abundance, have undergone important changes. Before North and South America were on the maps of technologically capable Europeans, the vast shallows of the greater Caribbean were crowded with green turtles, seagrass meadows surged with productivity from the continual cropping by serrated turtle beaks, and nutrients were spread widely with the cigars of dung that traced the movements of green turtles throughout their broad range. Today, many grazers of seagrasses remain, but the unique close-cropping grazing style of the green turtle is far less influential. On Caribbean seagrass pastures of today, one commonly sees long uncropped blades encrusted with surface-growing organisms. These grass blades often go ungrazed, brown with age, and detach to lock their nutrients within accumulating detritus. Much of the nutrient store held in the blades of seagrasses may be liberated only as the dead vegetation slowly rots away. Due to the decline of green turtles, an ecologically important short-circuit to the seagrass detritus cycle has begun to fail.

Sea turtles tend to be generalist feeders, with lists of food items that include many dozens of species. Even leatherbacks, with a narrow definition of what makes good food that includes only animals with the consistency of jelly, and green turtles, who as larger turtles eat mostly vegetation, have relatively wide preferences in terms of numbers of species eaten. These catholic tastes tend to minimize effects from sea turtle predation on any one organism (with the possible exception of the green turtle's favorite greens, turtle grass, *Thalassia*), but spread the influence of sea turtles around the breadth of the ecosystems they inhabit.

Green turtles eat mostly seagrasses and algae but will feed opportunistically on animals including jellyfish.

As prey, hatchling sea turtles fit into the diet of 100 or more species of fishes and marine birds. But as sea turtles attain size, fewer and fewer predators at sea are able to eat them. One ocean predator that stands out as equipped to eat large sea turtles is the tiger shark (*Galeocerdo cuvier*). These grand fish have the gape, jaw strength, and robust tooth shape that make them a specialist in chewing large chunks off big tough animals, including sea turtles. A tiger shark's teeth have a thick broad base and a laterally directed point that creates a V-shaped serrate cutting edge. Their advantage allows the shark to easily remove limbs or extract a mouthful of bony carapace from large turtles either living or dead. Although it is not uncommon for living adult sea turtles to have a broad crescent-shaped piece missing from the edge of their shell, or to have a missing chunk of carapace correspond with a flipper amputation, predation by sharks and mortality from their attacks are by no means rampant. In sea turtles that achieve adult size, predation other than by man is probably a rarity. Many turtles that are attacked by sharks survive even after the shock and blood loss of a ragged limb amputation, an astounding feat that seems near the pinnacle of toughness in the animal world.

Relationships between sea turtles and their world extend to a variety of animals that call a turtle their home. Most species of sea turtles have at least a few tag-along species growing on them. These tag-alongs are commensals — animals and plants that gain by living on a turtle but that have little effect upon their host, either positive or negative. Loggerhead sea turtles are exceptional for their tolerance of a diverse array of clinging commensal creatures. On a single loggerhead, one might find dozens of hitchhiking species.

Perhaps it is the relative sluggishness of loggerheads relative to the other sea turtle species. Or, perhaps it is the crusty irregularity of a loggerhead's carapace, a surface not unlike the hardened benthic substrate over which they commonly feed. But whatever traits bring about their propensity to host rides, many loggerheads find themselves as a living, traveling reef. To pore over a loggerhead's encrusted carapace is to witness an entire community of normally bottom-growing organisms — barnacles of several species, long tufts of colonial hydroids, thumbnail-long amphipods with leg specializations for clinging and lashing at tiny prey that flow by the turtle, shelled mollusks of all types, marine worms, small to hand-sized crabs, sea urchins, sea cucumbers, many species of macro algae, and even stony corals.

At least one barnacle species is almost obligated to be on a sea turtle — the turtle barnacle, *Chelonibia testudinaria*. All sea turtle species are known to sport these sessile crustaceans, which are seldom found anyplace else. Whereas turtle barnacles typically grow on a turtle's shell or head and become as large as half a golf ball, other smaller species are also common. One group of barnacles has members that embed themselves in a sea turtle's skin or that thrive attached to the turtle's bulbous tongue.

It seems clear that the barnacles benefit from easier access to items of food that are either disturbed by the feeding turtle or that flow with the sheet of water over the turtle as it swims. Heavily fouled turtles, as some loggerheads can be, probably suffer some decrease in swimming speed. This added drag would probably matter most for the smallest turtles, which have yet to outgrow the mouths of potential predators. Yet, these smallest turtles are also the fastest growing, and in frequently shedding their shell scutes they may be able to keep their backs clean by periodically ridding themselves of their acquired hangers-on.

Even fish capitalize on the habitat that sea turtles have to offer. Suckerfish (remoras) may be so numerous that they drape a large turtle like a flowing cloak. Small green turtles I have seen have had suckerfish as large as themselves suctioned to their plastron. Sometimes, the presence of these fish appears a bit annoying to the turtle, who may squirm to no avail in attempts to detach its unwanted fishy appendage. But other relationships between fish and turtles seem beneficial to both parties. Hawksbills and green turtles are known to frequent predetermined stations on a reef and assume a neck-out and flipper-spread posture in order to invite visits by cleaner fishes. With the dreamy look of a cat having its chin scratched, a supplicant turtle receives attention from a crew of wrasses, gobies, or tangs, which glean algae and tiny invertebrates with precise nibbles.

Suckerfish rely on a passing leatherback for safety and feeding opportunities.

The Species

How Many Kinds of Sea Turtles are there?

There are seven species of sea turtles... or perhaps eight. It is a debate that reaffirms the uncertainty of science, and it is a controversy that adds a bit more ambiguity to an already mysterious group of animals.

When most people think about species, they think of organisms with a particular look that are grouped together because they are similar. But the concept of a species is broader and more detailed than this, and it is an integral component to understanding how living things evolve, fit into their worlds, and interact with each other.

In practice, sea turtles and most other creatures are divided into species by two general sets of criteria: how they look and how they act. The look of a sea turtle involves much about its form – ranging from highly variable traits like size and color to less variable traits like bone sutures, scale counts, and the presence or absence of unique structures. How a sea turtle acts, or has acted, applies to whether turtles from a recognized group would ever, could ever, interbreed with turtles from another recognized group and make little turtles that themselves grow up to breed. Underlying each of these concepts is the genetic makeup of a sea turtle. Genes, of course, determine how a sea turtle looks and acts, but they also reveal a turtle's history. Studying the genetics of a group of sea turtles can reveal roughly how long the group has been separated (reproductively isolated) from another sea turtle group, how great that separation is, and whether it is enough to warrant labeling the group a separate species.

The first taxonomists to begin classifying sea turtle species used common sense to guide them and did not have access to information about genetics. Thus, sea turtles that looked different were often labeled as being different. However, some species were lumped together because rare turtles were thought to be variants of more common ones. In the eighteenth and nineteenth centuries, it was difficult to determine how different a group of turtles had to be in order to be a species.

The olive ridley has an open-ocean lifestyle that differs from its cousin, Kemp's ridley.

To truly represent a group of animals well, taxonomists like to study many individuals throughout their range. Yet, many sea turtles are large animals with wide distributions. One doesn't just fill up museum drawers with dozens of sea turtles like a curator can with pinned butterflies and stuffed mouse skins. So on occasion, a great deal of inference about species was made from a single specimen, or from just a few of them coming from a narrow slice of a turtle's range.

The green turtle is a widely distributed species with much variation in adult size and appearance.

With all the obvious limitations of studying specimens throughout their range at the time of the mid eighteenth century, Carl Linnaeus (considered the father of taxonomy) recognized three sea turtle species (the only three he had opportunity to study) and lumped them into a single genus grouping along with all the other turtles. Since then, five additional species have been recognized (or

Hawksbills occasionally hybridize with loggerheads or green turtles.

discovered). It is both remarkable and reassuring that the common-sense species descriptions from limited assessments made about 150 to 250 years ago apply to many of the species commonly recognized today. However, one of the eight species recently described has retained a controversial status and is widely believed to be a set of populations with unique traits rather than a separate species. This controversial species is the east Pacific green turtle (or black turtle), *Chelonia agassizii*, a sea turtle that many maintain is just a smaller and darkly pigmented green turtle. In deference to the majority opinion that black turtles are a variation of the green turtle, more discussion of this controversy is within the green turtle account on page 70.

Sea Turtle Hybrids

Sea turtles, it seems, hybridize. Reports have described turtles captured from the wild that by all appearances, and by examination of their genetics, are offspring of green turtles and loggerheads, of green turtles and hawksbills, of loggerheads and hawksbills, and of loggerheads and Kemp's ridleys. This in itself does not break the species rules, unless these hybrids go about reproducing themselves, which apparently happens.

To completely comprehend the shock one should feel at this revelation, one needs to understand the distance separating the species of sea turtles involved in these hybrid pairings. Depending on the pairing, these hybrid offspring had mothers and fathers whose lineages have differentiated from each other over 10-75 million years of evolution. It is equivalent to the distance separating horses and dogs, mice and monkeys, or cats and rabbits. Quite possibly, sea turtles are distinguished among the vertebrates in having the most distantly related lineages capable of producing successful hybrids in nature.

Sea turtle hybrids are odd and seem to be rare. Yet, whatever disadvantages hybrids possess have not kept some from reaching adulthood. In at least one instance, probable hybrids have laid eggs on nesting beaches, and those eggs have produced living hatchlings. This does break the species rules (as if we should expect the natural world to follow our rules), but more importantly, it raises questions about whether declines in sea turtle abundance and rarity of mates may be changing the very integrity of the species we think we know.

It is not easy to place sea turtles into simple, neat, species categories.

Green Turtle

Scientific Name

Chelonia mydas.
Named for the Greek roots for turtle and for the king of Phrygia to whom Dionysus gave the power to turn all he touched to gold.

Other common names

Other English names given the green turtle include green sea turtle, greenback turtle, soup turtle, and edible turtle. The distinctive form in the eastern Pacific is known as the black turtle. In Latin America, common names include tortuga verde and tortuga blanca (Spanish). Hundreds of other common names vary among cultures.

Size and weight

Adult female green turtles weigh between 175 and 485 lb (80 and 220 kg), with a shell straight-length of 30 to 47 in (80 to 120 cm).

The largest green turtles reach 153 cm in straight shell length and 650 lb (295 kg) in weight. Adult males are slightly smaller than females.

Distribution

Tropical and warm temperate marine waters worldwide. Nesting occurs on beaches mostly in the tropics, the major nesting beaches lying within latitudes 20° north and south.

General Appearance

Green turtles are sleek, powerful swimmers that grow to the largest size of any of the hard-shelled sea turtles. Contrary to the suggestion of color in their name, green turtles do not appear very green. Their common name comes from a description of their appearance on the inside rather than on the outside. When the insides of a green turtle are brought into the light, the fatty tissues show a greenish hue. The name is testament to how green turtles first came to be known, namely, as food. In fact, the greenest thing about a green turtle is likely to be green turtle soup. The broth is rendered from the calipash, a light green, fatty, gelatinous meat lined in irregular patches inside the carapace, and calipee, a similar light yellow-green meat attached to the interior of the plastron.

On the outside, green turtles are lovely animals. Their shells are often un-fouled by barnacles or other clinging creatures, which allows the coloration of their patterned shell to be clearly visible.

Adult green turtles vary in shell coloration between populations. A typical carapace coloration is a brown or olive background blotched with lighter patches and spattered with occasional dark brown or black. Variations in this pattern include mottling of brown, yellow, olive, and gray throughout nebulous background color. In the east Pacific green turtle, the adult's carapace is dark olive, dark gray, or black. Plastron coloration in adult green turtles ranges from blotched olive gray in east Pacific turtles, to butter yellow or dark amber in most other populations.

Juvenile green turtles are often vibrantly patterned. Carapace scutes and larger scales of the head and flippers typically show streaks of brown, olive, gold, black, and reddish brown, streaks that radiate as sunbursts from the rear margin of each scale. An imperceptibly thin film of algae may make some turtles appear greenish; although the upper sides of most turtles seem brown from a distance. Juveniles have a lighter yellow plastron than adults do, and the plastrons of the smallest

Adult green turtles feed on marine plants and reach an average weight of about 350 lb (160 kg).

juveniles (from the oceanic stage) are immaculately white.

In most green turtles, the scales crowning the head and on the upper surface of the flippers match the coloration of the carapace. Outlines of the scales (the seams) are lighter than the scales themselves. These light olive or yellow scale outlines are often the same color as the skin covering the shoulders and neck, which has sparsely scattered small scales.

Hatchlings are about 2 in (5 cm) in shell length. Their coloration is dark blue-gray to black on their upper surface and pure white below. A hatchling's carapace and flippers are thinly rimmed with white, and dark centers of their lateral head scales often give an appearance of having freckled cheeks. The skin covering a hatchling's shoulders and neck ranges from olive to blue gray.

The shape of a green turtle's shell is a teardrop, flattened below, domed above, and slightly flanged at the sides. The shell's surface is smooth, with scutes that do not overlap and that are typically shed in one piece as the turtle grows. The number of carapace scutes is almost invariable in green turtles, making these counts useful in helping to separate green turtles from other sea turtle species. Green turtles have four lateral (also called costal) scutes on either side of the midline of their carapace. Their head scales are also distinctive in that there are only two elongate scales (called prefrontals) between the turtle's eyes.

Although there is noticeable variation in size, shape, and color among green turtle populations throughout their worldwide range, green turtles of the eastern Pacific seem the most different. East Pacific green turtles are considered by some biologists and many casual observers to belong to a different subspecies of green turtle, or even to a different species altogether. East Pacific green turtles are also known as black turtles, or in western Mexico where they nest, as tortuga prieta or tortuga negra.

Among the characters separating east Pacific green turtles from other green turtles around the world, the most vivid separator is the black turtle's coloration. Black turtles are as dark as their name suggests, having gray, dark gray, or black coloration over their entire body as adults. These turtles are also smaller as adults than are green turtles from other populations, averaging only 155 to 265 lb (70 to 120 kg), and their number of eggs per clutch is also small, averaging about 70. Black turtles have a slightly different shape to their carapace, which is more vaulted and narrower at its rear than in other green turtles, and which has arched indentations over its rear flippers.

Although the physical attributes of black turtles hint that they are distinct from other green turtles, their genes tell us this is not necessarily so. Careful examinations of their genetics reveal that black turtles are no more separated from the global group of green turtle assemblages than are many other populations of green turtles. However, many biologists agree that the black turtle is isolated in its distribution, is significantly different from other populations, and may at least be an incipient species; that is, one that may be in the process of emerging as a unique and reproductively isolated form.

All green turtles have a blunt head and a rounded leading edge to their beak. Their lower jaw sheath is coarsely serrated and has a sharp cusp at its tip. The upper beak has ridges on its inner cutting edge, which with the serrated lower beak make for an efficient set of seagrass clippers. If perturbed, a green turtle may clench its jaws, grinding together the rough edges of its beak to make a creaking sound.

Although a relatively good look at a green turtle is possible in shallow clear waters, a surfacing turtle is likely to offer only a brief glimpse before disappearing beneath a boil. The closest most of us are likely to get to a green turtle is on a nesting beach. On a nesting beach at night, one can identify a green turtle by the silhouette of her domed shell and small head. As adults, green turtles have the smallest head in proportion to their body size of all the sea turtles. But even if one arrives too late to see

The algae growing on a green turtle's shell provide a grazing opportunity for gold-ring surgeonfish living on a Hawaiian reef.

a green turtle attempting to nest, her tracks on the beach are enough to determine that a green turtle has visited. A green turtle's track is a symmetrical series of flipper gouges a little over 3 ft (1 m) in width. Diagonal marks on the track's edge are from the turtle's long front flippers, and parallel marks on either side

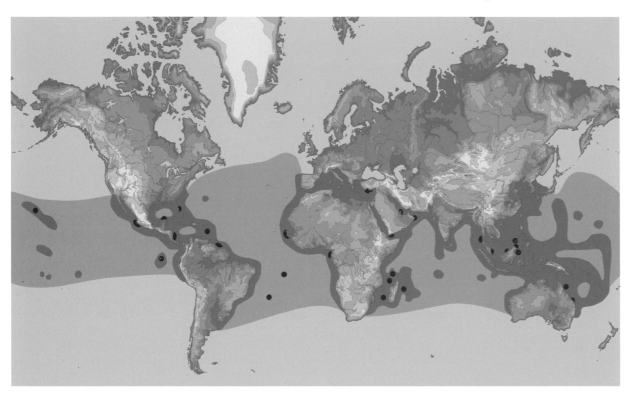

■ *Major Nesting Beaches*　　**■** *Large Juveniles & Adults*　　**■** *Oceanic Juveniles*

of the midline are from the simultaneous push from the turtle's rear flippers. Along the track center is commonly a pencil-thin tail drag punctuated by points where the turtle rested between each simultaneous heave from her flippers. A green turtle's nest site appears as if it were the result of a subsurface explosion. On soft sand beaches, a nesting green turtle leaves a pit 7 ft (2 m) in diameter and more than 20 in (0.5 m) deep. The pit lies at one end of an oval mound of sand as wide as the pit and up to several feet long.

Distribution and Movements

Green turtles swim in all of the world's warm-water oceans (Atlantic, Indian, and Pacific) and are most common within and just outside of the tropics. Although green turtles are found feeding in shallow waters as far north as Bermuda and as far south as Brisbane, Australia, they are essentially tropical sea turtles. They are known from the waters of roughly 140 countries and have been recorded to nest in 80 of these. Their nesting beaches are also mostly within the tropics, with all of the major nesting beaches lying between latitudes 20° north and south.

Within their global range green turtles make extensive movements but are unlikely to pass between oceans. Green turtles from temperate waters are known to migrate north and south with the seasons, although turtles in more tropical locations may remain within the same waters for years. Females migrating from feeding areas to nesting beaches make the most directed movements. A green turtle migrating to nest may swim dozens of miles a day to reach a familiar 110 yd (100 m) stretch of beach lying 1240 miles (2000 km) or more away from where she feeds.

Life History

Like the other sea turtles, a green turtle begins its life as a hatchling escaping from a sandy nest. After they enter the sea as hatchlings, green turtles are seldom seen until they reappear as dinner-plate sized juveniles swimming in shallow near-shore waters. Their absence during a period of growth out in deep ocean waters has been described as the 'lost year', although biologists now feel that this oceanic stage is probably 2 to 7 years. The size of green turtles when they leave the open ocean is known to be about 8 to 14 in (20 to 35 cm) in shell length, but their rate of growth is unknown, which leaves the precise duration of this oceanic stage a mystery. During the oceanic stage, it is thought that green turtles circle ocean basins riding upon their sluggish swirl of surface currents. It is interesting that Atlantic green turtles exit the open ocean at about 10 in (25 cm) shell length, and Pacific green turtles, which may have circled an ocean twice the size of the Atlantic, do not appear in coastal waters until they are 14 in (35 cm) in shell length.

Green turtles become better known to biologists as they forage on seagrass and algal pastures around islands and within coastal lagoons, bays, and reef tracts. Some juvenile green turtles live in areas where larger green turtles occur, and other green turtles tend to segregate their feeding areas by size. For instance, only juveniles between 8 and 28 in (20 and 70 cm) in shell length are found in shallow Florida coastal waters. Turtles ready to take the next step to maturity apparently leave Florida for the western Caribbean. Green turtles tagged in eastern Florida by Doc Ehrhart and his students at the University of Central Florida have shown up off Nicaragua, where green turtles larger than 28 in (70 cm), including adults, commonly feed on vast seagrass pastures.

A green turtle's growth rate slows greatly as it ages. Its mass increases 100-fold during the turtle's first few years, between hatching and the turtle's return to shallow waters. Over the following two decades or so, a juvenile green turtle's mass will increase about 20-fold. Then, at about half of its adult weight, a green turtle will spend the next two or more decades doubling its mass. At adulthood, growth is almost imperceptible even over periods of many years. Based on rates of growth seen in wild turtles from many locations, green turtles reach mature size in 20 to 50 years – the longest generation time of any of the sea turtles.

Adult females migrate to reproduce about every 2 to 4 years and lay eggs in 1 to 7 nests separated by roughly two-week intervals. Green turtle eggs are white spheres that average

Adult green turtles from the Galapagos are smaller and have darker pigmentation than those from other ocean regions.

about 2 oz (45 g) and produce a hatchling that averages about 1 oz (25 g). The number of eggs in a green turtle's clutch varies between populations, mostly according to the sizes of nesting females. A population with females maturing at a small size (for example, 30 in /80 cm in shell length) may average only 80 eggs per clutch, whereas a population with larger females (45 in / 115 cm shell length) may average 145 eggs per clutch. Males generally intercept females to mate along migration pathways or just off the nesting beach.

Green turtles are the lawn mowers of the sea.
They maintain close-cropped plots of seagrass that are more productive
and more nutritious than that of ungrazed areas.

Diet

Green turtles begin their lives as omnivores feeding opportunistically in the open ocean. There are few observations indicating what the smallest green turtles feed on. In young-of-the-year turtles that had been swept by tropical storms onto Florida's Atlantic coast, little green turtles were found to have eaten plants and animals, including tiny hydroids, crustaceans, bryozoans, and algae that are common from the floating patches of golden sargasso weed adrift in the Atlantic's currents. Slightly larger green turtles, those that have grown to nearly 8 in (20 cm) in carapace length but still bear the brilliant white plastron of an oceanic turtle, are occasionally found with open-ocean animals such as by-the-wind sailors (*Velella*, a colonial hydroid) and purple sea snails (*Janthina*) in their stomachs.

When they settle into shallow coastal waters, green turtles take up a vegetarian diet. As herbivores, green turtles feed on a wide variety of algal and seagrass species. A rich community of microbes that they maintain in their gut aids their digestion of this plant material. Like animals that graze on land, green turtles are not able to break down the polymer chains of plant cellulose, and without the tiny symbiotic organisms living within them, they would starve. The bacterial and protozoan gut flora of green turtles is thought to be specific to the cellulose of particular plant groups. Thus, individual green turtles are often found to specialize on only algae or on only seagrasses.

Green turtles in the wild eat little animal material, but occasionally take in sponges and small invertebrates that might be consumed incidentally. However, when given the opportunity to eat animals in captivity, green turtles can survive for years on nothing else. Growth rates for green turtles fed fish and squid in captivity are apparently higher than in the wild, but such a high-protein diet has been seen to bring about pathological conditions and occasional death.

Unique Traits

Green turtles are fast, agile swimmers and may be the swiftest of all the sea turtles. Their speed is such that a powerboat might have difficulty keeping up with a small green turtle even in clear shallow water. They startle easily, and when chased, a green turtle the size of a large Frisbee can surpass 12 miles (20 km) per hour, porpoise from the water during breaths, and dart at sharp angles to instantaneously change its direction. Especially in young green turtles, their seabottom-colored camouflage, vigorous swimming, and propensity to startle, reflect an animal that is probably exposed to occasional risks from large predators.

The excitability of a juvenile green turtle in the water belies its behavior when brought aboard a boat. Taken from their element, other sea turtles can be expected to crawl about, flap, and make attempts to bite their captors. But a captured green turtle quickly becomes calm and submissive, resting upon the deck with a bowed head while biologists make their measurements. Green turtles almost never attempt to bite the hand that studies them. But their serenity ends when they are brought near the water for their release. The sendoff typically results in an explosion of flapping and spray as the turtle enters the water.

Individuals in some green turtle populations show a behavioral trait that is unique among the sea turtles; they crawl upon land in daylight to bask. It is a trait seen only in turtles living around remote islands such as the Galapagos, Australia's Bountiful Island in the Gulf of Carpentaria, and the westernmost islands of the Hawaiian archipelago. Although it is not known exactly why green turtles bask, or why individuals from most populations do not, it is easy to see how the trait would be relegated to places that were only rarely visited by humans. Serenely soaking up sunshine on a beach is a behavior that would have been rapidly extinguished as the local native people partook of the easy harvest.

Conservation Status

We have only guesses about the historical abundance of green turtles, but they are believed to have been one of the most common large animals on the planet. Today, they are much more rare following profoundly rapid declines. Green turtles have been eaten by people for thousands of years, but we can be relatively

This tiny hatchling green turtle will not reach adulthood for about 30 years.

sure that the last few hundred years have taken the greatest toll on green turtles. Over this period, human population growth, technological advancement, and a specific taste for green turtles have led to a high risk of green turtles becoming extinct.

The carrying capacity of the Caribbean's seagrass pastures suggests that 30 to 40 million adult green turtles once filled this sea. But even if this estimate is high, harvest records of green turtles kept by Europeans reveal that they drew from a Caribbean population of at least a few million individuals. Today, only a thin fraction of this abundance remains.

Green turtles worldwide are depleted and most populations are continuing to decline. A recent global assessment of the green turtle by Jeff Seminoff describes how the world's green turtle population has declined by about half over the last three generations (about 140 years). Some populations have declined over 90 per cent during this period and several green turtle rookeries have been extirpated.

Some green turtle populations measured at their nesting beaches have been protected from harvest and are now beginning to show signs of recovery. But superimposed on our attempts to protect green turtles are numerous threats that have only been recognized recently. One of these new threats is a mysterious skin-tumor disease called fibropapillomatosis. In specific locations that are now spread throughout the turtle's range, green turtles have been appearing with warty growths as large as grapefruit on their skin and eyes. Such individuals frequently become entangled in debris, starve to death, or succumb to associated internal tumors that crowd major organs and blood vessels. A herpes-like virus is thought to cause the tumors, but the role of the turtle's environment in making them susceptible to the virus remains unclear.

The green turtle is considered by the IUCN, The World Conservation Union, to be Endangered. This status means that they face a very high risk of extinction in the wild in the near future, with 'very high risk' and 'near future' defined in terms of percent population decline over time measured in green turtle generations.

Green turtles were formerly one of the most common large animals on Earth.

Loggerhead Sea Turtle

Scientific Name

Caretta caretta.
New Latin modification of the French word *caret* for turtle.

Other common names

Other English names include loggerhead, loggerhead seaturtle, and logrit (Caribbean). In Latin America, common names include caguama and cabezona (Spanish). Many other common names vary among cultures.

Size and weight

Adult female loggerheads weigh between 155 and 375 lb (70 and 170 kg), with a shell straight-length of 30 to 43 in (80 to 110 cm). Adult males are slightly larger than females.

Distribution

Warm temperate marine waters and into the tropics, but only occasionally found within 8 degrees of the equator. Most nesting occurs on warm temperate beaches or just inside the tropics.

General Appearance

Much of a loggerhead's appearance gives the impression of a tough, worn, weathered brute of a turtle. If the smooth, rounded, unfettered form of a green turtle can be said to be feminine, then a typical loggerhead, scarred, notched, and bedecked with barnacles, might be described as having a decidedly masculine roughness around the edges. Yet, many would argue that loggerheads have a noble beauty all their own.

The coloration of an adult loggerhead's shell is often partially obscured by a carpet of macroalgae, large barnacles, and a varied host of clinging tagalongs. Where the shell is visible, it is dark reddish brown. On close examination, the brown color can be seen to come from a radiating pattern of orange, red, brown, and black smears within each shell scute. The shell scutes are frequently fragmented and peeling where many old thin layers of keratin flake away as new scutes grow from underneath. At whatever rate a loggerhead is able to shed its acquired load of commensal organisms by losing its shell scutes, it is not frequent enough to keep many loggerheads from looking much like the seabottom they rest on.

The scales atop the head of a loggerhead typically take the reddish-brown coloration of the turtle's shell, although the sides of the head and neck are nearly always a bright golden yellow. This same yellow coloration covers the shoulders and the entire underside of the turtle. The upper surfaces of the flippers have coin-sized scales that are most frequently orange-brown and outlined in yellow.

The loggerhead's shell is a stout wedge shape with a width about three-quarters its length. Loggerheads have five lateral scutes on either side of their carapace midline. On the head, loggerheads are distinguished from other sea turtles in having two pairs of prefrontal scales between the eyes, which often have one or two intervening scales.

The loggerhead's massive head is its namesake. The width of the average head is often substantially larger than our own. A loggerhead's upper jaw sheath is highly thickened, with a curved leading edge and a blunt cusp. The lower jaw is sheathed in equally thick keratin and has a broad crushing surface at its cusped end. Bulging jowls betray a robust machinery of bony framework and muscle for pulverizing the hardest of mollusk

Adult loggerhead sea turtles feed on slow-moving, hard-shelled animals and reach an average weight of about 240 lb (110 kg).

shells. A perturbed loggerhead will occasionally grind its jaws and produce a sound like the creaking of a strained timber.

Hatchlings are about 2 in (4.5 cm) in shell length. Their coloration varies greatly from light (tan or pale gray) to dark (brown, charcoal, or black). Most hatchlings are countershaded light below and dark above, but others may be uniformly pigmented. The trailing margins of the shell and flippers are often lighter than

Loggerhead hatchlings vary in coloration from blonde to black.

the hatchlings' background color. The lightest hatchlings often have darker centers to their cheek scutes, giving them a freckled look. The carapace is lumpy with the raised scutes that will later become thickened keels as hatchlings grow into juveniles.

As a young loggerhead grows to be larger than a handful, its carapace and other dorsal scutes take on an orange-brown color with faint patterns of radiating streaks within each scute. Their lower surfaces become amber yellow, the hue of vibrant *Sargassum* weed. During the first half of their development, a period that corresponds with life in the open ocean, juvenile loggerheads bear thick, rear-pointing spiny keels on their shell. Three keels above and

two below, in addition to serrations at the rear margins of the shell, must make a young loggerhead a tough target for oceanic sharks.

Larger juveniles, those greater than 18 in (45 cm) shell length, have begun to grow out of their thickened shell scutes. Toward adulthood, their shells elongate, scutes become thinner and flaky, marginal serrations disappear, and the only remaining topography to the shell is a pronounced hump toward the rear over the turtle's sequestered hips. Larger immatures and adults also differ from small juveniles in having three thickened traction scales on the underside of each rear flipper and two to three similarly callused scales under the wrists of their fore-flippers. These scales are testimony to the propensity of larger loggerheads to occupy shallow waters where they crawl along the seabottom.

A casual observer seeing a loggerhead breathe at the surface will recognize the turtle by its large golden and orange-brown head. On occasion, mariners may have the opportunity to pass closely by a loggerhead seemingly sleeping at the surface. There, an observer can be relatively certain that a large-headed orange and brown turtle with scattered barnacles is a loggerhead. On a nesting beach at night, a female loggerhead can be identified by the silhouette of her somewhat straight-backed shell and large head. The track left by a nesting loggerhead is an asymmetrical series of paisley swirls from the rear flippers on either side of a flat, smooth, wavy center mark. A typical track is a little less than 3 ft (1 m) in width and is usually without a tail drag down the center. A loggerhead's nest is generally a 7 ft (2 m) wide circular mound of sand next to a slightly smaller hemispherical pit. Loggerhead nest pits and mounds are much less extensive than those at green turtle nest sites.

Distribution and Movements

Loggerhead sea turtles inhabit the temperate and tropical waters of the Atlantic, Indian, and Pacific oceans. Their foraging range during the summer months extends well into New England in

North America, although the species is most common between latitudes 40 degrees north and south. Loggerheads are rare in the central tropics. Nesting beaches are distributed throughout roughly 50 countries but about 80–90 percent of nesting occurs in only two, the United States (southeast only) and Oman (mostly the island of Masirah).

The greatest voyages made by loggerheads are when they are small. Because these turtles spend such a long time as juveniles out in the open ocean (about a decade), they have ample opportunities for travel. Researchers believe that little loggerheads may travel tens of thousands of kilometers around their ocean's basin before they settle into a life closer to shore. Like other sea turtles from temperate waters, loggerheads tend to migrate north and south with the seasons, but turtles in warmer waters may stay put throughout the year. Females migrate from their feeding areas, which are typically located in subtropical waters, to nesting beaches lining more temperate regions.

Life History

Loggerhead hatchlings dispersing from their natal beaches begin an open-ocean life stage that lasts from 7 to 12 years. During this time young loggerheads feed near the surface and do a great deal of floating while ocean currents disperse them. But in-between bouts of laziness, young loggerheads can be surprisingly active.

Oceanic juvenile loggerheads large enough to require two hands to lift have been tracked using satellite transmitters attached by researchers working in the central Pacific and in the eastern Atlantic near the Azores and Madeira. In the persistent eddies that occur near the Azores, loggerheads were found

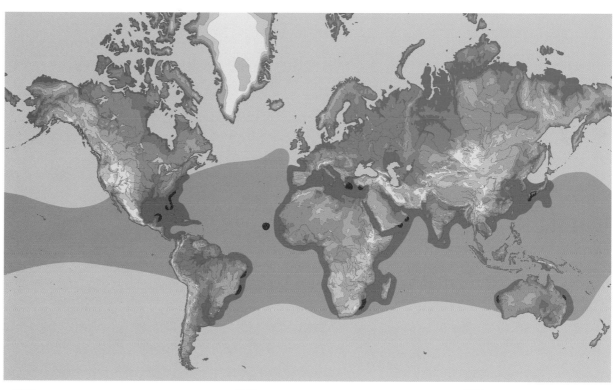

◼ *Major Nesting Beaches*　　◼ *Large Juveniles & Adults*　　◼ *Oceanic Juveniles*

to linger for months within the swirling waters above regional sea mounts waiting to become islands. Although the Azorean loggerheads spent 80 per cent of their time within 16 ft (5 m) of the surface and seldom averaged greater swimming than 800 yd (750 m) per hour, turtles would occasionally dive to 330 ft (100 m) or more. At Madeira, loggerheads were found to be more directed in their swimming and to eventually move far westward from where they were first satellite tagged. In the central Pacific, loggerheads were tracked as they moved along

A loggerhead sea turtle in shallow Bahamian waters crushes a
tulip shell formerly protecting a hermit crab. These turtles are able to feed on
a variety of hard-shelled animals that are armored against most predators.

oceanic fronts lying between water masses of high and low concentrations of plankton. In all cases, it seems that little loggerheads in the open ocean position themselves or are carried by currents into concentrations of floating and subsurface food in the open ocean.

From growth studies done by Karen Bjorndal and Alan Bolten of loggerheads at sea, it is apparent that they outgrow their ability to forage efficiently in the open ocean. The largest oceanic loggerheads have lower growth rates than do similar-sized loggerheads that have shifted to coastal foraging. So it seems that a loggerhead's dramatic change in habitat is driven by food opportunities. Although the wide ocean's surface may suit little loggerheads that can survive off the small drifting creatures swept into oceanic fronts, larger loggerheads require more substantial meals that can only be easily found only in shallower coastal waters.

Loggerheads settling into shallow waters near coastlines inhabit lagoons, bays, channels, and reefs ranging in depth from 330 ft (100 m) deep to less than 3 ft (1 m). As in green turtles, these larger juveniles may live for many years in habitats and regions where no adolescent or adult turtles are found. Nearing maturity, many loggerheads migrate closer to the tropics and reach pubescence and adulthood far from where they first encountered shallow water as juveniles.

Estimating from the rate at which loggerheads grow, adult size is reached in roughly 20 to 40 years. As in most other sea turtles, adult loggerheads nearly stop growing such that adult turtles observed over 20 years scarcely change in size beyond the error range in their shell measurement. From hatchling to adult, a loggerhead multiplies its mass by a little over 6000 times.

Female loggerheads migrate to breed at their nesting beaches about every two to four years and lay eggs in one to seven nests separated by roughly two-week intervals. Their eggs average about 1 oz (33 g) and a hatchling fresh from the nest is about 1/2 oz (20 g). The number of eggs in a loggerhead's clutch is fairly constant between populations, averaging about 115. Males generally intercept females to mate along migration pathways and are seldom seen near the nesting beach.

Diet

Loggerheads take their first bite of food out in the open ocean and their early tastes are not discriminating. A little loggerhead's meals are likely to include hundreds of items found amongst the patches of algae and flotsam they live by, including plants, invertebrate animals, dead insects, and many other slow-moving and inanimate things. As oceanic loggerheads grow, they become able to catch larger prey, but they remain dependant upon sluggish sea creatures such as jellyfish, salps (translucent, free-swimming sea squirts), floating sea snails, and goose-neck barnacles.

Juvenile and adult loggerheads that have begun feeding in shallow coastal waters eat a wide variety of local seafood. Although preferred species vary by region, typical loggerhead food consists of large, bottom-crawling or attached, hard-shelled invertebrates like marine snails, clams, non-swimming crabs, and sea pens (pen-like colonies of coral-related animals). Occasionally, loggerheads eat softer foods such as jellyfish, sea squirts, and anemones.

Unique Traits

To catch their food, loggerheads are known to muscle through whatever obstacle keeps them from their prey. This means mashing a wooden-slatted trap to bits in pursuit of a captive spiny lobster, consuming the sponge and coral concealing a cowering crab, and flipper-plowing through bottom sediment to get at burrowing bivalve mollusks.

Loggerheads do not swim as swiftly as the other sea turtle species. They are mild-mannered creatures, but if directly confronted with a threat, they are not shy about using the crushing power of their enormous jaws. In responses to the unwelcome attention from a potential predator or to the competing affections offered by a rival male, a loggerhead's tendency is to bite decisively and let go eventually.

Conservation Status

This captive loggerhead participated in tests of turtle excluder devices (TEDs).

There are only two places in the world where loggerheads breed in abundance. One area is along the southern Florida Peninsula, USA, and the other is on Masirah Island, Oman. Elsewhere, loggerhead nesting is much less common, even rare, and many of these smaller populations are in perilous decline.

Loggerheads in the Pacific are in particular trouble. In about a generation, nesting loggerheads in Japan are down to about 10 per cent of their numbers when counts first began. And in Queensland, Australia, nesting loggerheads have declined to about 14 per cent of their abundance only half a generation ago. In Florida, the loggerhead population once thought of as stable has begun to decline. In Oman, uncertainties over trends in nesting numbers leave it unclear how loggerheads there are doing.

In general, loggerheads have not suffered from the intense commercial harvests that some other sea turtle species have experienced. But this does not mean that loggerheads have avoided human threats. This species has had the misfortune of positioning itself between us and the seafood we wish to harvest. Juvenile loggerheads forage and float precisely where long-lines (series of baited hooks) are set to catch oceanic fishes, and larger loggerheads feed within areas of fertile seabottom trawled for shrimps (prawns). At these intersections, loggerheads perish by the tens of thousands each year after being hooked, tangled, and drowned. Good news for loggerheads and other sea turtles is that progress is being made to reduce this mortality by modifying the gear that fishermen use. Unfortunately, open ocean fisheries lag far behind in this effort compared to coastal fisheries. Although the threats per hook and per trawl have great potential to be reduced, the overall number of hooks and trawls is increasing. This leaves the fate of the world's loggerheads in question.

The loggerhead sea turtle is considered by the IUCN to be Endangered. This status means that loggerheads face a very high risk of extinction in the wild in the near future.

The distributions of loggerheads and humans commonly intersect. Loggerheads are frequently tangled, hooked, and drowned by commercial fishing operations, and are struck and crushed by vessels and dredges.

Hawksbill Turtle

Scientific Name

Eretmochelys imbricata.
Named for the Greek roots for 'rowing turtle' (turtle with oars) and the Latin root for 'covered with overlapping scales' (likely pertaining to the hawksbill's overlapping shell scutes).

Other common names

Other English names given the hawksbill turtle include hawksbill sea turtle, hawksbill, and hawksbill seaturtle. In Latin America, the turtle is known most often as carey (kä-râ'). Many other common names vary among cultures.

Size and weight

Adult female hawksbills weigh between 88 and 176 lb (40 and 80 kg), with a shell straight-length of 30 to 35 in (75 to 90 cm).

Distribution

Tropical marine waters of the Atlantic, Pacific and Indian oceans. Nesting occurs almost exclusively on tropical beaches. Mexico, the Seychelles, Indonesia and Australia have the most significant nesting beaches, although they breed on beaches of about 60 countries.

General Appearance

Hawksbills are strikingly beautiful turtles. Although much of their beauty lies in their intricately patterned shell, a hawksbill's flippers and head also reflect the theme of colors that the turtles carry on their backs. A hawksbill's shell colors seem magnified, perhaps by the thickness of the translucent scutes covering their carapace. The tough, plastic-like scute plates are as thick as about 20 of these book pages and are imbedded with a myriad of colors. From a distance, hawksbill shells range in appearance from blonde with chocolate drippings to black with golden sunbursts. Up close in daylight, a hawksbill shell can be seen to have colors such as cream, amber, rusty reds, browns, and black, occasionally all together, in rich patterns ranging from overlapping bursts and radiating zigzags, to irregular superimposed splotches. Given this variation, no two hawksbills are quite the same.

Typically, a hawksbills underside is much paler than its topside. In many young hawksbills, the scutes covering the plastron are a patternless, thick cream color, although these belly scutes may have dark corners in some turtles. In adults, the plastron becomes a deep amber. Depending on the life experiences of an individual turtle, some of the beauty of a hawksbill's shell may be hidden by coarse sandpaper-like scratches from rocks and coral.

Hawksbill shell scutes are imbricate, meaning that each slightly overlaps the scute behind it. The center-line vertebral scutes overlap the most, such that they taper rearward into sharp Vs or Ws. Faster-growing young hawksbills have the sharpest rear margins to each of their imbricate scutes.

Young hawksbills have a heart-shaped shell with sharply serrate rear margins. In oceanic-stage turtles, the shell appears lumpy from the thickened scutes that form three longitudinal ridges on the carapace and two on the plastron. Hawksbills larger than a shovelhead have only a hint of these ridges. As hawksbills age into maturity, their shell elongates, and in the oldest individuals, the shell is smooth and the serrate rear margins have largely worn away.

The head and flipper scales of a hawksbill keep with the general color theme of the carapace but are likely to show greater

Adult hawksbills feed mostly on sponges and reach an average weight of about 150 lb (70 kg).

contrast. Frequently, an amber background separates dark-brown scale centers. Darker colors are much more dominant in the upper surfaces than they are beneath.

Hawksbill turtles have four lateral scutes on either side of their carapace midline. On the head, hawksbills are similar to loggerheads in having two pairs of prefrontal scales between the eyes, often with an intervening scale or two.

A hawksbill's narrow beak and long neck allow
it to probe reef crevasses for food.

A narrow raptor-like beak is the hawksbill's namesake. With the slightly cusped bill arching into an overbite and extending about half the length of the head, the turtle's profile is decidedly bird-like. The beak is strong, sharp, slender, and in a form designed for probing and extraction from the stony crevices of coral reefs. Hawksbills also have a longer neck than the other sea turtles, which may allow an extended reach into a reef's more secluded spots.

Hatchlings are about 2 in (4 cm) in shell length. Their coloration varies between light and dark, and browns and grays. Most hatchlings are slightly lighter below. Their carapace has the three thin longitudinal ridges that will thicken as they grow at sea.

In a cursory glimpse of a hawksbill from the water's surface, one could easily make identification from the head profile and shell colors. In the water, the same characters give the turtle away, but noting the presence of the turtle's sharply overlapping shell scutes can make a confirmation. Older hawksbills have often collected a scattering of large *Chelonibia* barnacles but are not often as fouled as a typical loggerhead.

Hawksbills nesting on beaches are not readily observed and commonly leave only obscure traces. Often, the only evidence from a nesting is a short track disappearing into thick beach vegetation. Hawksbills leave an asymmetrical series of flipper prints in the sand spanning about 2 ft (0.75 m), typically with a zigzagging tail-drag mark down the center of the track. Their nests are a pit with an adjacent mound 5 ft (1.5 m) or so in width, but this evidence is frequently obscured by dune undergrowth and beach wrack.

Distribution and Movements

Hawksbills are largely restricted to the tropics and are known from the Atlantic, Indian, and Pacific oceans. Their distribution in the water mirrors the distribution of the planet's great coral reefs. Although immature hawksbills do wander between reef sites, it is unlikely that these movements are seasonal. Although it was once thought that hawksbills migrated little after settling into coastal waters, we now know that they make punctuated shifts between habitats similar to other species of sea turtles. Hawksbills are observed again and again over many years resting under the same coral ledge but are also known to travel hundreds of miles between reef habitats. Adult hawksbills may forage within 60 miles (100 km) of the beaches where they nest, or they may travel as far as 1240 miles (2000 km) between their foraging and breeding sites.

Nesting occurs principally on island beaches and is far more scattered than in the other sea turtle species. Although hawksbills breed on the beaches of about 60 countries, none has any great concentration of this activity. Mexico, Seychelles, Indonesia, and Australia have the most significant nesting of hawksbill turtles. The largest population of nesting hawksbills may be at Milman Island, within Australia's northern Great Barrier Reef.

Small oceanic hawksbills drift in ocean currents but are seldom known to cross entire oceans. Larger juveniles and adults spend most of their lives in waters less than 100 ft (30 m) deep and may frequent habitat that is barely wet at low tide.

Life History

Hawksbills leave their natal beaches as hatchlings and disperse into oceanic waters where they are believed to forage within surface weedlines. Because hawksbills appear in shallow coastal waters when their shells are only 8 to 12 in (20 to 30 cm) in length, they are thought to spend only a few years out in the open ocean.

Young hawksbills just entering coastal waters have a limited band of suitable reef habitats dotting the tropics and near-tropics. Thus, it would seem to behoove a little hawksbill not to stray too far into temperate waters as they are carried within ocean currents. Although it is uncertain how long little hawksbills spend in the open ocean, the small size at which they leave this habitat suggests that

their oceanic stage is vastly reduced in comparison to loggerheads, as is the risk of being carried too far from tropical waters.

Juvenile hawksbills settling into coastal waters occupy reefs of all kinds. Although living corals are not a requirement for hawksbill habitat, they do characterize the reefs where hawksbills are most

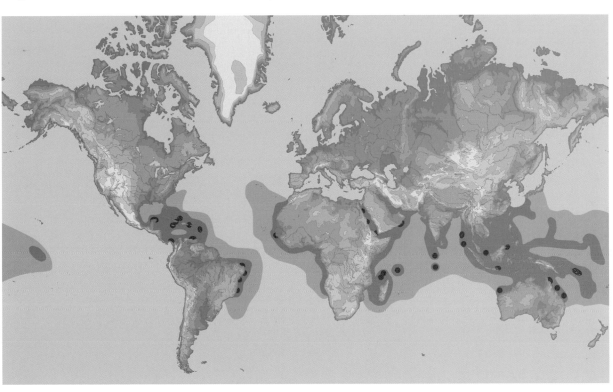

■ *Major Nesting Beaches*   ■ *Large Juveniles & Adults*   ■ *Oceanic Juveniles*

commonly found. In addition to favoring the organisms on which hawksbills feed, the hard and irregular features of reefs also provide ledges and caves within which hawksbills rest and avoid predators.

Just outside the tropics, there are areas of hardbottom and coral reef where mostly juvenile hawksbills are found. But within the tropics, deep hawksbill habitat often has a complete array of hawksbill sizes from plate-sized juveniles to full-sized adults. Growth of hawksbills from hatchling to adult is thought to take 20 to 40 years. Female hawksbills migrate to breed at their nesting

beaches about every two to four years. Hawksbill nesting often has a peak during the rainy season but could occur throughout the year. During a nesting season, most hawksbills will put an average of 130, 1-oz (27-g) eggs into each of two to four nests. Successive nestings are separated by intervals of about two weeks. Eggs incubate roughly 60 days before hatchlings emerge from the nest. Hatchlings average about 1/2 oz (15 g).

Diet

Although the diet of little hawksbills living in the open ocean is uncertain, these smallest hawksbills are thought to feed on surface-drifting organisms just as the youngest loggerheads do. Soon after settling onto shallow reefs, juvenile hawksbills are thought to undergo a profound transition in diet. Although some of the smallest coastal hawksbills are found to eat a wide variety of invertebrate animals and algae, most juveniles and adults assume a more parochial diet. For most of their lives, hawksbills are spongivores – specialists on eating sponges.

Sponges are an unusual food choice in that they possess substantial defenses against would-be predators. By lacing themselves with toxic chemicals and dangerously indigestible silica spicules, many sponges are not the favored item on most animal menus. Yet, hawksbills quickly acquire a taste and tolerance for sponge, and after a short initiation period, sponges are likely to make up 95 per cent of their diet. A limited number of species belonging to the order of demosponges are the hawksbill's favorites. Although this is the order that gives us the familiar bath sponge, these friendly and caressing sponges made of flexible

spongin are generally shunned by hawksbills. Many of the sponges eaten by hawksbills are held together by lacy, glass-like silica that you would no more want near your bare skin than shredded glass.

A hawksbill's tolerance for a diet of glass is largely a mystery. Occasionally, hawksbills do eat less toxic fare such as sea cucumbers, mollusks, anemones, sea urchins, crabs, and algae, but

Hawksbills have an amazing ability to eat and digest toxic sponges.

the rarity of these substitutes points to a clear preference for sponges. It is a wonder what benefit from eating sponge could possibly outweigh the difficulties of such a diet.

Unique Traits

Hawksbills are nimble turtles that seem unafraid of obstacles. At home on the reef, they are commonly found wedged into

As protection against the many rough, pointed, and stinging features of a coral reef, hawksbills have thick shell coverings and tough skin.

crevasses and beneath ledges from which they seem barely able to extricate themselves. Perhaps more than the other sea turtles, hawksbills make a practice of jamming themselves into tight spots and knocking about on rough, wave-swept reefs. One function of a hawksbill's thick shell scutes may be to protect them from the jabs they are likely to get as they poke about the sharp corals and rocky projections looking for the next meal of

Hawksbill hatchlings on a Mona Island beach in the Caribbean.

sponge. It is a protection needed especially by nesting female hawksbills, which occasionally crawl over the gothic projections of fringing reef to access a sandy beach. Once on a beach, hawksbills are even less intimidated by the tangle of branches and vines on the upper beach where eggs can incubate away from the tide. Hawksbills probably surpass the other sea turtles in their maneuverability on land, and are able to employ a tactic largely unheard of for a sea turtle out of its element – hawksbills can back up.

Conservation Status

The best guesses of biologists are that the world's hawksbills have declined by 80 per cent or more during the past century. Given the direction of current population trends and the continuation of threats faced by hawksbills, most believe that this slide toward extinction will be difficult to reverse. Because hawksbills are widespread in the tropics there is an illusion that the species is holding its own. But most of these populations are either declining or are mere shadows of their former abundance. Fewer than 15,000 females nest on beaches worldwide each year, and this nesting is stretched between hundreds of small and vulnerable nesting populations. The Caribbean now has about a third of the world's hawksbill nesting. In this region, one possible bright spot is the Yucatan Peninsula of Mexico where about a thousand hawksbills nest each year and where the nesting trend seems to be increasing.

Like the green turtle, the hawksbill has suffered the fate of a commercially harvested species. For many decades, hawksbills have been harvested for their shell scutes. These scutes as a trade commodity are known as tortoiseshell, bekko, or carey. The malleable, plastic-like plates are fashioned into jewelry, hair combs, eyeglass frames, and varied ornaments. Shell scutes from 30,000 or more hawksbills per year were imported into Japan alone during the period of 1970 to 1992. Currently, trade in tortoiseshell has diminished following adherence to an international convention (CITES) to protect endangered species, but substantial illegal harvest and trade still occurs. Domestic harvest of hawksbills remains common in Fiji, the Solomon Islands, Cambodia, Indonesia, the Dominican Republic, Cuba and throughout Central America.

The hawksbill is considered by IUCN to be Critically Endangered. This status means that hawksbills face an extremely high risk of extinction in the wild in the immediate future.

Unfortunately for hawksbills, their beautiful shell scutes, known as tortoiseshell, are used to make commercial products and ornaments.

Olive Ridley

Scientific Name

Lepidochelys olivacea.

Named for the Greek roots for 'scaly turtle' (perhaps from the turtle's extra carapace scutes) and the Latin root for 'olive-like' (likely pertaining to the turtle's coloration).

Other common names

Other English names given the olive ridley include olive ridley sea turtle, olive ridley seaturtle, Pacific ridley, and olive loggerhead. In Latin America, the turtle is known most often as tortuga golfina. Many other common names vary among cultures.

Size and weight

Adult female olive ridleys weigh between 77 and 100 lb (35 and 45 kg), with a shell straight-length of 25 to 30 in (60 to 75 cm).

Distribution

Tropical marine waters of the Atlantic, Pacific and Indian oceans. Nesting occurs on beaches mostly in the tropics. In the eastern Pacific they nest on several beaches in Mexico and Central America, but are almost completely absent from islands in the central Pacific. In the Indian ocean they nest in large numbers only in eastern India and Sri Lanka. Occasional nesting in the Atlantic occurs in Brazil and Western Africa.

General Appearance

The ridleys are the smallest sea turtles. Each of the two species has a relatively large head with a cusped upper beak and each has a heart-shaped, almost circular shell. In a head-on view of an olive ridley, one can see the vaulting of that circular shell, topped by a flat peak and looking overall a bit like a 1950s representation of a flying saucer.

The topsides of olive ridleys tend to be the drab color that their name suggests, but they can also show an overall gray, brown, or black coloration. The underside of an adult is generally yellow. Smaller juveniles are pure white beneath and hatchlings are most commonly gray to black overall.

One unusual character shown by olive ridleys is a tendency toward having extra shell scutes. The number of plates on an olive ridley's back is greater and more variable than the number covering either Kemp's ridley or the other sea turtles. Most olive ridleys have six to nine pairs of lateral scutes on either side of their carapace midline (Kemp's ridleys typically have five pairs), and some turtles may have one or more lateral scutes on one side than on the other. Most olive ridleys also have six to nine vertebral scutes along the midline length of their shell (Kemp's ridleys generally have five vertebral scutes). In additional comparisons to Kemp's ridley, olive ridleys have a slightly more triangular head, subtly larger eyes, and a shell that has both less breadth and more height.

Another character of both ridley species is the presence of four conspicuous pore openings on each side of their lower shell. The pores are openings for the mysterious Rathke's glands (also present but inconspicuous in hawksbills and green turtles), which may secrete pheromones or anti-fouling substances, or perform some other function that has thus far escaped the imaginations of biologists.

Because ridleys are small, they leave fainter tracks on nesting beaches than the other sea turtles. Having emerged onto a beach, ridleys leave an asymmetrical series of swirls from the rear

Adult olive ridleys feed on a variety of hard- and soft-bodied invertebrates and reach an average weight of about 90 lb (40 kg).

flippers on either side of a flat, smooth, wavy center mark. A typical track is a little less than 2 ft (0.66 m) in width and has no tail drag mark down the center.

Distribution and Movements

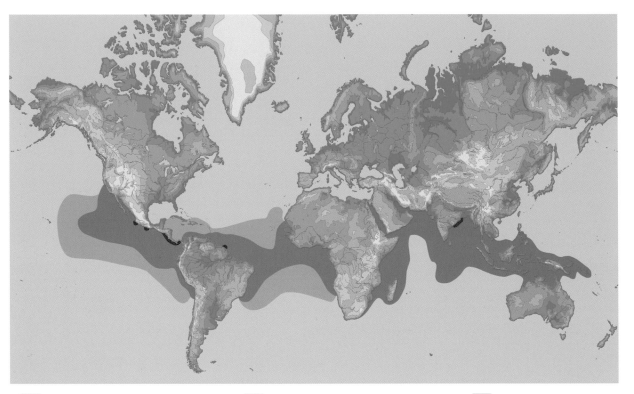

Major Nesting Beaches   *Large Juveniles & Adults*   *Oceanic Juveniles*

Guianas Coast (Guyana, Surinam, and French Guiana). Occasional nesting in the Atlantic occurs in Brazil and western Africa.

Hatchling olive ridleys enter the sea and are presumed to disperse with oceanic currents. Only rarely are small juvenile olive ridleys observed at sea. But there are occasional sightings of juveniles at the surface of the open ocean having shell-lengths between 8 and 24 in (20 and 60 cm), which suggest that olive ridleys have a multi-year early oceanic stage similar to loggerheads.

Most of what is known about movements of olive ridleys comes from studies of adult female turtles approached by researchers on nesting beaches. At the well-studied beaches of Pacific Costa Rica, tens of thousands of adult female olive ridleys have been tagged with flipper tags so that their identities would be known if the turtles were seen again far from their nesting beach. The locations where these tagged turtles have been recovered are a function of both where the turtles go and where they are likely to be recognized by someone. As it turns out, the vast majority of tag recoveries of these Costa Rican nesters were made as the turtles traveled south, to the waters of coastal Ecuador, where hundreds of thousands of adult olive ridleys were harvested in the 1970s to be turned into leather boots and handbags.

Better detail on movements has come from turtles equipped with radio transmitters capable of delivering location data to orbiting satellites. Tracks of these turtles show them leaving the

Olive ridleys are almost exclusively tropical sea turtles. They occur in Pacific, Indian, and Atlantic oceans, but their distribution is patchy. In the eastern Pacific, olive ridleys nest in impressive numbers on several Mexican and Central American beaches. Elsewhere in the Pacific they nest in low numbers, and they are almost completely absent from the islands of the central Pacific. In the Indian Ocean, olive ridleys nest in abundance only in eastern India and Sri Lanka. In the Atlantic, olive ridleys are uncommon, although they were formerly abundant nesters on the

Olive ridleys commonly forage near the surface
in deep oceanic waters where they are attracted to floating debris.
They seldom stray outside the tropics.

*This female laying her eggs at sunset on a beach
in Surinam is one of few olive ridleys remaining in a western Atlantic
population that is close to regional extirpation.*

Pacific waters near their Costa Rica nesting beaches and traveling north to Mexico, south to Peru, and west into the Pacific as far as 1800 miles (3000 km) from land. Most of these adult olive ridleys appeared to be nomadic and did not remain within a single foraging area.

Sometimes, olive ridleys travel within large flotillas. Such aggregations suggest social relations that are unusual for turtles, but they reveal a tendency to group that might be expected from a turtle that assembles in mass *arribadas* during nesting.

Life History

Olive ridleys may spend nearly all of their youth, perhaps a decade or more, out in the open ocean. This remoteness in their lives adds mystery to how they go about living them. We do not know how quickly olive ridleys grow, and we do not know exactly how long they take to reach maturity.

Adulthood is reached at about 24 to 28 in (60 to 70 cm) in shell length. As adults, olive ridleys spend at least some time in coastal waters where they feed on bottom-dwelling creatures. Even in shallow waters near land, olive ridleys seem to show no allegiance to specific home foraging grounds. Often, olive ridleys are observed to be associated with transitory upwelling events that provide pulses of nutrients and explosions of life. They also are found foraging among rafts of floating debris drifting in ocean currents. Because these ridley 'smorgasbords' either grow or assemble, fade or disperse, and then appear again elsewhere, reliance on these events would seem to require a life spent wandering.

Reproduction occurs either within mass *arribadas* or as solitary nestings. Within populations of sufficient size, perhaps hundreds, most female ridleys choose to nest in the company of others.

An individual olive ridley is likely to nest one to three times in a season, with each nest containing approximately 100 to 115 eggs that each weighs about 1 1/4 oz (35 g). The period between successive nests is about 14 days when a turtle nests by herself but can be as long as 48 days for females holding their clutches of eggs for *arribada* events. It is likely that olive ridleys nest almost every year. Hatchlings emerge from nests in 50 to 70 days and weigh approximately 1/2 oz (17 g).

Diet

Olive ridleys eat a wide variety of invertebrate animals from a range of ocean habitats. This diet includes oceanic animals such as pelagic red crabs, jellyfish, salps, and flotsam-attached barnacles, and it includes bottom-dwelling animals like crabs, mollusks, sea urchins, sea squirts, and shrimps. Various algae are eaten, either incidentally or deliberately, and on occasion, benthic fishes are found in the stomachs of olive ridleys stranded dead. Some of these fishes may be eaten as carrion, perhaps being discards from near-shore shrimp trawling. Frequently, olive ridleys become hooked on pelagic long-line fishing gear that has been baited with fish or squid.

Unique Traits

Ridleys may be the most social sea turtles. The behavior that best shows their gregarious nature is the *arribada*. For olive ridleys, these mass nesting events occur at night, which contrasts with the daytime *arribadas* of Kemp's ridley. Olive ridley *arribadas* may involve just a few hundred females nesting on one or two consecutive nights, or they may involve hundreds of thousands of females nesting over several nights. At Orissa, on India's northeast coast, approximately 600,000 turtles once nested in a single week-long *arribada*. Despite the size of the mass-nesting events at Orissa, the normally annual phenomenon was conspicuously absent for two recent years following severe erosion of the nesting beaches. As beaches re-formed, mass nesting returned. Such intensive synchronous nesting, unanimous abandonment, and return of the multitudes show a tremendous mass concurrence in the reproductive decision-making of olive ridleys.

Within each nesting season, *arribadas* are thought to be

orchestrated by climatic and celestial events such as winds, tides, and moon phase, but the occurrence of the events often defies prediction. Frequently, *arribadas* seem to be brought about by strong offshore winds that arrive on the waning (or sometimes the waxing) quarter moon. The wind conditions make evolutionary sense in that an offshore breeze would blow the smell of turtle eggs away from land predators. But the adaptive advantages of

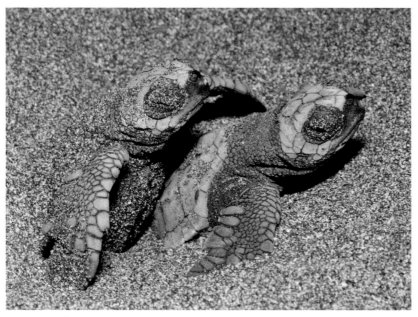

Two olive ridleys begin their life's journey.

nesting by a quarter moon have yet to be explained by storytelling. Because the *arribada* is believed to surprise and saturate egg predators, it makes sense that the nesting turtles benefit from some level of unpredictability, as long as they themselves could recognize and agree upon the appointed time to nest.

Among the hard-shelled sea turtles, olive ridleys are also unique for their open ocean lifestyle. Both juveniles and adults are seen at the surface over deep ocean waters. More often than not, these turtles are found near floating logs, escaped buoys, and other drifting buoyant items. An attraction to life rafts has resulted in olive ridleys playing a role in the survival of sailors adrift at sea. In accounts such as Dougal Robertson's *Survive the Savage Sea,* sea turtles, almost certainly olive ridleys, were caught by hand as they lingered near the rafts of desperate, hungry castaways.

Conservation Status

Olive ridleys are the most abundant of the world's sea turtles, but an illusion of their unending abundance has driven mass harvests that threaten this species' existence. In modern industrial times, the olive ridley has been by far the most commercially exploited sea turtle. They remain numerous despite some drastic declines, and yet, the species' status is questionable. Like the once super-abundant (now extinct) passenger pigeon, olive ridleys may require a critical level of abundance to function as a population.

In the 1970s, approximately one million olive ridleys were taken from the waters off the Pacific coasts of Mexico and Ecuador and turned into leather goods. This pressure, in addition to extensive harvest of eggs on Pacific nesting beaches, resulted in the collapse of nearly all of the populations breeding on the beaches of Mexico. One remaining mass-nesting beach suffered severe declines, but has recently begun to recover following bans on sea turtle harvest.

In the Indian Ocean, the Orissa population of olive ridleys averages about 400,000 turtles nesting per year. However, many tens of thousands annually are drowned off these nesting beaches by fishing trawlers. In the Atlantic, the highest nesting occurs on the central north coast of South America in the Guianas, where nesting has declined 80 per cent since the 1960s.

The olive ridley is considered by IUCN to be Endangered. This status means that olive ridleys face a very high risk of extinction in the wild in the near future.

Olive ridleys grow up in the open ocean over a period of many years.

Kemp's Ridley

Scientific Name

Lepidochelys kempii.

Named for the Greek roots for 'scaly turtle' (perhaps from extra carapace scutes of the turtle's sister species) and the proper name 'Kemp' with the Latin genitive ending, from Richard M. Kemp, a fisherman who submitted the type specimen described by Harvard's Samuel Garman in 1880.

Other common names

Other English names given Kemp's ridley include Atlantic ridley, bastard ridley turtle, bastard turtle, and ridley (likely from the vernacular of fishermen, who considered the turtle's identity to be a riddle – thus, ridd-lee. Similar uncertainty about parentage brought about the term 'bastard turtle'). In Latin America, the turtle is known most often as tortuga lora.

Size and weight

Adult female Kemp's ridleys weigh between 75 and 100 lb (35 and 45 kg), with a shell straight-length of 25 to 28 in (60 to 70 cm).

Distribution

The Gulf of Mexico and warm temperate waters of the western North Atlantic, along the coast between Florida and Cape Cod, Massachusetts. Rarely in the eastern Atlantic, and unknown in the south Atlantic. Nesting occurs almost exclusively on the beaches of Tamaulipas, Mexico. Since the 1970s most Kemp's ridleys have been born in protected hatcheries in Mexico and Texas, and later released into the Gulf of Mexico.

General Appearance

As adults, Kemp's ridleys are about the weight of a large German shepherd dog. The turtle's overall coloration is olive gray above and yellowish cream underneath. Their shell is more circular than the shells of the other sea turtles and its flanged edges often make it wider than it is long. For someone who is used to seeing other more common species of sea turtles in the water, a Kemp's ridley seems unusual. The impression given by a passing Kemp's ridley is that of a ghost-like gray disk gliding by.

Kemp's ridley has a large head and a cusped parrot-like beak. Compared to the olive ridley, Kemp's ridley has a broader, less triangular head, and a flatter, broader shell. The plates covering the shell are less abundant than in the olive ridley. Kemp's ridley most often has only five pairs of lateral scutes on either side of its carapace midline and only five vertebral scutes along the midline length of its shell.

Hatchling Kemp's ridleys are dark gray all over and weigh about 1/2 oz (17 g) fresh from the nest. As hatchlings grow they develop three pronounced ridges on the middle length of their carapace and two similar ridges on the plastron. Nearing adulthood, only a thin remnant of the center carapace ridge is evident. An adult's carapace is smooth and generally un-fouled by barnacles and other opportunists.

Because Kemp's ridleys nest on dry blustery days, very little is left of their track and nest site that would allow identification. Under some circumstances, one can recognize the alternating flipper marks and narrow width – less than 25 in (65 cm) – of a ridley track leading to and from a shallow pit and low nest mound.

Adult Kemp's ridleys feed mostly on crabs and other hard-shelled animals and reach an average weight of about 90 lb (40 kg).

Distribution and Movements

Nearly all Kemp's ridleys have the same hometown beaches, those surrounding the Mexican pueblo of Rancho Nuevo, in the state of Tamaulipas. The rarity of this species and its reliance on a single basket for nearly all its eggs have raised concern

the surf and taken to a sea turtle husbandry laboratory at Galveston, Texas. There, ridleys spent their formative first year in individual buckets, growing to the size of salad plates (10 in or 25 cm in shell length). After about a year, these 'headstarted' ridleys were taken from their buckets, transported by trawlers, and released offshore into the Gulf of Mexico.

Regardless of the circuitous route and helping hands that delivered young ridleys into the Gulf of Mexico, the yearling turtles are likely to spend another year or so drifting within currents. Most ridleys are found within the Gulf of Mexico and may live out their entire lives there. But many exit the gulf as juveniles and are known throughout the Atlantic coast between Florida and Cape Cod, Massachusetts. Kemp's ridleys are rarely sighted in the eastern Atlantic and they are unknown from the south Atlantic. The habitats where large juveniles and adults are typically found include turbid coastal and estuarine waters with seagrasses, mud banks, and oyster bars.

Both juveniles and adults are known to move with the seasons. Ridleys along the Atlantic coast move south as winter approaches, but turtles in the Gulf are also known to move into deeper, warmer waters as cold weather arrives. Adult female Kemp's ridleys come from the northern, southern, and eastern Gulf of Mexico to converge at their western Gulf nesting beaches.

■ *Major Nesting Beaches*　■ *Large Juveniles & Adults*　■ *Oceanic Juveniles*

among sea turtle conservationists. As a result, a great deal of attention has been paid to the ridley nests at Rancho Nuevo.

Many Kemp's ridleys have had the first legs of their life's journey determined by human intervention. Since the 1970s, most have emerged from nests in protected hatcheries. Some have emerged within hatcheries near Rancho Nuevo and some have come from eggs that were transported north to hatcheries near the beaches of Padre Island, Texas, USA. Of these relocated hatchlings, some were released on Padre Island beaches only to be recaptured in

Life History

Although biologists believe that Kemp's ridleys live near the sea surface within convergence zones, these youngest turtles are rarely observed. A rough guess is that ridleys spend one-and-a-half to two years on the open seas before they settle into shallow coastal waters.

Kemp's ridleys that leave the Gulf of Mexico were once thought to be lost. Upon further evidence, it now seems that these turtles from the eastern US coast are better able to determine their own fate than they had been credited. Yes, they are far from where they would breed as adults, but the noticeable lack of mature turtles in this wayward group would seem to indicate that they eventually depart these Atlantic waters. In fact, a continuum of small juveniles in the north and larger juveniles in the south seems to fit the story that young turtles swept out of the gulf by the Gulf Stream slowly work their way down the coast and around the peninsula of Florida.

Several Kemp's ridleys that were tagged as yearlings have been seen as adults on nesting beaches. Judging from these records and from how quickly ridleys grow, this turtle likely reaches adulthood in 10 to 15 years.

Like the olive ridley, most Kemp's ridleys breed within *arribadas*. But because of the present rarity of this turtle, the largest mass nestings involve only a few thousand turtles. The season for nesting is April through July.

An individual female is likely to nest one to three times in a season, with each nest containing approximately 100 eggs that each weighs about 1 oz (30 g). The period between successive nests is about 14 days when a turtle nests by herself but can be 30 or more days when females wait for the conditions prompting an *arribada*. It is likely that most females nest every year. Hatchlings emerge from nests in 45 to 60 days and weigh approximately 1/2 oz (17 g).

Diet

The youngest ridleys are presumed to feed on the same associates of drifting *Sargassum* that form the diet of young loggerheads. This would include a wide variety of small, slow-moving or attached organisms such as copepods, snails, and hydroids.

Larger Kemp's ridleys love to eat crabs and they seem to occupy areas where they can get the most of them. A ridley's favorite meal is the blue crab, *Callinectes sapidus*, a sprightly swimming and fast-clawed resident of secluded bay waters. Other seafood popular with Kemp's ridley includes small marine snails

Kemp's ridleys hunt blue crabs in shallow coastal waters.

and clams, and occasional jellyfish. Because balls of mud have been found in the stomachs of some ridleys, it is thought that they may take in bites of the seabottom in efforts to consume the small invertebrates hidden within.

Kemp's ridleys may also feed on the discarded bycatch from the shrimp trawlers that so commonly traverse their habitat. Stranded ridleys are commonly found to have fishes in their stomachs that are probably too fast for them to catch but are common components of the sea life tossed dead from trawl vessels.

A Kemp's ridley flings sand over her nest at Rancho Nuevo, Mexico.
Their nesting also includes bouts of rapid rocking from side to side, which produces
a distinct thumping and compacts the sand over the eggs.

Unique Traits

The largest Kemp's ridley is just small enough for a strong person to pick one up and carry it. But in doing so, one might find oneself slapped, bitten, and generally regretful for the attempt. Although Kemp's ridley is small relative to the other sea turtles, their scrappy nature makes them seem comparatively substantial.

Kemp's ridleys are fast and mean. Larry Ogren, a colleague who certainly knows ridleys better than most, has wondered aloud whether anyone would be as mean if they had to eat things that pinched their face. Certainly, having to deal with a face full of darting, slashing blue crab during every meal would favor those both nimble and determined.

The turtle does seem to have quickness beyond what most other sea turtles can show. Their disk-like shell allows a ridley to pivot on a dime and almost instantaneously change direction. In this respect they seem to be rivaled only by a green turtle of similar size.

The obstreperous nature of a ridley is easily seen in a turtle that is out of its element. Having been captured, Kemp's ridley will often thrash until exhaustion. In its attempts to deter its captors, a ridley will take every opportunity to bite them with its robust, parrot-like beak.

Kemp's ridley is also known to dance. On the nesting beach, female ridleys in the process of covering their eggs can be seen to raise their shells and rapidly thump the lower edges of their plastron against the sand. This vigorous dancing seems to be a startling departure from the way that a turtle is supposed to act. An explanation for it is that the behavior comes at a time in a turtle's nesting sequence when it might be adaptive to tamp down the sand covering her clutch of eggs. In part, ridleys may do this dance because they can. The rest of the sea turtles may be too large to lift their own weight and pull off such a routine.

Conservation Status

On a June morning in 1947, a Mexican engineer named Andres Herrera visited a beach in Tamaulipas where he and his companions stumbled upon a Kemp's ridley *arribada*. The film that Herrera made of this event stands as one of the most important clues to understanding this enigmatic species. The flickering images reveal

Presently, most Kemp's ridley hatchlings come from a single protected beach.

that Kemp's ridley was once an abundant sea turtle.

Tens of thousands of nesting ridleys were captured in time. In the film, the camera pans the stretch of coast near what is now Rancho Nuevo. What initially appears to be a boulder-strewn beach is actually a tide of turtles enveloping every available sandy space. Amidst the antics of Herrera's traveling companions stepping from turtle to turtle, it is clear that the beach was literally filled with ridleys. From the foreground to the horizon, there are turtles — crawling to and fro, throwing puffs of dry sand into the breeze, and thumping out their rocking dance moves.

The Herrera film remained unknown to biologists until 1960, when Dr. Henry Hildebrand, University of Corpus Christi, Texas, heard of the film's existence and sought out the information it contained. Upon a systematic count and careful extrapolation from the turtles visible in the film, it is estimated that 42,000 ridleys took part in that 1947 *arribada*. Only a few years after this revelation, it became clear to biologists that Kemp's ridley was in

A Turtle Excluder Device (TED) is a grid and trap door that allows turtles to escape from a shrimp trawl net.

rapid decline. By 1968, the *arribada* at Rancho Nuevo comprised only 5000 turtles, and by the 1980s, *arribadas* rarely involved more than 200 turtles. Kemp's ridley was disappearing

Years before Herrera made his film, the Rancho Nuevo ridley population was discovered by economic enterprise. Starting in the 1940s, trains of burros burdened under swollen sacks of eggs were run by *hueveros* who brought the fruits of ridley reproduction to the Mexican marketplace. For 20 years or more

the annual harvest of eggs was extensive. Recognizing this threat, the Mexican government in 1966 posted army troops at the beach to protect the ridley nests at gunpoint.

But Mexican soldiers could not guard Kemp's ridley from an even more severe threat that killed turtles before they could arrive at their beach. Following World War II, shrimp trawlers plying the Gulf of Mexico began using ever more powerful diesel engines that allowed the pulling of larger trawl nets. With the expansion of this industry, principally a fleet out of US ports, a growing expanse of shrimp habitat in the gulf was strained through the nets of trawlers.

Shrimp habitat and ridley habitat are largely one and the same. The nets that drew shrimp from the gulf also contained drowned Kemp's ridleys. By the 1960s the largest shrimp trawling effort in the world intersected perfectly with the distribution of the rarest sea turtle. For years, ridleys were known to shrimpers as a creature that clogged their nets and smashed their harvest. The incidental killing of ridleys continued for decades until roughly 1990 when shrimpers began using mandated turtle excluder devices (TEDs), which allow captured turtles to escape through a door in the net.

In the past decade or so, the future of Kemp's ridley has turned rosier. There has been an upturn in nests through the 1990s and recently the number of turtles in a single *arribada* has passed 1000. The number of nests made along Texas beaches has increased from one to two per year to dozens annually. It is uncertain whether this expansion of range is due to a general population increase, to efforts toward imprinting hatchling ridleys on Texas sands, or to both. Nonetheless, the status of Kemp's ridley remains perilous, with the world's population at only about 5000 adult females.

Kemp's ridley is considered by IUCN to be Critically Endangered. This status means that Kemp's ridleys face an extremely high risk of extinction in the wild in the immediate future.

Though still perilous, the survival outlook for the world's rarest sea turtle has improved by recent efforts to protect them.

Flatback Turtle

Scientific Name

Natator depressus.
Named with the Latin roots for a swimmer and for depressed (that is, low, which is likely to be a reference to the turtle's flattened carapace).

Other common names

Other English names given the flatback include Australian flatback and flatback seaturtle.

Size and weight

Adult female flatbacks weigh approximately 155 to 175 lb (70 to 80 kg) and have a shell length of 33 to 37 in (85 to 95 cm). Adult males are slightly smaller than females.

Distribution

Tropical marine waters between northern Australia and New Guinea. Nesting is known only from Australian beaches that are within or just outside the tropics.

General Appearance

As adults, flatbacks have the shell length of an average loggerhead but are generally only three quarters of a loggerhead's weight. Flatbacks are indeed flat. The turtle's shell is an oval with a low dome pressed downward to give a nesting turtle the appearance of being flush with the beach. The edges of the shell are depressed into flanges that upturn slightly like a hat brim. In large turtles the shell surface and edges are smooth and the turtle is generally unfettered by barnacles and other commensal growth.

The coloration of this turtle is olive gray above and cream beneath. Hatchlings are also shades of olive gray and are highlighted by bold dark outlines to their carapace scutes. A hatchling's serrated shell margins become smooth with age. The eyes of hatchlings have a turquoise glint.

At one time, flatbacks were believed to be a compressed version of a green turtle (and were placed in the same genus). Like green turtles, flatbacks have one pair of elongate prefrontal scales between the eyes and four pairs of lateral scutes on either side of the upper shell. But in addition to their low-domed appearance, flatbacks are very different from green turtles. In comparison to a green turtle, a flatback's head is much larger and triangular, and its flippers are shorter. A flatback's shell is distinctive in having thin, oily scutes that one could easily scratch through. By the time a flatback reaches adult size, the seams separating its thin carapace scutes virtually disappear, such that the shells of the oldest turtles seem covered only by skin. The flippers are distinctive in having large scales only at their margins. The remainder of each flipper is covered by supple skin with small thin scales.

Flatbacks leave tracks on their nesting beaches that look much like green turtle tracks. The turtle walks with a quick-paced butterfly gait and leaves a track of parallel flipper marks roughly a meter wide. The nest is an oval mound near a circular pit.

Distribution and Movements

This sea turtle comes closest to being endemic. It is thought that all nesting of flatbacks occurs in Australia and that many of these turtles live their entire lives in Australian waters. The complete range of the flatback stretches no farther northeast than Papua

Adult flatback turtles feed mostly on soft-bodied animals like sea cucumbers and reach an average weight of about 165 lb (75 kg).

New Guinea, no farther northwest than the eastern Indonesian islands near Timor, and no farther south than the warmest temperate waters of Australia. Flatbacks are most common on the Arafura Shelf in Tropical Australia. The turtle prefers shallow, turbid waters with soft seabottom away from coral reefs.

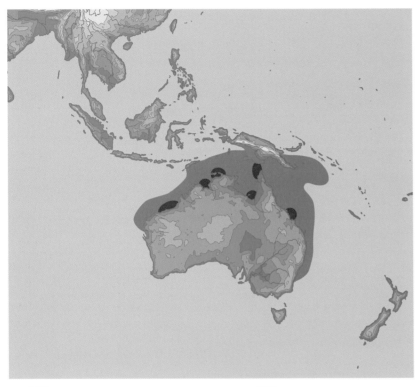

■ *Major Nesting Beaches*   ■ *Juveniles & Adults*

Because of their limited range, it would seem as if flatbacks don't travel much. However, it is likely that flatbacks ready to breed often find themselves hundreds of miles away from their nesting beach. Nesting migrations between foraging areas and beaches are known to span well over 600 miles (1000 km), although these trips are not likely to take turtles far from land or over deep waters. Like most of the other sea turtles, tagging studies have shown biologists that flatbacks are faithful both to their nesting beaches and to their foraging grounds.

Being sea turtles, it is astounding that flatbacks disperse as little as they do. In each of the other sea turtles, the initial scatter of young turtles within open-ocean currents ensures that they see a great deal more of the world than their own backyard. In flatback turtles, this oceanic stage is evidently lacking in their lives (see the discussion on life history below).

Life History

In the other sea turtles, much of their mysterious lives remains elusive because of the remoteness of the open ocean. But in the flatback turtle, mysteries are concealed within the turbid waters off the wild north Australian tropics.

Only recently did clues arise indicating that newborn flatbacks, unlike every other sea turtle, stayed close to land within shallow shelf waters. A principal clue came as biologists recognized pieces of hand-sized flatbacks beneath the feeding stations of white-bellied sea eagles, a raptor that seldom strays far from shore. Although sightings and strandings of flatbacks remain rare, turtles of every size are known from the same region. Age at maturity is only a guess for flatbacks, but based on limited growth information, they are likely to reach adulthood only after 20 years or more.

The absence of an oceanic dispersal stage explains why flatbacks are so restricted in their distribution. In order to bypass this stage, flatback hatchlings are substantially larger than all other hatchling sea turtles except the leatherback. At 1 1/2 oz (40 g), a flatback hatchling is nearly half again as large as a green turtle hatchling. A larger hatchling means that flatbacks are able to outsize the bites of coastal predators and reach the size for bottom feeding more quickly.

The flatback nesting season reaches peak activity during the austral summer between November and December. A female will lay an average of 50 billiard ball-sized eggs in each nest.

*Flatback turtles nest almost exclusively on the beaches
of northern Australia. They are unique among sea turtles in having
hatchlings that remain relatively close to shore.*

Hatchlings emerge from the nest in about 50 to 55 days. The number of eggs in a clutch is small and the size of eggs is large compared to other sea turtles. Nesting flatbacks make an average of three nests per season and migrate to nest about once every one to three years.

Seafood in this category includes sea cucumbers, soft corals, bryozoans, squid, and jellyfish. Their particular fondness for sea cucumbers matches the abundance of this resource within the turtle's soft-bottomed foraging habitats.

This flatback returning to the sea from Crab Island, Queensland, shares its beach with crocodiles large enough to eat it.

Diet

The smallest flatbacks are believed to feed on small planktonic invertebrates that collect near the surface over the Australian continental shelf. Most of the food items chosen by larger flatbacks are mouth-sized, soft-bodied invertebrate animals.

Unique Traits

Many of the observations of flatbacks at sea are of turtles basking at the surface. On calm days a turtle may spend hours at the surface and provide appreciated perches for tired seabirds. Speaking fancifully, it may be a fondness for sun that prompts a significant number of nesting flatbacks to crawl onto beaches during the day. Although most flatbacks choose the nocturnal nesting pattern favored by most sea turtles, a small percentage labor at their reproductive task under the burning tropical sun.

Despite their turbid habitat, flatbacks may be the cleanest of all the sea turtles. Their sleek, un-fouled, barnacle-free appearance may be due to compounds they exude through their skin or that make up their thin covering of scutes.

The shell of a flatback has a greasy or waxy feel that may result from anti-fouling substances, which prevent clinging algae, barnacles, and other hangers-on from gaining a foothold on the turtle.

Conservation Status

The flatback is ensconced within a corner of the world that has remained wild and largely unaltered by industrial human beings. Like no other sea turtle, the fate of the flatback lies in the hands of a single nation. Fortunately, both the turtle's life history and the wise stewardship of the Australian people have allowed the majority of flatbacks protection within either marine parks or world heritage sites.

Owing to the turtle's inconspicuous haunts and habits, the historical abundance of flatbacks is unclear. However it is evident that at least some populations have declined. Old photographs from the early 1900s depict large numbers of flatbacks nesting on islands near the more modern settlements of central Queensland, halfway down the Great Barrier Reef. On a number of these islands today, nesting by flatbacks is rare.

For many centuries, the aboriginal peoples of Australia have consumed and used sea turtles, including the flatback. Given that this relationship has persisted so long, it seems unlikely that this subsistence harvest has had any profound effect on the risk of flatback extinction. To the aboriginal peoples, sea turtles remain not only food, but also dreamtime ancestors. Community elders have enforced rules governing this special relationship and have determined who could catch turtles and how many turtles they could take. This traditional wisdom may serve as an explanation for the common occurrence of flatbacks in areas where industrial Europeans have not displaced the indigenous inhabitants of the Australian tropics.

One relatively new threat to flatbacks is from commercial fisheries. Trawlers, which tow nets through flatback habitat to harvest prawns (shrimp), have drowned thousands of sea turtles annually, the majority of which are flatbacks. But the recent (2000) requirement for trawlers to use TEDs (Turtle Excluder Devices) is hoped to substantially reduce this threat.

The hatchlings of flatbacks are larger than those of most other sea turtles.

Flatbacks are generally well protected in Australia by the Environment Protection and Biodiversity Conservation Act of 1999. The flatback is considered by IUCN to be Data Deficient in status. This means that there is inadequate information to assess the flatback's risk of extinction. Most biologists feel that this sea turtle's limited range makes it vulnerable to habitat changes, over-exploitation, and incidental mortality from human activity.

Leatherback Turtle

Scientific Name

Dermochelys coriacea.
Named with Greek roots for leathery turtle and the Latin descriptor for leathery skin.

Other common names

Other English names given the leatherback turtle include leatherback, leatherback seaturtle, leathery turtle, trunkback, trunk turtle, and coffin-back. In Latin America, the turtle is known as canal, tinglado, baula, and tortuga laud. Many other common names vary among cultures.

Size and weight

Most adult female leatherbacks weigh 440 to 1320 lb (200 to 600 kg) and have a shell straight-length between 4 ft 9 in and 5 ft 7 in (145 and 170 cm).

Distribution

Tropical and temperate marine waters worldwide and into the sub-arctic. They have the broadest distribution of any sea turtle. They forage as far north as British Columbia, Newfoundland and the British Isles, and as far south as the Cape of Good Hope and New Zealand. Nesting occurs on beaches mostly in the tropics.

General Appearance

Foremost, leatherbacks are magnificently large. The largest leatherback known was a male weighing 2019 lb (916 kg). It was found dead on a Welsh beach open to St George's Channel between the Atlantic Ocean and the Irish Sea. The turtle had a curved carapace length of 8 ft 5 in (2.56 m) and its flippers spanned 8 ft (2.41 m) Most leatherbacks are considerably smaller, but the average female on an Atlantic nesting beach is still impressive in having a shell length of about 5 ft 3 in (1.6 m), which would put her in the 880 lb (400 kg) weight class. Pacific leatherbacks average smaller at about 4 ft 7 in (1.4 m) in shell length.

Adult leatherbacks are dark, streamlined, scaleless turtles with long, broad flippers. Their topsides are black with random white or light gray splotches, and their undersides are splotched almost equally by black and white. While on a nesting beach, the turtle's light undersides often blush to pink. But the most conspicuous dash of color a leatherback sports is an irregular pink spot at the crown of the turtle's head. Apparently, no two spots are the same exact shape.

A leatherback's body is a barrel-shape elongated into a streamlined teardrop. They are broad-shouldered beasts, with the leading edge of their teardrop torso bulging with the muscle that powers their massive fore-flippers. Seven distinct ridges extend the length of the turtle's naked carapace and fade together at the rear, which tapers into a pointed projection. Five less-distinct ridges run most of the length of the lower shell.

Both the stiff, wing-like front flippers and the broad, rudder-like rear flippers are larger in proportion to the turtle's body than in the other sea turtles. Although front flippers are highly tapered in adults, those in hatchlings are more of a paddle shape. In larger turtles, a broad web of skin connects the rear flippers to the tail. Unlike the other sea turtles, none of the leatherback's flippers has claws.

Except in the hatchlings, leatherbacks have no scales and are covered with tough, thick, rubbery skin. The turtle's head

Adult Leatherbacks eat an array of jelly-like sea animals and reach an average weight of about 880 lb (400 kg).

is large and triangular, and the mouth is without a horny beak. A leatherback's jaws are weak by sea turtle standards and the lower jaw closes within the upper jaw in a tight scissor-like manner. Leading the upper jaw, a deep notch separates two fang-like cusps, and the lower jaw ends forward with

■ *Major Nesting Beaches*   ■ *Juveniles & Adults*

a robust pointed hook. Leatherbacks have thick eyelids that close to a vertical slit.

Hatchling leatherbacks are black with white highlights and are covered with tiny, thin, bead-like scales. The white highlights trace the margins of the flippers, the seven longitudinal shell ridges, and an imaginary continuation of these ridges down the turtle's neck. The fore-flippers of a hatchling span one-third greater than the turtle's length, and are so large as to appear cumbersome. Of the other sea turtles, leatherbacks

have the only hatchlings that crawl down the beach with a simultaneous butterfly stroke.

Nesting leatherbacks also crawl with a simultaneous gait and leave a track on the beach showing clear parallel marks from both front and rear flippers. A straight central tail-drag mark is also conspicuous. The width of a leatherback track is almost always greater than 7 ft (2 m). The turtle's nest site is most often a confused array of two or more sets of mounds and pits left as the turtle turned and crawled about while covering her nest.

Distribution and Movements

Leatherbacks are dispersed throughout the world's tropical and temperate ocean waters. The turtle is distinguished in having the broadest distribution of any sea turtle or of any reptile. This extent of range is greatly expanded by the occurrence of leatherbacks in cold waters. These turtles are known to forage as far north as British Columbia, Newfoundland, and the British Isles; and as far south as southern Chile, central Argentina, the Cape of Good Hope, and New Zealand.

The leatherback's nesting distribution is largely restricted to the tropics. Principal remaining nesting beaches are located in northern South America and the Caribbean; on Africa's Gulf of Guinea south to Angola; in the Andaman and Nicobar Islands; in Indonesia and West Papua; and on the Pacific coasts of southern

Mexico and Costa Rica. Some significant nesting occurs as far north as central Florida, USA, and as far south as South Africa. Many once important nesting areas have greatly diminished.

Leatherbacks have expansive migrations. An individual turtle might travel through the waters of both the southern Caribbean and eastern Canada in the span of only a few weeks. Once, all we knew of leatherback travels came from chance recoveries of turtles bearing stainless-steel flipper tags. But today, greater details of leatherback wanderings are revealed by the broadcasts of turtles bearing satellite radio-transmitters. This tracking has shown that in both the Atlantic and the Pacific, foraging leatherbacks wander over enormous looping paths that span entire oceans. There are some patterns to the turtles' journeys, such as high to low latitude migration preceding winter, and movement vice versa in the advance of summer, but leatherbacks are seldom faithful to geography except to nest. If foraging patterns do exist in leatherbacks, they may follow oceanographic events rather than geographical landmarks.

Like other sea turtles, leatherbacks show fidelity to their nesting beaches. Often, familiar females are seen repeatedly over many years of nesting seasons on the same small stretch of beach. Pinpoint nesting on a few miles of sand is remarkable given that leatherbacks travel many thousands of miles to get there.

Although the commutes of females are best known because we can see them at their nesting beaches, male leatherbacks are the ones best known from the coldest extent of the species' range. It is possible that females choose to limit the extent of their high-latitude wanderings during years that they return to the tropics to nest.

Life History

Leatherbacks live nearly all of their lives in waters that we generally see only from the railings of ocean-going ships. This remoteness and the turtle's recent rarity leave many questions about how leatherbacks live their lives.

A life of mysterious wanderings begins when a leatherback

A leatherback hatchling reaches wet sand during its critical crawl from nest to sea.

hatchling enters the water off its natal beach. Like older leatherbacks, young leatherbacks search for food in the open ocean. Because small turtles may have trouble diving deeply, biologists assume that neonate leatherbacks make a living near the sea surface.

Only on rare occasions are juvenile leatherbacks seen by the people desperate to study them. These juveniles are almost never observed at sea but are recovered on beaches either dead or in poor condition. In reviewing these recovery records, it was observed that juveniles up to 3 ft (1 m) in shell length came only from tropical waters. Thus, it seems that the penchant for cold water foraging begins in, and only may be possible for, leatherbacks at or near adult size.

Leatherbacks grow into adults more rapidly than other sea

Leatherbacks nest in the tropics but may travel far to feed in productive waters near the Arctic.

chronological layers in the bones of dead leatherbacks. The research was successful in estimating ages of variously sized leatherbacks using annual rings laid down within small bony plates that encircle the pupil inside the turtle's eyeball. The technique gave an estimated age of maturity of 5 to 14 years.

If these maturity estimates are correct, leatherbacks increase in size 10,000 times in about a decade. For a reptile, this is unprecedented growth. But leatherbacks are not typical reptiles at all, as is described in the section on Unique Traits below.

Leatherback nesting reaches a peak most often during the months preceding the tropical wet season, or during what would be spring in the temperate climates of the hemisphere. Females typically lay 65 to 85 eggs in each of about four to nine nests throughout a season. Nesting events are separated by 9 to 10 day intervals. Along with the eggs in each nest, the nesting female intersperses many yolkless 'eggs' that are merely spheres of clear albumin packaged in papery eggshell. These ancillary nest

turtles do. In captivity, young leatherbacks have been seen to double their weight every one to three months. Yet, a captive leatherback has never lived more than a few years and growth rates in the wild are unknown. To answer the important question of maturation in leatherbacks, George Zug with the National Museum of Natural History, USA, examined

contents, which tend to be deposited on top of the clutch, vary greatly in individual size and total number but each is normally smaller than a typical egg. The purpose of these infertile 'yolkless eggs' is widely speculated either to provide a moisture source for developing embryos, to satiate egg-predators that dig into the nest, to fill gaps between the leatherback's large eggs at the top of the clutch and prevent sand from filling the airspaces, or all of the above. They all seem like plausible explanations.

Eggs are billiard-ball-sized spheres weighing about 3 oz (76 g) and produce a hatchling weighing an average of 2 oz (44 g). Incubation periods vary greatly with temperature but most beaches have nests producing hatchlings in 55 to 70 days.

Like other sea turtles, leatherbacks may reproduce over many decades. For a female, reproduction occurs every two to three years. The reproductive habits of males are unknown.

Diet

The world's largest turtle lives and grows on a diet of clear, watery, jelly-like animals. The revelation is a bit like hearing from a champion weightlifter that they have never eaten anything but cucumbers. How could a leatherback be the biggest and grow the fastest by feeding on animals that are 96 per cent water? The answer is that leatherbacks apparently eat a lot.

Juvenile leatherbacks that have lived briefly in captivity were able to eat twice their body weight in jellyfish every day. It is possible that leatherbacks of all sizes in the wild are just as ravenous. Given the poor nutrition offered by the turtle's gelatinous food, quantity must make up for quality.

Leatherbacks are specialist feeders on slippery critters with strange names like moon jellies, cannonball jellies, and lion's mane jellies. They are also fond of similarly gooey animals like ctenophores (comb jellies), salps, and siphonophores such as the Portuguese man-o-war. Some of these menu items are spiced by stinging nematocysts potent enough to send a human to the hospital.

Leatherbacks have many adaptations that allow them to consume their squishy prey. For example, the turtle's upper jaw cusps can pierce and hold the most elusive jelly blobs. And for snacks larger than a single bite, scissor-like jaws can slice larger jellyfish – some are 18 in (0.5 m) across – into consumable pieces. Lining nearly the complete length of a leatherback's throat, rows of stiff, overlapping, 1-in (3-cm) long, cone-shaped papillae point toward the turtle's stomach. The grip of these backward-pointed spines, coupled with strong throat muscles, enable a leatherback to wring out its food and expel the excess seawater the turtle slurps in.

Unique Traits

Leatherbacks are the least turtle-like of the sea turtles. In fact, many of their traits are much more mammal-like than reptile-like.

One mammal-like trait leatherbacks have is a tendency toward being warm-blooded. To be more specific, leatherbacks are endotherms (their body heat can raise their body temperature) that remain poikilothermic (having a body temperature that varies with their surroundings). This trick is critical for an animal in need of vigorous activity while enveloped in water near 32° F (0° C). Although the turtle's body temperature varies, its internal warmth, in addition to a series of heat conservation measures, allows a leatherback to have a core temperature as much as 64° F (18° C) above the surrounding seawater.

Heat conservation measures used by leatherbacks include bundled blood vessels leading into and out of the flippers, located in the turtle's shoulders. The bundled vessels serve as counter-current heat exchange units that warm blood that has circulated through a cold flipper. The result is a conservation of heat within the organs and muscles of the trunk. The trunk is of course surrounded by a shell, which in leatherbacks is a mosaic of bone, connective tissue, and blubber-like fat lying under thick skin. Just as a marine mammal's blubber insulates in cold water, so does the fatty layer surrounding a leatherback sea turtle. Each of these thermal adaptations is enhanced by the turtle's large size. Similar to many of the larger dinosaurs, leatherbacks capitalize on gigantothermy, that is, a low ratio of their surface area to body volume (that all big animals have), which reduces the heat escaping through their skin.

A warm body opens many unique possibilities for a reptile. Leatherbacks can maintain high activity in cold surroundings, dive to chilly depths, and grow amazingly fast. These traits allow leatherbacks to perform and distribute themselves in sea-mammal-like ways. But one of the oddest turtle-mammal parallels is the leatherbacks' tendency to breech. Like the behavior seen in the great whales, leatherbacks (generally when they are

For a reptile, leatherbacks grow amazingly fast, increasing in weight by a factor of 10,000 in the span of about 10 years

perturbed by something) launch themselves vertically into the air, nearly clear the water, and come crashing down on their sides.

Conservation Status

Leatherbacks are greatly reduced from historic levels. Pacific populations, once the world's largest, are now close to being extirpated. Judging by a recent precipitous drop in nesting numbers, leatherbacks face extinction from threats that have become magnified only in the last few decades.

Before the latest declines, leatherbacks were already in trouble from threats that had taken their toll for many years. A large threat has been egg harvesting. By the 1990s, leatherback populations that once nested on the beaches of India, Sri Lanka, and Malaysia were essentially harvested to death. Today, threats more profound and insidious than egg collecting occur out in the open waters where leatherbacks forage. Chief among these is the threat from long-line fishing gear set to catch pelagic fishes such as tunas and swordfish. Leatherbacks become hooked and entangled in these lines and drown in great numbers.

Conservationists have identified long-lines as the principal reason for Pacific leatherback declines. During a time of unprecedented expansion of long-line fishing in the Pacific, the principal nesting beaches of the Pacific in Costa Rica and Mexico saw the number of visiting females drop by 90 to 99 per cent. Once, leatherbacks nesting in Mexico made up two thirds of the world's population for the species. Today, only about 1 per cent of the Mexican population remains.

Perhaps more than any other sea turtle, leatherbacks are threatened by persistent marine debris such as discarded lines and plastics. Being an open-ocean animal, leatherbacks never evolved the maneuverability needed to disentangle themselves from an obstacle. This penchant for getting tangled in things, in addition to the resemblance of plastic bags to a leatherback's favorite food, make the synthetic cast-offs of fishing activity and everyday life especially pernicious for leatherbacks.

The leatherback is considered by IUCN to be Critically Endangered. This status means that leatherbacks face an extremely high risk of extinction in the wild in the immediate future.

Leatherbacks are superlative turtles. They dive deeper, swim farther, and become larger than any other sea turtle.

Sea Turtles and Humans

Human beings have known, pondered, worshipped, and used sea turtles for many centuries. Many relationships between people and sea turtles have persisted, but many more have ended poorly for sea turtles.

Although it is romantic to think of humankind's first relationship with sea turtles as having achieved a natural balance, it is likely that as soon as we began using sea turtles, we began to use them up. Yet, in archeological evidence one finds many clues that early cultures did not take sea turtles for granted, and that these animals meant more to people than just another consumable.

Five to six thousand years ago on the Arabian Sea coast in what is now Oman, people lived with sea turtles. Remains of green turtles at many sites in this region suggest that the turtles were valued not only as food but in a spiritual context as well. Green turtles are frequently found buried in Arabian graves, often having been positioned head to head with the human occupant. Although this type of burial with animals was common through the Bronze Age in coastal Arabia, sea turtles are reported to be the most common animal used in this practice.

Continuing to the present time and throughout their global range, sea turtles have retained a spiritual value to people. Some of the mystic attributes of sea turtles seem widespread if not almost universal – representation of long life, prosperity, protection, fertility, guidance through the afterlife, general good luck, and prominence in the Earth's creation.

The most profound changes in our relationship to sea turtles came with commercial trade and the enhancement of trade by technology. One finds the most telling examples of these changes in the descriptions of Caribbean colonization by Europeans. The beginning of these colonization efforts, a cascading invasion force from Europe, came to depend on sea turtles for their very survival.

Through the sixteenth and seventeenth centuries, the Spanish, British, Dutch, and French sailed throughout the Caribbean, vied for island colonies, fought with local populations of Arawak and Carib Indians, and became very hungry. By the time that Europeans arrived in the Caribbean, much of the food providing protein to ships' crews had rotted away and the livestock familiar to continentals was ill suited for survival in the cramped holds of ships. Such a dire need for protein that could persist through lengthy sea voyages was met by the discovery of a profoundly abundant local resource – the green turtle.

Europeans discovered green turtles almost immediately upon their entry into the New World. In 1503, Christopher Columbus was toward the end of his final, disastrous voyage. Two worm-holed ships, the only remnants of a proud Spanish fleet that had left the port of Cadiz a year before, were making a desperate run from the far western Caribbean to Hispaniola and on to home. The sluggish, waterlogged vessels never made the Hispaniola port-of-call. After being blown by a tropical storm far off course to the north, Columbus found his beleaguered ships in the waters between Cuba and Jamaica and within sight of two small islands. Columbus noted that the islands were '…full of tortoises, as was all the sea about, insomuch as that they looked like little rocks…' He named the islands 'Las Tortugas' after the abundance of turtles, a name that was later changed by the British to Cayman Brac and Little Cayman, two of the three Cayman Islands.

Columbus and the remaining expedition continued on as far as Jamaica, where they were rescued after several months. Of the many discoveries heralded upon his return to Spain, tiny islands surrounded by turtles seemed insignificant. Yet, in

This olive ridley may excite European tourists, help feed a Costa Rican village with its eggs, or be worked into shoe leather in rural Ecuador.

revealing what is now thought to be the largest green turtle nesting colony ever known, Columbus began a pivotal historical role for sea turtles in the events that would shape the colonization of the wider Caribbean.

Columbus' lookout had sighted the presently known Cayman Islands on 10th May, which was probably at the beginning of the nesting season when a great annual convergence of Caribbean

The green turtle played a pivotal role in the European colonization of the Caribbean.

turtles was occurring. We can only imagine the likely scene — female green turtles, each between 220 and 440 lb (100 and 200 kg), in a sprawling aggregation filling up the shallow waters around the islands, and male-female couples bobbing at the surface in such a density as to make the sea seem like a vast field of boulders. Haphazard discovery had revealed to Europeans the hub of green turtle abundance in the Western Hemisphere -- two tiny islands that were the breeding grounds for millions of turtles.

To hungry sailors and colonials, the nesting green turtles of the

Caribbean were as profound an example of divine providence as anyone could hope for. It was a resource that could not help but be devoured. The turtles that crawled onto beaches in mass-nesting forays could be readily flipped in their tracks, carted to a ship, and stacked among the other provisions below decks. By reptilian persistence, the harvested turtles could live on their backs in a ship's hold for months, without food or water, until their butchering could yield fresh meat to a hungry crew.

The European sea captains set to the task of empire building were astounded at the limitless abundance of the Caribbean green turtle. Like the turtles' persistence as living cargo, the Cayman green turtle population seemed unending. But as provisioning turned to commerce, and as harvest turned to plunder, the deceptively abundant green turtles of the Caymans were to dwindle.

By the late seventeenth century, scores of British sloops and barques were shipping an estimated 13,000 turtles each year from the Caymans to the home Isles and to colonies elsewhere in the Caribbean. For decades during which nearly every turtle ashore was carted away, somehow, green turtle nesting on the Caymans had persisted. But in what could be predicted now but not then, the Cayman Island green turtle began a steady slide into oblivion.

One of the most important characteristics to understand about sea turtles, if we are to continue to live with them, is their time scale. Most sea turtles have a generation time that spans many decades. It is a lengthy period throughout which every turtle driven to nest on her beach might be slaughtered without any substantial evidence that the population is crashing. As decades of maturing turtles in the pipeline reach adulthood and arrive for harvest at the nesting beach, they continue to provide the illusion of an infinite resource. Just as we might continue to witness the flicker of distant stars extinguished long ago, so too can we continue to take our fill of nesting sea turtles... for a time. By the late 1700s, at a time when taste for green turtle soup at fancy British dinner parties had peaked, the Cayman nesting colony had

A farm for sea turtles. Since 1968 green turtles have undergone a process of domestication at a farm in the Cayman Islands. The effort began with adult turtles and eggs taken from Caribbean beaches outside the Caymans. The farm is now self-sufficient in that no eggs or turtles are taken from the wild to replace turtles that are either released or slaughtered for food. Those juxtaposed fates – captive turtles set free and others made into turtle burger – describe the controversial nature of the farm. It is a major tourist attraction that brings the international public into roles as both consumers of sea turtle charisma and of sea turtle meat.

Cayman farm green turtles surge toward their source of pelletized 'turtle chow.' They grow to about 4.5 pounds (2 kg) in a year and are either released into nearby Cayman waters (about 40 percent), kept on as breeding stock (about 1 percent), or grown into meat supplying local markets (about 60 percent). This demand for green turtle meat lingers in the shadow of the largest harvest of wild green turtles in history. Once, the Caymans were the breeding islands for millions of green turtles. Today, despite the release of about 30,000 farm-raised turtles since 1980, the number of female green turtles using Cayman beaches is believed to be only ten.

The olive ridley egg harvest at Ostional, Costa Rica, is a clear example of the relationship between sea turtles and humans. The harvest takes place during the first day of a multi-day arribada (mass arrival). If these first eggs were not harvested, many of them would be destroyed by the digging of nesting turtles later in the event. Some argue that the harvest removes eggs that are least likely to produce hatchlings.

Eggs harvested at Ostional are bagged, given a registered seal, and transported throughout Costa Rica. Although the eggs were historically an important protein source in the local diet, most eggs today end up in bars as an accompaniment to beer and liquor. Administered as such it is easy to imagine how the eggs have come to be regarded as an aphrodisiac. Many believe that the regulated egg harvest has minimal effects on the olive ridley population and adds incentive to protect this resource by other means. About a third of egg-sale proceeds is directed toward beach protection, research, and education. Turtle tourism also flourishes at the village of Ostional. Visitors participate in walks guided by local biologists and can be on hand when hatchlings scramble from their nests 7-8 weeks after an arribada. Although unregulated egg harvest has been implicated in the decline of many sea turtle populations, the Ostional experiment is held out as a model for sustainable use and conservation.

been essentially extirpated. Today only a handful of green turtle nests are recorded in the Cayman Islands each season.

After centuries of struggling to live on a human planet, our sea turtle species are depleted but still with us. Six of the seven extant species are threatened with extinction but none has disappeared. All over the world, sea turtles are still being consumed, but the global community has made recent progress with important international agreements to manage our consumptive relationships with sea turtles.

Apart from a continued use of sea turtles for food, adornments, and various luxury items, the most important modern threats to sea turtles come from them simply getting in our way. These threats are incidental, and mostly accidental, but they are often devastating. Foremost among these incidental threats is the capture and drowning of sea turtles by nets, lines, and hooks meant to catch fish. For most species of sea turtles, mortality from fisheries probably surpasses deaths from directed capture. For some species, especially the loggerhead, the leatherback, and Kemp's ridley, incidental mortality is by itself enough of a threat to result in extinction.

Sea turtle biologists and national governments have recognized the important role that fishery management plays in conserving sea turtles. As a result, national regulations and international agreements have begun to take reduction of sea turtle mortality into account. But the conservation task is difficult. Many of the fisheries that kill the most sea turtles, such as pelagic long-line and net fisheries for tunas and swordfish, have a high economic value and occur far from the watchful eyes of fishery managers. Thus, methods to minimize sea turtle mortality that also reduce fish catch rates are not embraced, and any enforcement of regulations is hampered by the vastness of the open oceans.

Apart from the incidental effects that we have on sea turtles, our purposeful relationship with them has begun a turn from largely predator-and-prey to substantially less harmful associations,

even to one of growing mutualism. Recently, the benefits we enjoy from living sea turtles have greatly expanded.

Some of what we receive from living sea turtles comes in the form of knowledge. Sea turtle research has yielded many recent discoveries; including how animals sense their world, migrate great distances, and live under challenging conditions. But sea turtles also leave us with many questions for the future; including how

A Kemp's ridley bound by an abandoned gill net.

they live so long, and what roles they play in our own ecology.

Humans also continue to receive spiritual and emotional benefits from living sea turtles. Many people seek them out in order to enjoy being with them. And sea turtles seem to allow this attention, at least to a limited extent; sea turtles are more approachable than most wild animals.

This approachability can be seen in the many ecotourism enterprises that feature sea turtles. Some of these allow glimpses of turtles in the water, but by far the most common tours facilitate sea turtle experiences on their nesting beaches. There, guides can bring visitors intimately close. With careful guidance, a small group of 'turtle-watch' participants can experience with all their senses an impressive wild sea animal. In these nocturnal encounters, one can taste the salt mist from the pounding surf, see the bulk of the turtle glistening in the moonlight, feel the spray of sand the turtle casts over her nest site, and hear the periodic air-rush with each labored breath, a sound that precedes the smell of low tide.

experiences, as spiritual ones do, leave us with more questions than answers. The turtles present themselves, only to re-enter the sea, glide away, and perform most of their astounding lives far from where we can conveniently watch.

This charisma and mystery have fostered an important mutualistic relationship between sea turtles and people. Sea turtle conservation philosophy and efforts have grown tremendously in recent decades. More than ever, programs are in place and organizations are working to understand and protect sea turtles. And this mutually beneficial relationship arrives none too soon.

In a way, one might consider the present period as being a golden age in our relationship with sea turtles. Although sea turtles have declined, our advancing technology allows us greater knowledge of them and an expanded (albeit often vicarious) familiarity with them. Even if we are never able to witness all that sea turtles do, we are able still to use our instrumentation, science, and imaging to learn from them and to share what we discover with others through a wide array of media (like this book).

An olive ridley arrives at dusk on a Pacific beach in Costa Rica.

Even if sea turtle breath has not the smell of roses, these magnificent animals certainly embody their own brand of charisma. Almost without exception, sea turtles evoke positive emotions from people. Hatchlings are perceived as cute, swimming turtles are graceful, and all seem to amplify our sense of wonderment. Sea turtles crawl onto land where we can comfortably watch their intricate process of reproduction; but the

Of course, sea turtles are likely to get more difficult to know the more rare they become. An intersection of lines describing disappearing sea turtles and advancing technology just may define a present-day peak in our opportunity to experience these animals. It may be that our descendants will both envy us for our capacity to experience sea turtles, and curse us for not doing more to save them. Perhaps, this golden age in our relationship with sea turtles could also be one during which a collective wisdom finds a way for this relationship to continue.

Sea turtles are mysterious and mystical, coveted and consumed. They serve us as inspiration, sentinel, commodity, and prey. Our greatest hope for a future with these animals may be in a full realization of their value and of the benefits in a world where sea turtles thrive.

RECOMMENDED READING: *The Biology of Sea Turtles*, ed Peter Lutz and John Musick, CRC Press, 1997. *The Biology of Sea Turtles*, Volume II, ed Peter Lutz, John Musick, and Jeanette Wyneken, CRC Press, 2003. *So Excellent a Fishe*, by Archie Carr, Scribner's, 1984. *The Windward Road*, by Archie Carr, University Press of Florida, 1979. *Biology and Conservation of Sea Turtles*, ed Karen Bjorndal, Smithsonian Institute Press, 1995. *Australian Sea Turtles*, by Robert Bustard, Collins, 1972. *Loggerhead Sea Turtles*, ed Alan Bolten and Blair Witherington, Smithsonian Books, 2003. *Fire in the Turtle House*, by Osha Davidson, Public Affairs, 2001. *Decline of the Sea Turtles*, by the National Research Council, National Academy Press, 1990. *Voyage of the Turtle*, by Carl Safina, Henry Holt & Co, 2006. *Sea Turtles: A Complete Guide to Their Biology, Behavior, and Conservation*, by James Spotila, Johns Hopkins University Press, 2004.

ACKNOWLEDGMENTS: I am indebted to the many friends and colleagues I've come to know through sea turtles. These include Allen Foley, Andrea Mosier, Anne Meylan, and Peter Meylan, who each provided helpful comments on the manuscript. I also thank my wife Dawn, who has contributed unique beauty to this book through her art. And for a splendidly rewarding life I thank my parents, who tempted me into a love of learning.

A
GARDEN
FOR ALL
SEASONS

A
GARDEN
FOR ALL
SEASONS

PIPPA GREENWOOD

headline

With lots of love to all at CTF, you are *My* Reason for All Seasons.

First published in 2002 by HEADLINE BOOK PUBLISHING
10 9 8 7 6 5 4 3 2 1

Cataloguing in Publication Data is available from the British Library
ISBN 0 7553 1081 0

Designed by Colin Walton, assisted by Tracy Musson

www.waltoncreative.com

Special photography by Peter Anderson

www.peteranderson.net

Picture research by Mel Watson

Edited by Anne Askwith

Index by Richard Downing

Also by Pippa Greenwood

Many, including:

New Gardener

Gardening Hints and Tips

Garden Pests and Diseases

Garden Problem Solver

Flower Gardener

Pippa's Organic Kitchen Garden

Printed and bound in Italy by Canale S.p.A

HEADLINE BOOK PUBLISHING

A division of Hodder Headline

338 Euston Road

London NW1 3BH

www.headline.co.uk

www.hodderheadline.com

contents

introduction

If you have a garden you are truly lucky. It can provide you with fresh air, freedom, flowers, fruit and a fantastic sense of achievement as you watch it grow and develop. In reality, though, all too often a garden is largely ignored for all but the warmest weather. But there is a lot you can do to turn your garden, however large or small, into a garden for all seasons. Once the gardening bug has bitten you, you will soon realise that you want to use it throughout the year: to tend it, watch it, sit out in it, enjoy it.

OPPOSITE Richly coloured paving creates an area of hard-standing around a well-planted pond and surrounding borders. Plants with stunning foliage such as variegated sage, bog iris and chives provide colour for much of the year without relying solely on flowers. Every planting opportunity has been used, even the walls have been planted up to add texture and colour.

Once the main part of summer is over, many flowers come to an ungracious and often unattractive end, temperatures drop and the garden seems less appealing. So you find yourself leaving it to look after itself until it perks up again the following year. Of course it is more likely that you will want to sit outside in the warmer summer weather. But it is not difficult to make your garden somewhere you want to spend time in at other times of the year too.

If you are planning an entire new garden from scratch, the need for it to look good and be as usable as possible throughout the year is something you should consider from the outset. Building a garden with year-round plant and feature appeal is much easier if the whole concept is well planned and thought out beforehand. But if your garden is already well established, that does not mean to say that it needs to remain a short-season-of-use garden, which only really looks attractive from late spring to mid-summer. By incorporating some of those special plants that help to provide 'off-season' colour, texture, outline or perfume, you will instantly improve its appearance.

You may feel strongly that you have no interest in a garden in winter perhaps but, if so, I would say think again. True, lower temperatures and a shorter day length will mean that there are fewer times when you are likely to sit outside for prolonged periods; but even a cup of coffee drunk hastily outdoors in winter sunshine whilst you sit wearing multiple layers of woolly clothing tastes better out in the open air – and it tastes better still when you are surrounded by a good-looking garden or even just a single, small flowerbed or border. For me the subtle flowers of witch hazel or winter jasmine, and, too, the smaller winter performers such as winter-flowering pansies or heathers, snowdrops or winter aconites, bring an unsurpassable delight to any garden: a classic case of how small is beautiful, illustrating that plants need not be showy to be effective. Even a handful of winter-interest plants can transform a garden from a bleak wintry blankness into somewhere truly beautiful.

You can also use a well-chosen selection of plants to keep your garden looking good in other slightly less inclement seasons than winter, by filling the late summer border and ensuring that your garden is

packed full of colour and charm from late winter throughout spring and
into early summer too. Suggested plants in shaded boxes in the plant
directories are cross-referenced where applicable. Other plants are
included to give you as wide a selection as possible.

It is not just with plants that you can make your garden a place to enjoy
throughout the year. Non-living structures such as arbours, arches, pergolas
and water features all help, especially if painted or planted to make them
look their best. Creating protected places to sit and enjoy what your garden
has to offer, regardless of the season, will mean that, even when there is
no weeding to do, there will always be a reason to escape outside.

I hope that in this book you will find a host of ideas for ways in which
you can transform your garden into somewhere that is special and has
great appeal, regardless of the time of year – a real garden for all seasons.

ABOVE In winter the garden takes on a whole
new look. Structure, form and texture become
all the more important. With the arrival of the
most bitterly cold weather some plants,
whether deciduous or evergreen, are transformed into beautifully decorated living
statues when covered with a hoar frost.

trees AND shrubs

In all but the smallest garden there is room for at least one tree or shrub but, if you can find the space, use more – it's as simple as that! For trees and shrubs are an important part of any garden. If a garden is largely made up of herbaceous perennials, perhaps with flowering annuals added during summer, come the back end of autumn and throughout winter there will be little of interest left. But trees and shrubs form a permanent 'framework', a solid background for the garden, providing structure that has an input all year and for at least one season becoming a focal point.

OPPOSITE Carefully chosen trees and shrubs are a fundamentally important ingredient of this garden, bringing height and structure to it throughout the year. When in leaf, trees such as this birch are a delight, but once the leaves have fallen, the bark appears in all its glory.

Trees and shrubs are of course important not only for their contribution to the seasons. Carefully positioned, a tree or shrub can be used to mask an eyesore or to create a screen between your garden and the adjacent road or neighbour's house. Most of us enjoy a bit of peace, or at least personal space in the garden and, if your plot is overlooked, or if the view over your garden fence consists solely of the neighbour's ugly garage, trees or shrubs can easily come to the rescue. Evergreens obviously work best in a situation like this but, if your garden is not used so much in the winter months (and after all, who sits outside for lunch when it is freezing cold?), a deciduous tree or shrub may actually have what it takes when it is really needed.

Even a single tree will help to give a new garden a more established feel. A collection of trees can be used to frame a particularly gorgeous view. Trees can also provide much-needed shelter from prevailing winds, allowing you to grow a wider range of plants in the area, or even cast dappled shade on an excessively sunny garden, enabling you to sit outside and enjoy your surroundings without being grilled to a frazzle in the height of summer. Most important of all, trees and shrubs usually offer an array of attractive features – foliage, flowers, berries, fruits, bark, or simply an unusual or dramatic outline – that bring your garden to life through all or at least most of the four seasons of the year.

I adore trees, but I am the first to admit that they are not necessarily the easiest ingredients of your garden to select. What will they look like 'off season'? Will they be a suitable height? For how much of the year will they make a significant and positive contribution to the garden? How many can you sensibly use? Perhaps most fundamental of all, how can you ensure that you are choosing a good one in the first place? To help you answer such questions, below are some of the issues to consider when choosing and buying trees and shrubs; and on pp. 32–63 I have suggested some of my favourites, outlining their characteristics and any particular needs. It is essential that you check out any tree or shrub's potential before you buy; whether you choose one of these or indeed anything else, do make sure that you know what you are planting, where it likes to grow and what it will eventually look

OPPOSITE Evergreens, including many of the dwarf conifers, make an important contribution to a garden for all seasons, their many foliage colours and textures being on display throughout the year. The bright-red, delicately divided leaves of the maple nearby may fall in autumn but put on a fabulous show earlier in the year.

like. I have listed the plants according to their main season of interest, but indicated if a plant is also attractive at another time of the year.

To make your garden look good for as much of the year as possible, you will need to consider whether to choose plants that are interesting for a large part of the year, or a few different trees or shrubs, which, between them, will provide that interest. Alternatively you may feel that you are happy to compromise and plant something whose season of appeal may be relatively short, but which is impossible to resist because it is so fantastic whilst at its best. To a large extent your choice will be determined by personal preferences and the plant's suitability for the site you have to offer. You may feel that you want to use a selection of plants of which one or more fall into each of the above categories; or you may prefer to create seasonal areas within your garden, so making a spectacular but limited-season tree or shrub easier to include. For most gardens, shortage of space will mean that you will be able to grow a wider selection of shrubs than you can trees, but there is no magic formula to help you decide on the proportion of trees and shrubs.

Sizing up before you buy

When choosing a tree, it is always worth considering what it will look like in a few years' time. That sweet and innocent little thing may look appealing now, but it may also have the potential to tower above your house, covering the garden in shade in the process. Some trees have a relatively upright habit, so, although they may ultimately grow to a fair height, they will not have such a dramatic effect on the rest of the garden and, if carefully positioned, could be a real asset. Others have a tendency to spread outwards, often making them less of a problem as far as blocking light from the house is concerned, but posing problems if the garden is tiny. Wide-spreading trees restrict the number that you can grow as, once fully grown, they will take up more soil space. Although you need to plan ahead when choosing, you could look upon a tree as being a wonderful asset for a certain number of years but then something you will need to remove before it swamps the garden or its roots encroach on the foundations of your house. Small, weeping forms

OPPOSITE Some trees, such as these flowering cherries, may have a very brief blooming period, but the beautiful display they put on in spring more than compensates for this. A classic case of short, but sweet! Underplanted with bluebells (*Hyacinthoides non-scripta*) they look all the more stunning.

of tree, such as the Kilmarnock willow (*Salix caprea* 'Kilmarnock') or *Prunus autumnalis* 'Pendula Rosea', may be the answer if space is really limited and, provided that you plant carefully near by, avoiding anything else that is particularly large, the tree will retain its position and give great impact. But beware: some weeping trees have such a wide-spreading crown that they take up too much space in a small garden.

Remember that some shrubs too can grow both tall and wide and end up closely resembling a tree. Some of the potential heights and spreads of the trees and shrubs on pp. 33–63 may seem quite scary, but bear in mind that these are ultimate dimensions, and for the vast majority it will take an awfully long time for something to get that big. To keep garden trees within bounds or to remove excessive growth or dead wood you may need to carry out some maintenance pruning (see p. 181).

Seasonal features – bark, foliage, flowers and berries

Trees and shrubs can bring a lot more than height and structure to a garden. Each tree or shrub has its own set of features and to create year-round interest in your garden you will need to decide which of these fits your plans and your garden the best.

In some cases it may be the tree's bark – several forms of birch (*Betula* spp.) and varieties, including the common silver birch, fall into this category, as does the totally touchy-feely *Prunus serrula*, which has gloriously shiny reddish-brown new bark. Bark is especially noticeable during the winter months, as is an attractive stem. If you are after bright colours, consider the dogwoods (*Cornus* spp.) and willows (*Salix* spp.), which, if regularly cut back or stooled, produce a fantastic display of red, orange or yellow stems.

Leaves can provide a wonderful array of shapes and textures and of course colour. Never forget that even the often-ignored colour green has an almost unlimited range of tints and shades and is extremely beautiful and calming. Also, of course, there are many trees and shrubs that have variegated, golden or red foliage. In a lightly shaded spot a golden-leaved tree or shrub will help to provide a lighter, less gloomy atmosphere. Some golden or variegated foliage will tend to become greener or less variegated if there is too much shade, but something like a variegated holly is better able to cope – try *Ilex* x *altaclerensis* 'Golden King' and you will see what I mean.

Deciduous trees and shrubs may have breathtakingly beautiful autumn foliage and, provided that you do not try to grow anything that drops its leaves too close to a pond, where the foliage will become a nuisance, a bright, colourful show of leaves can be just what your garden needs once the warmth of summer has gone. If you are choosing a plant for its autumn colour, make sure you buy it in the autumn. The precise colouring may vary from year to year and with the growing conditions but, if you actually see a plant in its full autumn glory, you can still have a pretty good idea about what you can expect to see once it is planted in your garden. Don't just go on other people's suggestions: their idea of a fabulous riot of colour may not be the same as yours. If you are planting a tree for autumn colour, it is worth planting it in a relatively protected site – otherwise one very windy day can bring all that colour to a hasty end. By giving the tree a bit of shelter you should be able to prolong the display for several weeks.

Some trees and shrubs have foliage that changes colour as it ages, not just as autumn approaches. I love the pinkish tinge of young beech foliage, although you will need a lot of space to even contemplate this particular tree. The rowan *Sorbus thibetica* 'John Mitchell' is near white, almost silvery as the foliage breaks in spring; it then turns green as the leaves enlarge, and in autumn you get a mouth-watering display of purple, pink and yellow. *Sorbus aria* 'Lutescens' also has delicately silvery young foliage. Many of the Japanese maples have particularly vibrant leaf tones shortly after the foliage breaks.

Evergreens, including conifers, are great if you want a living garden statue – yes they will increase in size but, other than that, you can be sure that they will keep their green, golden, blue-green or variegated foliage for twelve months of the year. This makes them especially useful as a backdrop, perhaps behind a border or as hedging; or a specimen tree can be planted in a prominent position where its colour and shape can be enjoyed. Take care to choose those that are said to stay

ABOVE Snake bark maples have something to offer at every season: once the foliage has finally fallen, the intricately patterned bark on the stems and trunks is beautifully revealed. Other trees with coloured or marked bark will also make a good contribution, but do ensure they are planted where they can be seen easily.

**TOP TREES AND SHRUBS
FOR AUTUMN COLOUR**

FOLIAGE ● FRUITS ●

Acer, including *A. palmatum* and
   A. japonicum varieties ● p. 48

Amelanchier lamarckii ● p. 36

Berberis, e.g. *B. 'Rubrostilla'* and
   B. thunbergii ● ● p.51

Callicarpa ● p. 51

Cotinus ● p. 52

Cotoneaster ● ● p. 52

Euonymus alatus ● ● p. 52

Euonymus europaeus ● ● p. 52

Fothergilla major ● p. 37

Malus (flowering and fruiting crab apples),
   e.g. *'Golden Hornet'* ● ● p. 49

Parrotia persica ● p. 50

Rhus ● p. 54

Rosa moyesii ● p. 54

Sorbus aria ● p. 50

Sorbus cashmiriana ● p. 50

relatively small, and you can then create wonderful mounds, spires and other bold, clear-cut shapes (see p. 27).

Some trees put on an exceptional display of flowers and, although this too may be quite short-lived, it is well worth the wait. Just think of the flowering cherries. More shrubs are grown for their flowers and, because they are generally held lower down and in a more sheltered spot, winds are less of a problem. If you can choose a tree or shrub that also has perfume or good autumn leaf colour or an attractive bark or stem, you are on to a real winner. In order to ensure that shrubs flower in profusion, you may need to carry out routine pruning (see p. 181).

Berries too can be a real bonus, providing added colour for the garden. The great thing about them is that they provide a seasonal display when the flowers or foliage have done their stuff. Plant trees or shrubs that bear berries, nuts or other fruits and you will also encourage wildlife, particularly if you use any native species such as oak (if you have the space), rowan or hawthorn. Berberis, pyracantha and cotoneaster will all produce many a good meal for the birds too.

Buying trees and shrubs

Trees and shrubs are most frequently sold 'container grown' – that is, having been raised and grown on in a pot. During the winter months you may also be able to buy some 'bare-root' trees; these have been grown in open ground and then carefully dug up and sold with their roots wrapped in hessian and compost or similar material. Bare-root plants can safely be planted only when the soil is neither too wet nor frozen and whilst the tree or shrub is dormant. They are generally less expensive than container-grown equivalents and, although they usually need a bit more care and attention initially, I often find that they establish and grow away very well. Whether the plant is bare-root or container grown, it is essential that the root system has never been allowed to dry out, so try to take a look if possible before you buy it. Once you have it at home, you will also need to take great care that it remains moist, so you will need to water it regularly, especially if it is a bare root.

It is difficult to generalise about what makes a tree or shrub a good specimen to pick but, if you are buying whilst the tree is in leaf, you should certainly check for pests and diseases and obvious signs of any nutrient deficiency – all these may pose problems in the future, and certainly indicate that the nursery or garden centre has not been looking after it too well. Some problems, such as powdery mildew, rarely have a significant effect in the long term, but others such as vine weevil are a potential disaster zone. If I spot any plants with the characteristic leaf-edge notching caused by this particular pest, I shop elsewhere, for if the weevil or its grubs are in one pot they may well be in others too; introduce it into your garden and you will regret it in the future. Healthy-looking branches and trunks are a must, so avoid those which have cracks, splits, snags (areas from which a branch has been torn or incorrectly sawn) or dead stems. If possible find one that has a good, open structure of healthy, undamaged limbs. The odd recently broken branch may be almost inevitable, but aim for as few as possible.

A container-grown tree or shrub that has a very congested root system, packed tightly within the pot so that little compost is even visible, is something I would avoid as well. Once really pot bound like this the plant may well have started to run out of steam, it is more likely to have suffered from drought from time to time and it may be harder to get it established, as the roots will be inclined to carry on growing round and round in the pot shape. I am sure that every garden centre must hate me for this bit of advice, but I always suggest carefully easing a plant from its pot to check the state of the root system. If it is too pot bound, if the roots are brown and soggy, or if there is a large quantity of spare compost (which usually lands on your foot), the plant is best left for someone else to buy. You want to choose one with plenty of firm roots but which has not been in the pot so long that it has become badly pot bound.

If you are not brave enough to do this, at least check the surface of the compost – if it is covered with weeds, algae or liverworts, I presume that the plant has not been very well cared for and may have been standing unsold for too long. After all, if the garden centre cannot be bothered to keep weeds down, do you really believe that the tree or shrub has been properly fed and watered? From time to time I have fallen

TOP TREES AND SHRUBS FOR FLOWERS

Amelanchier lamarckii p. 36

Berberis x *stenophylla* p. 37

Camellia p. 37

Ceanothus p. 43

Chimonanthus praecox p. 60

Cornus kousa var. 'Chinensis' p. 41

Corylopsis p. 37

Exochorda x *macrantha* 'The Bride' p. 44

Magnolia p. 32

Malus (flowering crab apples) p. 49

Philadelphus p. 46

Prunus (flowering cherries and almonds) p. 33

Rhododendron p. 38

Rosa p. 46

Viburnum p. 39

for a plant in a seriously weed-infested pot and decided that, providing that everything else is as it should be, I will turn a blind eye to the unwanted vegetation. So I have bought the plant, but only after I have removed every trace of weed from the compost. By doing this you will reduce the risk of introducing irritating new weeds to your own garden. It is also worth remembering that a plant in a pot is more prone to winter damage than one growing in open ground. If it is very pot bound it is all the more likely that the roots will be damaged by plummeting temperatures, as they are so close to the outside edges of the pot. I avoid buying new plants in the few months following extremely harsh weather, as the likelihood of their roots having been damaged is just too great. Obviously root-ball frosting or freezing can occur on any plant once you have purchased it, so it is essential to plant it promptly.

Positioning for best effect

With any tree or shrub, when you are considering where to plant it, always bear in mind its various assets – size, shape, whatever seasonal features it has to offer and whether it has impact for more than one main season of interest. Make sure that the relevant parts can be enjoyed at the appropriate season, and that they will not be masked by whatever else is planted close by. Position the plant in a place where it can be enjoyed to the full, where you can feast your eyes (or indulge your nose) at every opportunity – perhaps close to a path or seating area if it has a good perfume, or in a sheltered spot if it has short-lived blossom or fantastic but potentially short-lived autumn colour. Make sure that plants grown for their berries are placed close to a path or other point of access so that these generally relatively less flamboyant fruits cannot be missed. You may also want to consider what else will be looking good in that area of the garden at those specific times of year. Will it upstage another less showy plant, or will it be the one to come off worst in the battle of the seasonal good looks?

If you plant a single, specimen tree towards the corner or even in the centre of your lawn, it will in effect take centre stage because its outline and overall shape in winter, and its foliage in spring, summer and

OPPOSITE Any tree which has a good shape and attractive foliage with a seasonal sprinkling of pretty flowers needs to be put in a prime position. The circular bed beneath can be planted up with perennials or, better still, with a combination of bulbs and seasonal bedding to give a year round display.

autumn, will look all the better against a plain, green carpet of green grass – nothing to detract from its own, personal beauty. An interesting branch structure, perhaps a weeping shape such as that wickedly pretty weeping silver-leaved pear (*Pyrus salicifolia* 'Pendula'), is always shown off to best advantage when grown in isolation like this. In a tiny garden, a shrub grown in this way will have the same effect.

You may decide that you wish to create areas of your garden each with a different seasonal appeal. A winter garden will make a welcome sight and can have great impact too, provided that a good range of winter interest plants are concentrated together. There may be other parts of the garden where you may prefer to concentrate on height-of-the-summer colour, so ensuring that the area most used for sunbathing, sitting or eating over the warmer months always looks at its best when in use.

In smaller gardens it is often easiest and most effective to ensure that there are plants for all seasons in each area of the garden; by spreading the seasonal-impact makers widely, the garden as a whole should have something to offer throughout the year.

Evergreens are always useful when it comes to creating a garden for all seasons, as they will provide foliage throughout the year, often of good colour and with interesting textures too. Because the branches are never bare you can be sure that evergreens will provide reliable areas of colour and texture at all times.

The positioning of individual trees and shrubs is also important. You need to be sure that each is put to best use within your plan. Winter-interest trees and shrubs, for instance, are not likely to be seen or enjoyed much if growing in the far corner of the garden. Instead place these closer to the house or near to a pathway that you will still use regularly despite the weather. Make sure that something with a perfume is positioned so that you can enjoy this, and in winter remember that access to a perfumed shrub via the frosted grass makes little sense as far as the health of your lawn is concerned. Trees or shrubs with good autumn colour or those with eyecatching flowers make a bold seasonal statement, so make sure that these can be viewed to their full glory, preferably both within the garden and from at least one house window.

OPPOSITE A tree or shrub with flamboyant flowers often puts on a relatively short-lived display, so it is all the more important that when it does its stuff it can be enjoyed from every angle. With the hedge and lawn providing a perfect foil, this *Cersis siliquastrum* (Judas tree) looks its best.

Extending the season with climbers

Climbers are effective as they can be used not just in their own right, but also to extend the season of interest provided by other plants in the garden. Allow a climber to scramble through an existing tree, shrub or hedge, and this natural support system then plays host to a climber that is colourful at a different time of year.

If your garden already has several perfectly acceptable trees or shrubs but their peak-performance time is short-lived, why not add to what they have to offer by using them as a framework for something else? Shrubs can look great with a clematis, *Tropaeolum tuberosum* var. *lineamaculatum* 'Ken Aslet', the flame creeper (*T. speciosum*) or another scrambling plant grown through them. You could use temporary annual flowers, such as morning glory, sweet pea or the semi-evergreen, half-hardy Chilean glory vine (*Eccremocarpus scaber*) in the same way. For a sizeable tree, one of the more rampant clematis, such as *Clematis Montana*, or a suitable climbing or rambling rose will have the same effect. Whether you choose plants for flowering that coincides with that

ABOVE Climbers offer a great opportunity to introduce colour in a relatively small space. They take up little room in the garden and can brighten up an arch or pergola or, like this *Rosa* 'Madam Solvay' rose, be allowed to scramble through existing plants.

OPPOSITE I planted this young summer-flowering clematis at the base of a lovely dry stone wall in my own garden. It may have started out small, but within a season or two it should be romping through the rhododendron, decorating it with flowers in summer and doubling the display produced in one place.

of the main plant, or for flowering that brings colour when the others' flowers have faded, add-on planting like this works a treat.

When planting a climber to enliven a new tree or shrub, it is not difficult to plant so that each root-ball has adequate space and both plants can grow away well without either of them hindering the other. Planting close to an existing, well-established shrub or tree may, however, not be quite so easy. You need to give the new plant enough space and ensure that it has a plentiful supply of food and moisture; and you need to minimise the risk of the roots of the established plant being damaged.

Underplanting to add interest

You can also add colour and interest beneath a favourite tree or shrub by planting spring- or autumn-flowering bulbs, corms or attractive ground-cover perennials or other low-growing perennials, such as lungworts (*Pulmonaria*), epimedium or heuchera. The sight of a spirit-lifting spring underplanting of crocus, miniature narcissus or snowdrops is enough to make you do this for every tree or shrub you plant. If it is the autumn that needs a bit of additional colour, autumn-flowering crocus, such as *C. speciosus* and *C. kotschyanus* subsp. *kotschyanus* (also known as *C. zonatus*), work well, as do the bigger blooms of colchicum.

With spring bulbs, either choose those that are particularly well adapted to a life of dappled shade beneath trees, or plant them only beneath deciduous trees, where you should find that they receive adequate daylight to perform well – by the time the tree or shrub has developed a dense canopy of leaves, the bulbs will have already had a good amount of light. When you are creating a naturalised display of bulbs, it is usually easiest to use a trowel or bulb planter – making a larger hole when planting a sizeable area of bulbs can prove very difficult in (and potentially damaging to) the mass of tree roots beneath the plant. If the soil is naturally extremely free-draining or poor, it is especially important to try to improve it in the immediate vicinity of the bulbs. Adding garden compost will supply some food and also reduce the risk of the soil becoming excessively dry during the height of the summer.

ABOVE Trees and shrubs benefit from an area cleared of grass around their base. But plant this up with *Cyclamen coum* and enjoy their flowers and marbled foliage too.

OPPOSITE Topiary is the ultimate form of living sculpture, allowing drama and often plenty of humour in to your garden, twelve months of the year. Topiary works just as well on a small scale, or in good-sized pots.

Creating topiary shapes for year-round interest

Evergreen plants such as box (*Buxus sempervirens*), privet (*Ligustrum ovalifolium* and varieties, and *L. vulgare*), *Lonicera nitida*, holly (*Ilex* spp.), yew (*Taxus baccata*), bay (*Laurus nobilis*) and many of the conifers can be pruned to create fantastic topiary shapes. Box is perhaps the easiest to work with, as the new shoots are formed from the centre of the plant. Topiary shapes are a way to bring your individual style to life in the garden in the form of living architecture and geometry that lasts all the year round. Once clipped or trained into a ball, spiral or other shape, plants become a living sculpture, which you can use either in amongst other plants or as a stand-alone feature. Placed in a prominent position, perhaps on a terrace, patio or front steps, that topiary peacock or elaborate box spiral really can take on a life of its own!

Topiary frames are available from some garden centres or mail-order suppliers and, if you decide to give this art form a try, you need not worry that you will be taking on a life's work: with a small frame and a

well-chosen plant you could have a recognisable shape within a few years, although larger or more complex shapes will take much longer. If the idea of tackling even a simple piece of topiary sends you into decline, you can choose from the selection of ready-trained and near fully-grown topiary figures for sale at more and more nurseries and garden centres — all you have to do is clip your bear, peacock or aeroplane regularly to keep it in shape. Whether you buy a ready-trained and pruned piece of topiary or decide to start from scratch yourself, it is essential that you use really sharp shears or secateurs: nasty, chewed stems look awful and make the job take a lot longer.

If you buy a topiary frame, choose one that is well made, as it will be in place for several years and the last thing you want is for it to fall apart. It is possible to buy quite intricate wire shapes to create your own topiary animals (and indeed many other shapes). Whatever you choose, select a plant that is, if possible, a vaguely similar size and shape to the frame but certainly not a lot taller or wider. Next position the frame over the plant and clip off all stems that protrude from the framework. A dense piece of topiary always looks much more attractive, so at every opportunity throughout the first few years in particular, pinch out the tips of the stems, as this will encourage bushy growth. After the initial clipping you should only need to tackle it once a year, usually in early summer, each time clipping back protruding stems to the framework so that any new growth is kept within it. A large topiary shape may take a fair bit of time to maintain, but you can be sure that it will also leave you feeling very satisfied, and in a strange way I find jobs like this quite therapeutic — just don't risk trimming your topiary when you are in too bad a mood, or it may end up with a shorter, harsher hair cut than it really needs!

Making a simple cone shape

It is probably easiest to create a cone using a plant that tends naturally to grow in an upright or cone-like shape. *Cupressus macrocarpa* 'Goldcrest' or yew (*Taxus baccata*), for example, respond well. Choose a good, dense, healthy plant. Using secateurs, clip it into the approximate

OPPOSITE A simple topiary ball, like this one grown from box, is not even time-consuming to maintain. It can be clipped with a good pair of garden shears. For more intricate shapes such as elaborate animals, or other figures, topiary shears are advisable.

shape by eye. If you are not naturally good at this sort of thing, be cautious and take off less rather than more.

Later in the year or the following year in the summer, once new growth has been put on, you can then make a more accurate cone shape using a home-made template. Use three canes wired together at the top to form a wigwam shape. Then at approximately 7cm (3in) intervals attach circles of wire around the outside of the three canes. The wire circles need to be attached to the canes with care so that they do not get displaced and so that they retain their circular shape.

Place this cane-and-wire cone shape over the top of the plant, check that it is correctly angled and upright, and then using secateurs clip off any shoots that protrude out of the cone.

Once you have removed the template, the plant should have a good, even shape. It will probably need to be clipped twice a year, in late spring and mid-summer, if it is to keep its shape and look really neat and sculptural. Slower-growing plants such as yew can usually be kept looking good on just one clipping a year, whilst a faster-growing subject, such as *Lonicera nitida*, will need attention three times each year.

Creating a spiral from a cone

You will need a reasonable-sized (90cm/36in minimum), approximately cone-shaped evergreen plant.

Attach a piece of string to the very top of the plant. Loosely wind the string around the outside of the cone to create a spiral. Check that the string is neatly and evenly laid, and that the tiers of the spiral are even throughout. The string marks the upper edge of each turn of the spiral. Then attach the string firmly to its final point – either the main stem of the plant or a relatively sturdy branch.

Using sharp secateurs, carefully cut away the outer branches of the tree, following the spiral shape marked out by the string. You will need to cut away the branches to the mid-point between adjacent whorls of the spiral. By cutting right back to reveal the central main stem you will make the spiral look neater and more architectural.

ABOVE If clipped regularly a well-grown piece of topiary can provide a faultless, solid three-dimensional shape. These rounded *Buxus* (box) cones also provide a real touchy-feely element to this garden and are perfectly planted in an accessible spot.

OPPOSITE A topiary spiral may look difficult to achieve, but follow the advice opposite and you too could have a *Buxus* (box) spiral like this with surprisingly little effort, but this is definitely a case for buying some topiary shears!

springTREES

For me spring-interest trees are vital. With their blossom and delicate young foliage they remind me that yes, finally, winter has come to an end and the gardening year is about to unfold.

ABOVE RIGHT Magnolias like this *Magnolia stellata* exude opulence and luxury. In the spring they can put on a truly breathtaking display of their white, pink or purplish flowers and this one even has a delicate but distinct perfume. A real knock-out!

Magnolia

SPRING	SUMMER	AUTUMN	WINTER
flowers			

The magnolias come in a wide range of sizes and flower shapes, the most common resembling goblets, tulips and stars. Some, such as *M. grandiflora*, produce their blooms in summer (see p. 41), but many put on a terrific show in spring. True, their display of **white**, **pink** or **purple-pink** flowers may not last for long, but whilst it is there it will transform your garden into a palace! Many spring-flowering magnolias have their showy, waxy blooms severely damaged and spoiled by frosts, so wherever possible try to grow these trees in a sheltered spot. The vast majority also prefer dappled shade and need an acid soil.

M. stellata (star magnolia), **H** 3.6m (12ft), **S** 4.5m (15ft): from early to mid-spring this small tree is covered with a mass of star-shaped white blooms. They have a faint but delicious fragrance too and the plant looks all the more dramatic because the flowers are produced on the bare branches. Each flower measures up to 10cm (4in) across. Never getting too big, this magnolia is very slow-growing and so will take many years to reach its potential height, and it can often be grown successfully in a large tub such as a half barrel. It looks lovely in winter when the complex system of branches is covered in a hoar frost.

M. x soulangeana: this may grow to a height of about 9m (30ft), bears tulip-shaped flowers in mid-spring, sometimes also giving a second, sparser show towards the end of summer. It has many good garden varieties including 'Lennei', whose flowers, **pinky-purple** on the outside and white inside, appear from mid- to late spring.

Malus CRAB APPLES

SPRING	SUMMER	AUTUMN	WINTER
fruit			
flowers			

Few grow to more than 6–7m (20–22ft) in height; many are considerably smaller. There is a plentiful supply of very garden-worthy crab apples and these deciduous trees are easy to grow in pretty well any garden. Most look startlingly pretty in the spring, when they are covered with single or double, **red**, **pink** or **white** flowers. Later in the year these will be replaced by miniature apple-shaped fruits, which vary in colour from red to yellow or purple and in many cases either can be an ingredient for delicious crab apple jelly or left to decorate the tree throughout the autumn (see p. 49).

Malus APPLES

SPRING	SUMMER	AUTUMN	WINTER
fruit			
flowers			

Much as crab apples merit a place in your garden, it is worth mentioning that the flowers, and later the fruits, of both dessert and cooking apples are extremely beautiful too. Indeed those of plums, apricots, almonds, cherries and pears are delightful as well. So if space is really at a premium and you hanker after something truly scrumptious, why not grow a couple of fruit trees? Provided that they are supplied with the right pollinator, you should get a good crop of fruit once the trees are established and, if grown on a suitably dwarfing rootstock or trained as a cordon, espalier or fan, they need not take up much room at all.

Prunus FLOWERING CHERRIES AND ALMONDS

SPRING	SUMMER	AUTUMN	WINTER
foliage			
flowers			

If you want to produce a show of blossom in your garden in springtime, one of the prunus is a great choice. Most of these are flowering cherries and they vary greatly in size and habit. Most have a typical tree shape. Some are weeping, such as 'Cheal's Weeping', which produces masses of double, **rose-pink** blossom and reaches a height of only about 2.5m (8ft). Some

have a very upright or columnar habit, such as 'Amanogawa', which has slightly fragrant, semi-double, **pale-pink** flowers and grows to a height of up to 3m (10ft). Although these trees' display of blossom may not really be that long-lived (especially if the weather becomes windy), it is so fantastic that they are widely planted in gardens of all sizes. Most of the ornamental prunus also produce a good display of **yellow**, **gold** or **red** foliage in the autumn.

Although I often admire those huge plantings or avenues of pink flowering cherries, I am not always fond enough of the shade of pink to actually grow one myself. I prefer the really deep pink and single flowers of a variety such as 'Kursar'. This tree, which grows to a height of about 5m (16½ft), also produces stunning red and gold autumn foliage. I always enjoy the white-flowered prunus too. Again there are numerous different varieties to choose from.

One of my favourites is the double form of the wild cherry, *P. avium* 'Plena', H 12–15m (40–50ft). In late spring it is covered in closely packed bunches of pendulous double **white** flowers. It also gives good yellow and red leaf colour in autumn.

P. sargentii (Sargent's cherry) will ultimately grow to a height of up to 15m (50ft) and in mid-spring is covered in masses of pink flowers, each measuring about 4cm (1½in) across. In spring the young foliage is an attractive bronzy-green colour as it emerges, gradually turning green later in the spring. Come the autumn it will reward you with a great display of crimson and orange foliage.

P. tenella, by far the smallest of the flowering almonds, reaching a height and spread of only about 90cm (36in), is heavily decked with **bright-pink** flowers in mid-spring.

Pyrus salicifolia 'Pendula'

SILVER-LEAVED PEAR

SPRING	SUMMER	AUTUMN	WINTER
foliage			
flowers			

H 8m (26ft), **S** 3.6m (12ft). This plant always makes an impact because of its attractive weeping habit, which somehow looks less man made than many other weeping trees. The leaves, of a similar shape to those of a weeping willow, are covered so densely in tiny grey hairs that they look almost silver. In mid-spring the branches develop clusters of really pretty **creamy-white** blossom.

RIGHT Foliage is a fundamentally important element in any planting, especially if you want to make impact throughout the year. This *Robinia pseudoacacia* 'Frisia' is one of my favourites – with its stunning, yellowish green leaves it seems to glow in sunshine.

Robinia pseudoacacia 'Frisia'

FALSE ACACIA

SPRING	SUMMER	AUTUMN	WINTER
foliage			
flowers			

H 18m (60ft), **S** 15m (50ft). From the moment the much divided leaves emerge in the spring, they are a wonderful bright **yellowish-gold** colour. Provided that the tree is growing in full sun, this colour is retained well throughout the year and provides a warm glow in the summer garden. In early summer, 20cm (8in)

ABOVE Lilacs spell cottage garden loud and clear; this purple form is cleverly underplanted with delicate bluebells too.

ABOVE RIGHT Aesculus indica forms a relatively compact and slow-growing tree which looks great in spring and indeed for much of the year (see p. 40).

long clusters of white and faintly scented flowers are produced along the stems. A gorgeous tree, but beware: it has some really vicious thorns on it.

Sorbus aria 'Lutescens' WHITEBEAM

SPRING	SUMMER	AUTUMN	WINTER
foliage			
fruits			

H and **S** 10–12m (33–40ft). The young silvery foliage is especially beautiful when it appears in spring. A neat, almost conical-shaped tree, it provides another pretty display in autumn, when the leaves turn **brown** and **golden yellow**, and the deep crimson berries develop.

Syringa LILAC

SPRING	SUMMER	AUTUMN	WINTER
flowers			

H 1.5–4.5m (5–15ft), depending on which one you choose. In theory these do best in a sunny spot with well-drained soil, but one of the most handsome specimens I have ever seen grew in my mother's garden, its feet firmly in London clay. So if you have fallen for the charms of one of these perfumed beauties, improve a heavy soil as much as you can by adding copious quantities of grit and compost and then take the risk and get planting! The dense cone-like clusters of flowers are produced between mid-spring and early summer, depending on the variety. The

smaller ones could just as easily be classed as trees; the larger ones such as the traditional **white**-flowered S. vulgaris really do grow to tree-like proportions. The buds look great but, when they are replaced by star-like heavily perfumed flowers, lilac becomes completely irresistible. Choose from **white**, **pinkish-lilac** or **purple** flowers.

OTHER TREES WITH GOOD SPRING INTEREST

Acer, including A. rubrum p. 48

Aesculus indica p.40

Aesculus parviflora p. 40

Cornus mas

Davidia involucrata p. 41

Laburnum x watereri p. 41

Prunus x subhirtella 'Autumnalis' and 'Autumnalis Rosea' p. 58

spring SHRUBS

Fabulous spring-interest shrubs are a great way to ensure that the unfolding of the new season is as fantastic as possible, with that wintry garden suddenly springing into life.

Amelanchier

SPRING	SUMMER	AUTUMN	WINTER
foliage			
flowers			

A. lamarckii. This may ultimately reach a height of about 10m (33ft), but it can be pruned and grows slowly, so it is still a lovely garden shrub. It thrives in sun or part shade and prefers a lime-free soil – I have one that grows on chalk and is actually doing very well, but it is regularly mulched with acid material. In mid- to late spring it will be covered with clusters of small, white flowers. Each year mine is truly breathtaking, and the great thing about it is that the flowers are much tougher than many of the more widely grown spring blossom plants, such as the cherries, and so the display lasts a lot longer. The new foliage is also attractive at this time of year, being a warm, **coppery** colour. Throughout the summer the leaves become greener and then, in the autumn, the bush is transformed into a brightly glowing bonfire as the foliage turns bright **red** and **yellow**.

A. canadensis is also well worth a mention. It is smaller than A. lamarckii and less spreading, with the flower clusters held more upright.

RIGHT I must confess to being in love with Amelanchier. With its dense covering of longlasting white flowers in the spring, it would put even the most flamboyant wedding in the shade. Then come the autumn its foliage turns such rich colours it is as if in flames. Much better value than most of the more widely grown flowering cherries.

Berberis x stenophylla

SPRING	SUMMER	AUTUMN	WINTER
flowers			

H and **S** 2.5m (8ft). For much of the spring this shrub's elegantly arching branches are closely packed with masses of small, scented **golden-orange** flowers. It also makes a fantastic hedging plant.

Camellia

SPRING	SUMMER	AUTUMN	WINTER
foliage			
flowers			

Although many camellias have the potential to reach tree-like proportions, they are extremely slow-growing and will even thrive in a pot for many years. There are a huge number of different ones available with either single or double almost rose-like flowers. Choose from **white**, **red** or pretty well any imaginable shade of **pink** and, provided that they have an acid soil, they are not difficult to grow. These evergreens have very glossy green leaves, which provide a perfect foil for the flowers. Ideally you should choose a site fairly well protected from frost, as the blooms often coincide with frosts and look especially miserable when frosted. White blooms in particular look awful as the gingery brown damaged petals show up so much, but reds and pinks look slightly better.

Cersis siliquastrum JUDAS TREE

SPRING	SUMMER	AUTUMN	WINTER
foliage			
flowers			

The height is rarely more than 6m (20ft) in Britain, as this striking plant really needs a very warm, sunny garden with free-draining soil if it is to reach great heights. In late spring the stems are completely covered with **rose-purple** flowers – the first time you see this plant you may think it is not real, so stunning is the display.

Corylopsis willmottiae

SPRING	SUMMER	AUTUMN	WINTER
foliage			
flowers			

H 3m (10ft), **S** 2.5m (8ft). Prefers a lime-free soil in sun or part shade. Because the flowers appear whilst frosts are likely, this fantastic plant will look best if planted in a fairly protected site in amongst other shrubs or near a south- or west-facing wall. In early and mid-spring the bare branches are decorated with 5–8cm (2–3in) long racemes of **pale yellow** and strongly and sweetly perfumed bell-shaped flowers. It also has a good autumn colour.

Fothergilla major

SPRING	SUMMER	AUTUMN	WINTER
foliage			
flowers			

H 2.5m (8ft). The flowers are a **creamy-white** colour, rather like elongated pompoms, have a delicate fragrance and are held in upright spikes. The autumn colour is also very showy with shades of **purple**, **red** and **orange**.

Kalmia

SPRING	SUMMER	AUTUMN	WINTER
flowers			

K. latifolia (sheep laurel), **H** 3m (10ft), **S** 3.6m (12ft), and *K. angustifolia* (calico bush), **H** 1.2m (4ft), **S** 1.2m (4ft), and their varieties both produce unusual flowers in late spring, each flower resembling an upside-down open umbrella. **Pink**, **red**, **purple** or **white** flowers are available, depending on the variety you choose. They prefer an acid soil.

ABOVE Space age and very unusual is the way I would describe the blooms on this *Kalmia latifolia*. Dare to be a bit different and grow one, but make sure it is in acid soil or lime-free compost.

Magnolia liliiflora 'Nigra'

SPRING	SUMMER	AUTUMN	WINTER
flowers			

H and **S** 3m (10ft). The flowers are tulip-shaped, a glorious rich **purple** colour and about 12cm (5in) long, held elegantly on this shrub from mid- to late spring.

Osmanthus delavayi

SPRING	SUMMER	AUTUMN	WINTER
foliage			
flowers			

H 1.8m (6ft), **S** 2.5m (8ft). Does well in sun or shade. From mid- to late spring this compact and bushy evergreen shrub produces small, elongated **white** fragrant flowers, each about 1cm (½in) long and often clustered together. In the autumn these are replaced by bluish-black egg-shaped fruits.

Pieris LILY-OF-THE-VALLEY BUSH

SPRING	SUMMER	AUTUMN	WINTER
foliage			
flowers			

Numerous species and varieties of these evergreen shrubs are readily available and make good garden shrubs on an acid soil or in a good-sized container of lime-free compost. Their pointed leaves are either green or variegated, but in the spring most, including the widely grown 'Forest Flame', produce new growth that is a really bright **red** or **orange** or **salmon** colour, depending on the variety.

Although this may sometimes be spoiled by frost, these shrubs continue to produce the striking new foliage for weeks on end, and so the display continues on and on. Many pieris also produce very attractive spikes of **creamy-white** bell-shaped flowers in the spring.

Rhododendron and *azalea*

SPRING	SUMMER	AUTUMN	WINTER
foliage			
flowers			

There are far too many brilliant garden rhododendrons and azaleas to list here; suffice it to say there is one for pretty well any size of garden. Some of the dwarf forms rarely grow more than 30cm (12in) or so in height, whilst others have the potential to be 6m (20ft) or more if given long enough. An acid soil is essential for almost all these shrubs, but sometimes they do surprisingly well in a neutral site. Shade or part shade suits these woodland plants well. Flower colour ranges from white through **yellow**, **orange**, **salmon**, **pink**, **purple** and **red** – between them they have enough colours to allow you to choose almost any conceivable shade you wish.

Stachyurus praecox

SPRING	SUMMER	AUTUMN	WINTER
foliage			
flowers			

H 2m (6½ft). Sun or part shade. An extraordinary shrub with bright-green

pointed leaves with prominent veining. From late winter and well into spring the branches are covered with elegant hanging spikes of **yellow** flowers. These look delightful in spring sunshine and also when topped with a dusting of snow. This is one of those shrubs which, to my mind, is simply not widely enough grown.

ABOVE One of the best plants for all seasons is this *Pieris* 'Forest Flame'. Glossy evergreen foliage is there for twelve months of the year and in spring there is a dazzling display of bright-red new leaves popping up in amongst the delicate, pendant white flower trusses.

OPPOSITE Who needs winter snowfall when you could have such as fabulous display as this in spring? When in full flower this *Viburnum plicattum* 'Mariesii' (Japanese Snowball) is decked with layer upon layer of flower-encrusted branches.

Viburnum

SPRING	SUMMER	AUTUMN	WINTER
foliage			
flowers			
fruit			

There are many specific forms and varieties of viburnums, which are readily available and which make great garden shrubs. See also p. 63.

V. x burkwoodii: ʜ 2.5m (8ft). This evergreen or semi-evergreen shrub has glossy leaves, which in some years and situations change colour slightly in autumn. The flowers are fragrant and **whlte-tınged pink** and are followed by berries, which usually change from red to black as the year progresses.

V. carlesii: ʜ 2m (6½ft). From mid- to late spring this deciduous shrub is studded with dense mounds of lovely, extremely fragrant flowers, each of which has a pretty **pink** flush.

V. opulus (Guelder rose): ʜ 5m (16½ft). I am really fond of this rather rampant deciduous shrub. Later flowering than most, its flowers are also grouped in a lace-cap formation and are white, but it is only likely to come into flower towards the very end of spring or early summer. The flowers are pretty but it Is the clusters of really shiny, bright **red** berries that I adore. These develop from the end of summer into autumn and look like jewels nestled on the stems. Choose the

OTHER SHRUBS WITH GOOD SPRING INTEREST

Berberis darwinii

Berberis x ottawensis 'Superba'

Ceanothus impressus p. 48

Ceanothus thyrsiflorus var. *repens*

Other *Ceaonothus* p. 43

Choisya ternate, including 'Sundance'

Cytisus

Daphne mezereum p. 60

Daphne odora 'Aureomarginata' p. 61

Other *Daphne* p. 61

Enkianthus campanulatus p. 52

Forsythia

Garrya elliptica

Lavandula stoechas p. 45

Lonicera fragrantissima p. 62

Lonicera x purpusii p. 62

Mahonia japonica p. 62

Ribes sanguineum

Viburnum farreri p. 63

Viburnum x bodnantense p. 63

golden-leaved form 'Aureum', whose berries look even more opulent.

V. plicatum: ʜ 3m (10ft). This has deciduous leaves on layered branches. The **white** flowers are held in lace-cap-like heads, opening towards the end of spring; they are followed by **red** fruits. In the autumn the foliage turns a good **reddish-purple**. The cultivar 'Mariesii' has particularly large heads of flowers.

summerTREES

In some ways trees play a less important role during the summer months, because the chances are that your garden has other ingredients to provide plenty of colour. But there are still many trees worthy of a place in even the smallest garden.

Aesculus HORSE CHESTNUT

SPRING	SUMMER	AUTUMN	WINTER
foliage			
flowers			

A. indica (Indian horse chestnut) can reach a height of 20m (70ft) but takes many years to reach this. In mid-summer this tree produces breath-takingly beautiful **white** candles of flowers, often with a slight pink flush, each candle measuring 30–40cm (12–16in). The foliage is **yellowy-green** and has an interesting bronzish tinge when it first appears in the spring.

A. parviflora, **H** 4m (13ft), **S** 3m (10ft), is in some ways more of a shrub than a tree; this horse chestnut produces huge quantities of **white** flowers from mid- to late spring. These too are held in candles, this time about 30cm (12in) long. In autumn the foliage turns a brilliant warm **yellow**.

Catalpa bignonioides INDIAN BEAN TREE

SPRING	SUMMER	AUTUMN	WINTER
foliage			
flowers			

H 15m (50ft), **S** 12m (40ft). It may take many years for this plant to reach a stage when it produces its extraordinarily beautiful **white**, almost frilly, yellow- and purple-marked flowers in mid- to late summer, but in the meantime it is worth growing just for the look of its huge heart-shaped aromatic golden yellowish-green leaves. The form 'Aurea' is quite a bit smaller (10m/33ft) and has a much more

ABOVE If you love the look of horse chestnut trees, and all the happy childhood memories they bring but space is too limited, then how about growing *A. parviflora* instead, as it is much more suitable for the smaller garden.

yellow tinge to the foliage. Definitely a tree for a sunny site and it even thrives on a fairly heavy clay.

Cornus kousa var. chinensis
FLOWERING DOGWOOD

SPRING	SUMMER	AUTUMN	WINTER
foliage			
flowers			
fruits			

Slow-growing, but this shrub may reach a height of 6m (20ft) or more. It prefers a neutral to acid soil. The large **creamy-yellow** bracts are really showy, making this tree look as if it is covered in cream-coloured snow from late spring until mid-summer. In the autumn, good red fruits develop and then the autumn colour warms up to a rich **red**. A tree not to be missed.

ABOVE Guaranteed to draw attention to itself, the handkerchief tree is draped with huge creamy bracts in spring and summer.

Davidia involucrata HANDKERCHIEF TREE

SPRING	SUMMER	AUTUMN	WINTER
foliage			
flowers			

H 20m (70ft), **S** 12m (40ft). Grow this tree in a moist soil, as dryness around the roots often causes dieback, but make sure that it also has plenty of sun. The tree has an attractive domed shape and large 15cm (6in) long leaves covered in down. The **creamy** bracts, each measuring about 15 x 7cm (6 x 3in), look quite stunning as they adorn the tree from late spring right through into summer.

Koelreuteria paniculata GOLDEN RAIN TREE

SPRING	SUMMER	AUTUMN	WINTER
foliage			
flowers			

H 10m (33ft), **S** 5m (16½ft). Grow this tree in a miserable and dry soil and it will put on particularly good displays in autumn. From mid- to late summer it has numerous tiny **golden** flowers, each only 2cm (¾in) or so across, carried in sprays up to 30cm (12in) long. Red leaves emerge in spring which turn green as the season progresses. In autumn an extravagant array of yellow and red leaves appears.

Laburnum x watereri 'Vossii'

SPRING	SUMMER	AUTUMN	WINTER
foliage			
flowers			

H 6m (20ft), **S** 4.5m (15ft). For a truly gorgeous display of pendent clusters of rich **yellow** flowers from late spring, right through into early summer, a laburnum is the tree you should choose. This one in particular is my choice, as it very rarely sets seed and so the risk of children eating its poisonous seeds is obviously greatly reduced.

Magnolia grandiflora

SPRING	SUMMER	AUTUMN	WINTER
foliage			
flowers			

H and **S** 15m (50ft). This striking evergreen is often trained against a wall, but if you have the space it looks particularly stunning grown as a specimen tree. The large **creamy-white** flowers are cup-shaped and have a really strong fragrance as they appear from mid-summer to mid-autumn. One word of caution: most vegetatively raised plants, such as those you are likely to buy from a nursery or garden centre, will not flower until they are about six or seven years old. The variety 'Exmouth' also has very strongly scented **cream** flowers.

OTHER TREES WITH GOOD SUMMER INTEREST

Acer p. 48

Crataegus persimilis 'Prunifolia' p. 49

Malus p. 49

Robinia pseudoacacia 'Frisia' p. 35

summerSHRUBS

During the summer, some shrubs tend to take more of a back-stage role, but their shapes, colours and textures are still a vital ingredient of the garden; there are others that have a higher profile.

Abelia x *grandiflora*

SPRING	SUMMER	AUTUMN	WINTER
foliage			
flowers			

H and **S** 1.8m (6ft). This evergreen shrub has beautifully glossy and slightly toothed leaves, and from mid-summer to mid-autumn **white** flowers appear, with a slight pink glow to them and a delicate scent. Although this abelia is basically hardy, like all the others it will do best if planted in a sheltered spot, preferably close to a south- or west-facing wall in a sunny position.

Buddleja BUTTERFLY BUSH

SPRING	SUMMER	AUTUMN	WINTER
flowers			

There are several varieties of *B. davidii*, **H** 5m (16½ft) and **S** 4m (13ft), that are well worth a position in any garden, and because they are quite fast-growing, planting one is an excellent way of giving a brand-new and previously empty garden a fairly established feel quite rapidly and yet on a low budget. If they are to keep a fairly compact shape and flower well, buddlejas all need a sunny position. Between mid-summer and early autumn, they produce tremendous **purple** flower spikes, each consisting of huge quantities of really tiny flowers. This particular butterfly bush is the parent of a lot of cultivars that are easier to keep in some form of order in a smaller garden than their parent as they are slightly less vigorous and rarely grow to such a size. These include 'White Profusion' (**white** flowers with distinct yellow eyes), 'Nanho Blue' (**pale-blue** flowers) and 'Royal Red' (**deep-purple**

flowers in spikes up to 50cm (20in) long.

B. alternifolia, **H** and **S** 4m (13ft), is a rapid-growing deciduous shrub that is always particularly colourful towards the beginning of summer, when it is decked with perfumed **purply-lilac** flowers, all held in tiny rounded bunches slotted along the stems. The stems are arching and look very elegant, especially when topped with the flowers.

B. globosa (orange ball tree), **H** and **S** 5m (16½ft), is a semi-evergreen shrub bearing numerous **yellowy-orange** clusters of flowers in early summer each measuring about 2cm (¾in) across.

With the particularly vigorous and potentially large-growing buddlejas, it is worth remembering that if you need to keep them in check they can be cut back on a regular basis.

Ceanothus CALIFORNIA LILAC

SPRING	SUMMER	AUTUMN	WINTER
flowers			

A well-fed soil and a sunny position are necessary if you want to get the most from your ceanothus, and in the first year after planting it is worth giving it some winter protection, but after that it should survive without any serious damage. There are lots of different varieties of ceanothus that are fabulous in a garden situation, most of them topped with dense, near-spherical

clusters of **blue**, **purple** or **pink** flowers, which have a wonderful and quite strong honey-like scent acting as a magnet for bees throughout the flowering period.

C. *impressus*, **H** and **S** 2m (6½ft), has clusters of rich **lavender**-coloured flowers from late spring into early summer.

C. 'Puget Blue', **H** and **S** 3m (10ft), is my favourite, with its really bright **blue** flower clusters, produced mainly in early summer and then spasmodically through the rest of the summer. It is evergreen and so provides an attractive backdrop throughout the year.

The deciduous C. x *delileanus* 'Gloire de Versailles', **H** 1.8m (6ft), **S** 1.2m (4ft), has big clusters of pale, almost **powder-blue** flowers from mid-summer to the beginning of autumn.

All these and indeed the other ceanothus that you are likely to come across can be grown as freestanding shrubs, but often look particularly good if loosely trained against a wall.

Cistus SUN ROSE

SPRING	SUMMER	AUTUMN	WINTER
foliage			
flowers			

Once again, there are lots of different cistus that are worth growing in a garden, all displaying ostentatious, delightfully delicate-looking flowers,

looking as if they are made from crushed silk. Do make sure that you choose the hardy ones and that you grow them in a really sunny spot, with a very free-drained and, ideally, poor soil. Some favourite varieties include: C. *crispus*, **H** and **S** 60cm (24in) – **cerise** flowers; C. 'Elma', **H** and **S** 2m (6½ft) – big **pure-white** flowers; and C. 'Silver Pink', **H** and **S** 60cm (24in) – **silvery-pink** flowers.

Exochorda x *macrantha* 'The Bride'

SPRING	SUMMER	AUTUMN	WINTER
flowers			

H and **S** 2m (6½ft). The display produced by this plant in early summer may not last very long, but it is really fantastic, as the arching branches are covered with pendent clusters of **white** flowers, each individual flower measuring up to 3cm (1¼in) in diameter. It is quite slow-growing, and does well in all but

the chalkiest of soils, provided that it has plenty of sun or just a little bit of light shade.

Hebe SHRUBBY VERONICA

SPRING	SUMMER	AUTUMN	WINTER
foliage			
flowers			

Every time I go into a garden centre or nursery there seem to be several new varieties of hebe available, but if you want to take the easy route make

ABOVE The geometrically positioned leaves of hebes make them worthy of a place in the garden, but when in flower they take on a whole new dimension.

OPPOSITE The show put on by this *Kolkwitzia amabilis* is breathtakingly pretty, and a close look at the individual flowers reveals their intricate patterns.

sure that you check that the varieties you have chosen are fully hardy, as not all of them are. They do well in any soil, even one that is very chalky, in a well-drained site in a sunny spot. Some varieties to look out for include: *H. albicans*, **H** and **S** 1m (3½ft) – **white** flowers in mid-summer; H. 'Blue Clouds', **H** 1m (3½ft), **S** 1.2m (4ft) – from early summer through to early winter producing **mauve** flower spikes up to 10cm (4in) long; and H. 'Pewter Dome', **H** and **S** 1m (3½ft) – big clusters of **white** flowers between mid- and late summer, which look particularly stunning against the greyish-green leaves.

Kolkwitzia amabilis BEAUTY BUSH

SPRING	SUMMER	AUTUMN	WINTER
foliage			
flowers			

H and **S** 3m (10ft). In early summer, the branches are densely covered with clusters of small, tubular, **pale-pink** flowers, each with a delicate orange speckling on the throat and resembling miniature foxgloves. The variety 'Pink Cloud' is a good deal smaller (**H** and **S** 2m/6½ft) and flowers equally profusely. It is essential to grow kolkwitzias in a sunny spot.

Lavandula LAVENDER

SPRING	SUMMER	AUTUMN	WINTER
foliage			
flowers			

This much-loved plant has wonderfully aromatic foliage and flowers. It needs a sunny site with a well-drained soil or it is inclined to rot off over the wet winter months. Regular pruning is essential if you are to keep it good and bushy and prevent it from becoming ugly and leggy.

L. angustifolia (old English lavender), **H** and **S** 60cm (24in), has fragrant **bluish-grey** flower spikes from late spring to the end of summer. Varieties include: 'Alba', **H** and **S** 50cm (20in) – **white** flowers from mid- to late summer; 'Hidcote', **H** and **S** 45cm (18in) – really **deep-blue** flower spikes from early to mid-summer; 'Hidcote Pink', **H** and **S** 45cm (18in) – **pale-pink** flowers in early and mid-summer; 'Loddon Pink', **H** and **S** 45cm (18in) – pale pink flowers in mid-summer; and 'Munstead', **H** and **S** 45cm (18in) – **lilac-blue** flowers from mid- to late summer.

L. stoechas (French lavender), **H** and **S** 45cm (18in), in late spring to early summer, produces elongated **pinky-purple** bracts that grow in tufts from the apex of the flower spikes. Very good drainage is particularly essential.

Philadelphus MOCK ORANGE

SPRING	SUMMER	AUTUMN	WINTER
foliage			
flowers			

If you fancy the appearance of what looks like an avalanche of snow in your garden in early or mid-summer, a philadelphus is a plant you must consider. The flowers are either **white** or **cream** and usually have a prominent cluster of golden stamens in the centre. The individual flowers are also a good size, usually 2.5–5cm (1–2in) in diameter, and have a gorgeous orange blossom-like scent. Pretty well all the philadelphus are worth growing, but here are some you really should look out for: *P.* 'Belle Etoile', **H** and **S** 2.5m

(8ft) – slight pink flush to the base of the white petals and good scent; *P.* 'Beauclerk', **H** 1.8m (6ft) **S** 1.5m (5ft) – single flowers on the arching stems, very good perfume and a slight cerise flush to the base of the white petals.

P. coronarius, **H** 3m (10ft), **S** 2.5m (8ft), has semi-double, **white** flowers, again with a strong perfume. This is a brilliant plant if you have particularly dry soil. *P. coronarius.* 'Aureus', **H** 2.5m (8ft), **S** 1.5m (5ft), has really bright **golden-yellow** foliage that is at its strongest colour in early summer and then gradually greens up as the season progresses. It is best grown in semi- or full shade.

Potentilla CINQUEFOIL

SPRING	SUMMER	AUTUMN	WINTER
flowers			

H 75cm–1.8m (30in–6ft), **S** 90cm–1.5m (3–5ft). The brightly coloured flowers in shades of **red**, **yellow**, **orange** and **pink** are guaranteed to bring warmth to a sunny corner of your garden from late spring, right through until autumn, depending on the variety or combination of varieties you plant. The flowers are carried in clusters and each individual usually measures about 2.5cm (1in) in diameter.

P. fruticosa shrubby cinquefoil flowers mainly in summer, but in mild seasons it will still be putting on a fair show come the autumn. The shrubby varieties will probably be of most use in your garden, including 'Red Ace', bright **vermillion** flowers with a yellowish back to them; 'Abbotswood', **white** flowers; and 'Beesii', beautifully silvered foliage and good-sized **bright-yellow** flowers.

Rosa ROSE

SPRING	SUMMER	AUTUMN	WINTER
flowers			
fruit/hips			

The rose must be one of the best-known and indeed most widely planted shrubs in English gardens. Provided that roses are given a site in full sun (or failing that partial shade) and a fairly moisture-retentive but not

waterlogged soil, they are not difficult to grow. Give them a bit of regular feeding and prune according to their specific requirements and they should put on a brilliant display for much of the summer. The range of roses – from single through to double, from flowers held on a single stem to several flowers per stem, in pretty well every colour and shade of **white**, **cream**, **yellow**, **orange**, **red** and **pink** – means that there is definitely one to suit your personal taste and your garden. The most important thing to look out for when buying roses is a good healthy plant initially and, if possible, one that has a degree of disease resistance. For such information, check individual labels.

Weigela SPP. AND THEIR VARIETIES

SPRING	SUMMER	AUTUMN	WINTER
foliage			
flowers			

These shrubs produce a reliable show of flowers during the summer months. Individual flowers are shaped rather like miniature foxgloves and sometimes have attractively patterned throats to them. They do best in a sunny or partially shaded site and appreciate regular feeding.

    W. florida, **H** and **S** 2m (6½ft), has 2.5cm- (1in-) long **pink** flowers, held in clusters on elegantly arching branches. If you fancy a bit of variegated foliage, take a look at *W. florida* 'Aureovariegata', which has similar-coloured flowers and a beautiful cream edging to each leaf; *W.* 'Bristol Ruby' has bright **crimson** flowers; and *W.* 'Abel Carrière' has large **pinky-carmine**-coloured flowers that fade as they age.

ABOVE Most of the weigelas, including this *W.* 'Bristol Ruby' can be relied upon to make a mass of colour for much of the summer, their foliage is good looking too, particularly the variegated forms.

OPPOSITE Those perfect, pure colours, white and gold, are combined to perfection in the flowers of this *Philadelphus* 'Beauclark' AGM and as an added bonus the perfume is, well, out of this world.

OTHER SHRUBS WITH GOOD SUMMER INTEREST

Amelanchier lamarckii p. 36

Azalea p. 38

Berberis 'Rubrostilla' p. 51

Berberis wilsoniae p. 51

Callicarpa p. 51

Callistemon

Caryopteris x *clandonensis*

Ceratostigma willmottianum

Convolvulus cneorum

Cotinus p. 52

Daphne p. 60

Enkianthus campanulatus p. 52

Erica varieties (summer-flowering) p. 147

Escallonia

Fuchsia

Hibiscus syriacus p. 53

Hydrangea p. 53

Hypericum calycinum p. 54

Hypericum forrestii p. 54

Kerria japonica

Nandina domestica p. 63

Olearia x *haastii*

Perovskia varieties

Phormium tenax

Romneya coulteri

Rosa moyesii 'Geranium' p. 54

Rosa 'Sealing Wax' (moyesii hybrid) p. 55

Rhododendron p. 38

Rubus cockburnianus p. 63

Spirea

Syringa p. 35

Viburnum opulus p. 39

Yucca filamentosa

Yucca flaccida

autumnTREES

Autumn is a time when many trees really earn their crust. No floral display can top the rich, glowing warmth of good autumn foliage. Shiny, succulent berries – and sometimes flowers – are a crowning glory. Dwarf conifers also help to add colour and structure.

Acer

SPRING	SUMMER	AUTUMN	WINTER
foliage			
bark			

A. palmatum, *A. japonicum* and other Japanese maples (see also pp. 56 and 160) are delicately attractive trees. Once again there are simply too many of these to list: almost every one produces good autumn colour and in spring and summer the divided foliage clothing the branches is a real delight. Although ultimately they become tree-like in stature, the Japanese maples are extremely slow-growing and so are well suited to a smaller garden or even a good-sized container. To minimise the risk of the foliage showing scorching, it is best to plant these in a moist yet free-draining soil and in dappled shade out of the way of winds. Yes, admittedly this may make them harder to place, but once you have found the right spot they will reward you well.

Of the *A. palmatum* varieties, 'Bloodgood' has a lovely **purple** leaf colour and in the autumn it develops red-winged seed capsules. The Dissectum Atropurpureum Group has finely divided leaves that turn **reddish-crimson** in autumn. Var. *dissectum* (also known as *A. palmatum* 'Dissectum') has delicate green, very finely divided leaves and in autumn these turn **reddish** or **yellow**, depending on the precise weather that year and the growing conditions. 'Osakazuki' has lobed green leaves transformed into a mass of bright **reds** in autumn. 'Sango-kaku' (also known as *A. palmatum* 'Senkaki') (coral bark maple), perhaps more like a shrub than a tree in its stature, has bright **coral**-coloured twigs, which show up particularly well in the winter months; the bright green leaves turn a pretty **yellow** in the autumn.

A. japonicum 'Aconitifolium' is slow-growing but has the potential to reach eventually a height of about 15m (50ft). The lobed leaves turn bright crimson in autumn and look especially gorgeous when combined with the winged **red** seeds.

A. rubrum (red maple), **H** 20m (70ft), is impossible to ignore once autumn arrives and the lobed leaves turn a bright **reddish-orange** colour. In spring it bears tiny but attractive flowers on the bare stems. It is too large ultimately for most gardens, but plant it if you have the space, for it is truly fantastic.

Arbutus unedo STRAWBERRY TREE

SPRING	SUMMER	AUTUMN	WINTER
foliage			
flowers			
fruits			

H 10m (33ft). Slow-growing but it can also be pruned into a standard sphere with great effect. In the coldest parts of Britain it may prove to be slightly tender, but it survives well in most areas. In the autumn numerous clusters of small **white** or faintly **pink** flowers develop. These later form near spherical and bright orangey-red, long-lasting fruits. In many years the faintly honey-scented flowers will be present at the same time as the fruits from the previous autumn.

Crataegus persimilis 'Prunifolia'
HAWTHORN

SPRING	SUMMER	AUTUMN	WINTER
foliage			
flowers			
fruits			

H 3m (10ft). This will do best in a sunny spot. In autumn the shiny green leaves become rich **scarlet** and **orange**. It produces plenty of **white** flowers in the summer and these then form red haws that are often still present as the leaves change colour.

Malus FLOWERING CRAB APPLES

SPRING	SUMMER	AUTUMN	WINTER
foliage			
flowers			
fruits			

As well as having good spring blossom (see p. 33), many of the crab apples produce attractive fruits in late summer and autumn. *M.* 'Golden Hornet', **H** 4m (13ft), has numerous **bright-yellow** large fruits that seem to have little appeal to the birds and so often still

ABOVE Always looking as if man made, the strawberry tree is guaranteed to cause a few raised eyebrows, particularly since the fruits and flowers are both likely to be on the plant in autumn.

OPPOSITE The glow given off by the autumnal foliage of a maple like this *Acer palmatum* helps to bring warmth to the most miserable autumn day. When touched with sunlight the effect is even better.

decorate the tree in mid-winter. *M.* 'John Downie', **H** 6m (20ft), is covered with large **bright-red** and **orange** fruits in the autumn, which you may be tempted to make into crab apple jelly.

M. x *robusta* 'Red Sentinel', **H** 12m (40ft), **s** 10m (33ft), has large shiny rich **red** fruits that are also inclined to be long-lasting, often into late winter. The varieties 'Yellow Siberian' and 'Red Siberian' have prominent **yellow** and **red** fruits that seem to be not particularly attractive to birds and so are likely to stay on the trees into winter.

ABOVE The foliage of the Kashmir rowan looks good as soon as it appears, but in autumn it becomes golden-yellow as the tree is decorated with clusters of bright white berries.

Parrotia persica PERSIAN IRONWOOD

SPRING	SUMMER	AUTUMN	WINTER
foliage			
flowers			

H 12m (40ft). A truly remarkable tree. In autumn the leaves turn from green into a flamboyant mixture of **red**, **amber** and **gold**, positively glowing on the spreading branches. Then in winter the bare branches are adorned with tiny **red** flowers. Once established and a considerable size, the bark of the trunk flakes in an attractive way, adding another dimension to its winter appeal.

Sorbus

SPRING	SUMMER	AUTUMN	WINTER
foliage			
flowers			
berries			

S. aria (whitebeam) **H** 15m (50ft), has **brown** and **gold** autumn foliage and deep **crimson** berries. Many of the whitebeams provide useful food for the birds. However, many people report that those with **white** or **yellow** berries usually seem slightly less appetising and so are longer-lasting.

S. cashmeriana (Kashmir rowan), **H** 7m (22ft), has large clusters of bright white fruits in autumn, which remain on the tree even once the leaves have fallen.

S. vilmorinii, **H** 4.5m (15ft), has leaves that in autumn develop shades of **red** and **purple**. It also forms white berries, each with a distinct pink flush.

OTHER TREES WITH GOOD AUTUMN INTEREST

Acer griseum p. 56

Aesculus parviflora p. 40.

Cercidiphyllum japonicum

Cercis siliquastrum p. 37

Cornus kousa var. *chinensis* p. 41

Koelreuteria paniculata p. 41

Liquidambar

Magnolia grandiflora p. 41

Photina davidiana (also known as *Stransvaesia davidiana*)

Prunus avium 'Plena' p. 33

Prunus 'Kursar' p. 33

Prunus sargentii p. 33

Prunus X *subhirtella* 'Autumnalis' and 'Autumnalis Rosea' p. 59

Many other *Prunus* pp. 33, 58

Sorbus aria 'Lutescens' p. 35

autumnSHRUBS

If space is limited, all the merits of autumn trees can still be enjoyed by choosing some of the glorious autumn-interest shrubs that will bring warmth and colour to a garden of any size.

Berberis

SPRING	SUMMER	AUTUMN	WINTER
foliage			
flowers			
berries			

Many of the deciduous berberis produce gorgeous bright leaf colour in the autumn and a number also have attractive berries at this time of year.

B. 'Rubrostilla': **H** and **S** 1.8m (6ft). In autumn this shrub has screaming **red** foliage and clusters of **coral**-coloured berries hanging from arching stems. In early summer it has **pale-yellow** flowers.

B. thunbergii: **H** 2m (6½ft), **S** 2.7m (9ft). In autumn the near-round green leaves turn bright shades of **orange** and **red**, and this display is made all the more flamboyant by the arrival of the small, but bright **red**, berries. The variety 'Bagatelle' is the smallest deciduous berberis; it takes about ten years to achieve a height and spread of 30cm (12in). The foliage

is an attractive **purply-bronze** colour for much of the year and then in the autumn it develops a fuse of really brilliant **red**, **orange** and **crimson**.

B. wilsoniae, a partially evergreen shrub, is also relatively small, reaching a height and spread of about 1.2m (4ft) in ten to twelve years. The leaves turn rich shades of **orange** and **red** in the autumn and good-sized drooping clusters of berries develop towards the end of summer and into autumn. In early summer the plant produces clusters of pretty **yellow** flowers.

Callicarpa BEAUTY BERRY

SPRING	SUMMER	AUTUMN	WINTER
foliage			
flowers			
berries			

H and **S** 3m (10ft). After the pale **lilac**-coloured flowers appear in mid-summer, this shrub becomes literally encrusted

RIGHT Did Mother Nature have to spend hours on end gluing these clusters of brightly coloured fruits on to these stems? Her efforts were well rewarded when the job was finished and she had created this weird but wonderful *Callicarpa bodinieri giraldii*.

with tightly packed clumps of near spherical bright **violet** fruits – it looks as if someone has been busy with beads and glue. The foliage of *C. bodinieri* var. *giraldii* 'Profusion' turns a **purplish** colour in the autumn, having started out with a bronze tinge in spring and gradually progressing through shades of green in the summer months.

Cotinus SMOKE BUSH

SPRING	SUMMER	AUTUMN	WINTER
foliage			
flowers			

There are several types of cotinus that are worth including in the garden; however, it is worth bearing in mind that all cotinus prefer a sunny spot and if the soil is too heavily manured or fertile the autumn colour tends to be paler.

C. coggygria 'Royal Purple', **H** and **S** 3.5m (11ft), has **dark-purple** foliage throughout the year that turns a bright **red** come the autumn. Plumes of flowers appear in mid-summer and then turn grey, decorating the plant in attractive fluffy tufts of 'smoke'.

C. 'Flame', **H** 4m (13ft), has dark green foliage turning into a veritable bonfire of colours in the autumn. The fluffy flower plumes of this variety have an attractive **pinkish** tinge.

C. 'Grace', **H** 4m (13ft), has leaves with a rich **purple** tinge, which turn **scarlet** in the autumn.

C. obovatus, **H** 9m (30ft), **S** 6m (20ft), produces foliage with rich **red**, **purple** and **orange** coloration in the autumn. The fluffy flower plumes are up to 30cm (12in) long and have a distinct, pale **greenish** tinge.

Cotoneaster

SPRING	SUMMER	AUTUMN	WINTER
foliage			
flowers			
berries			

The berries of many cotoneasters make them extremely useful plants in autumn, and the deciduous ones such as *C. horizontalis* also produce exciting foliage colours at this time of year.

C. horizontalis is only about 60cm (24in) tall and has a spread of about 1.8m (6ft), making it perfect as a ground-cover plant or for hiding an otherwise boring bank. 'Variegatus' is also low-growing, only reaching a height of about 60cm (24in). The **white**-edged leaves take on **pink** tinges towards the end of autumn and into winter.

C. salicifolius 'Exburyensis' is usually regarded as an evergreen, although it may sometimes appear semi-evergreen, depending on the climate. It reaches a height and spread of about 3m (10ft) and in autumn is covered with **yellow** fruits.

There are many other cotoneasters that are well worth looking out for.

Enkianthus campanulatus BELL BUSH

SPRING	SUMMER	AUTUMN	WINTER
foliage			
flowers			

Quite a large shrub, reaching a height of 5m (16½ft), but if necessary an older and rather straggly plant can be cut back quite hard in the spring. It requires a neutral to acid soil, in a site in sun or part shade. In autumn the fairly dull green leaves turn bright shades of **yellow** and **red**. In spring and early summer the plant is decked with **cream** cup-shaped flowers, which often have pink or reddish coloration running through them; these are held in clusters and are fairly long-lasting.

Euonymus SPINDLE BUSH

SPRING	SUMMER	AUTUMN	WINTER
foliage			
berries			

E. alatus (the winged spindle bush) has interestingly winged corky outgrowths along the stems. It reaches a height of about 2.5m (8ft) and in autumn the leaves turn bright **red** and almost seem to give off a luminous glow. The fruits are divided into four lobes, each lobe containing a single orange seed, and when these open up they further add to the display.

E. europaeus, **H** 5m (16½ft), has foliage that, particularly in the variety 'Red Cascade', turns a rich deep **red** in autumn. This is improved further by the

appearance of the inky red-lobed fruits, which contain orange and white seeds.

Hibiscus syriacus ROSE MALLOW

SPRING	SUMMER	AUTUMN	WINTER
foliage			
flowers			

H 2.5m (8ft), **S** 1.8m (6ft). From late summer right through until early autumn, this completely hardy deciduous hibiscus produces beautiful **lilac** flowers with a dense purple eye. Although the flowers rarely last for long, a plentiful supply is produced.

Hydrangea

SPRING	SUMMER	AUTUMN	WINTER
foliage			
flowers			

Many of the hydrangeas produce a good display in summertime and for some this extends into autumn as well. These include *H. quercifolia*, whose flowerheads start off a **creamy-white** colour and then gradually develop into shades of **orange** and **purple** as the season progresses. The green leaves also change colour in the autumn, becoming a very showy **purple**, **orange** and **crimson**. This hydrangea, like all others, needs a moisture-retentive soil if it is to thrive. For this reason it is also best to plant it in a relatively shaded spot where soil is less likely to dry out.

ABOVE The spindle bushes such as this *Euonymus alatus* produce some of the hottest pinky-red colours in the garden in autumn; in sunshine or gloom they seem to glow and give out a much-needed warmth.

RIGHT Most trees and shrubs are used to provide good foliage colour in autumn, but with this hardy *Hibiscus syriacus* flowers can come in to their own too.

Hypericum ST JOHN'S WORT

SPRING	SUMMER	AUTUMN	WINTER
foliage			
flowers			

Many of the shrubby hypericums produce slightly **yellow** mottled foliage in the autumn, but some also have flowers, which may be present at this time of year too.

H. calycinum (rose of Sharon), **H** 45cm (18in), **S** 90cm (36in), starts to flower in early summer, but carries on well into the start of autumn, producing lots of rich **yellow** flowers, each with prominent stamens, measuring about 6cm (2½in) across. It is a great plant for ground-cover purposes and does extremely well in a rather miserable dry and shady spot.

H. forrestii, **H** 1.5m (5ft), **S** 2m (6½ft), has golden **yellow** flowers from the middle of summer into early autumn. Following flowering the plant produces really attractive bronzy-brown seedpods, which add further decoration.

Osmanthus heterophyllus

SPRING	SUMMER	AUTUMN	WINTER
foliage			
flowers			

H and **S** 4.5m (15ft). This osmanthus produces its clusters of fragrant flowers in both early and mid-autumn, and then goes on to produce sparse oblong **purplish-black** fruits. The foliage is very similar to that of holly and adds a

touch of spiky excitement! The variety 'Aureomarginatus' has golden **yellow** margins to the leaves.

Rhus SUMAC

SPRING	SUMMER	AUTUMN	WINTER
foliage			
fruit			

All the sumacs produce fantastic autumn colour. They seem to glow brightly wherever they are planted, but their colour tends to be best in free-draining soil in a sunny spot. In the autumn they also produce extraordinary upright and often rather furry conical fruits, which are a **crimson** colour. The only problem with the sumacs is that they tend to sucker and so can prove to be very invasive, often producing numerous shoots in nearby beds and lawn.

R. x *pulvinata* 'Red Autumn Lace' turns a rich fiery **red** in autumn and grows to a height of about only 4m (13ft).

R. typhina (stag's horn sumac), however, is likely to grow to 8m (26ft) but its autumn colour is particularly lovely.

Rosa ROSE

SPRING	SUMMER	AUTUMN	WINTER
flowers			
fruit			

R. moyesii 'Geranium', **H** 2.5m (8ft), **S** 2m (6½ft). I must admit that I think the single crimson flowers are gorgeous when they appear in summer, but it is for its autumn display of bottle-shaped **scarlet** hips that most people include it in their gardens. Unlike many rose hips, these seem to be relatively uninteresting to local wildlife and so often last well into winter, when they look startling covered with a hoar frost. The hybrid 'Sealing Wax', **H** 2.5m (8ft), **S** 2m (6½ft), with arching stems, has pretty **bright-pink** summer flowers, but again it is the flask-shaped scarlet hips that really win this plant points. These, too, often remain on the plant into autumn. Not the tidiest of shrubs, but who cares?

R. glauca, **H** 2m (6½ft), **S** 1.8m (6ft). This rose also produces hips, this time red, and likely to persist until early winter. These are set off beautifully in early autumn by **purplish-grey** leaves and **purple-red** stems.

ABOVE For some roses such as *Rosa moyesii* 'Geranium' deadheading is a definite no-no, as in autumn wonderful showy hips form.

OPPOSITE This sumac may have the potential to outgrow its space, but every inch it colonises will be pure delight in autumn.

OTHER SHRUBS WITH GOOD AUTUMN INTEREST

Abelia chinensis

Abelia x *grandiflora* p. 42

Amelanchier lamarckii p. 36

Aralia elata p. 60

Buddleja davidii p. 42

Calluna vulgaris

Ceanothus p. 43

Ceanothus x *delileanus* 'Gloire de Versailles' p. 44

Ceratostigma plumbaginoides

Ceratostigma willmottianum

Corylopsis sinensis var. *sinensis* (also known as *Corylopsis willmottiae*) p. 37

Cotoneaster x *watereri*

Fatsia japonica

Fothergilla major p. 37

Fuchsia varieties, including 'Mrs Popple' and 'Tom Thumb'

Gaultheria mucronata (also known as *Pernettya mucronata*)

Gaultheria procumbens

Hamamelis mollis p. 57

Other *Hamamelis* p. 57

Hebe – some later-flowering varieties, including 'Autumn Glory' and 'Great Orme' p. 45

Hebe albicans p. 45

Hydrangea 'Mariesii'

Hydrangea macrophylla varieties, including 'Blue Wave' and 'Hamburg'

Hydrangea paniculata 'Grandiflora'

Hypericum x *inodorum* 'Elstead'

Hypericum 'Hidcote'

Mahonia x *media* 'Charity' p. 62

Nandina domestica p. 63

Osmanthus delavayi p. 38

Perovskia, including 'Blue Spire'

Phlomis fruticosa varieties

Potentilla fruticosa, including 'Vilmoriniana' p. 46

Other *Potentilla*

Pyracantha

Rhododendron luteum

Rosa, including *R.* 'Fru Dagmar Hastrup'

Spiraea – later-flowering, including *S. japonica* and *S. japonica* 'Anthony Waterer'

Symphoricarpos albus

Viburnum x *burkwoodii* p. 39

Viburnum davidii

Viburnum farreri p. 63

Viburnum opulus p. 39

Viburnum plicatum p. 39

winterTREES

In winter many trees come into their own, as their silhouettes become prominent features.

Evergreens similarly bring a sculptural element to the garden which, because they retain their leaves, gives a solid feel and much-needed texture.

Acer

SPRING	SUMMER	AUTUMN	WINTER
foliage			
bark			

A. capillipes (snake bark maple), **H** 10m (33ft), has a domed shape that is attractive whatever the season, but it comes into its own in winter, when the trunk is clearly visible: **reddish-green** when young and marked with distinct white striping running up and down the trunk.

A. griseum (paper bark maple), **H** 12m (40ft), prefers a slightly sheltered spot out of the heat of the sun. It is possibly too tall for smaller gardens once it reaches its ultimate height, but pure joy all the time it is in position. In winter, once the leaves have fallen, the extraordinary peeling, **cinnamon**- and foxy-coloured bark is revealed in all its glory. Also a great tree for autumn when its leaves turn bright **red**.

Betula BIRCH

SPRING	SUMMER	AUTUMN	WINTER
foliage			
bark			

B. pendula (silver birch) – **H** 20m (70ft) ultimately, so too tall for all but the largest garden – is a fantastic tree in winter because the peeling, **silver-white** bark, marked with charcoal grey, looks so stunning. Although commonly found in non-garden situations, this British native is great in a garden. Try growing three saplings close together and allow them to form a group – a miniature woodland effect to die for. For smaller gardens try 'Youngii', which is a dome-shaped tree with a weeping habit that should grow no taller than 10m (33ft).

B. utilis var. *jacquemontii* and its varieties 'Silver Shadow' and 'Grayswood Ghost', **H** 18m (60ft), **S** 10m (33ft), are fantastic winter trees whose pure **white** bark creates an almost ghostly effect as they lurk at the end of your garden – spooky but very appealing.

ABOVE White on white may sound unappealing but one look at this trio of *Betula utilis* 'Jaquemontii' on a frosty morning should change your mind for ever.

Chamaecyparis CYPRESS

SPRING	SUMMER	AUTUMN	WINTER
foliage			

There are several of these cypresses and all help to provide shape, colour and texture throughout the year.

C. 'Aurea Densa', **H** 2m (6½ft), **S** 75cm (30in), has a fantastic near conical, compact shape, is extremely slow-growing and keeps its golden **yellow** colour throughout the year.

C. lawsoniana 'Minima Glauca', **H** and **S** 2m (6½ft), always reminds me of a frisky looking sea-urchin as it has a neat, compact sea-green globe shape.

C. obtusa 'Nana Aurea', **H** 1.8m (6ft), is quite a flat-topped tree in outline and has pretty, golden **yellow** foliage that tends to be somewhat greener if grown in shade.

Cornus alba RED-BARKED DOGWOOD

SPRING	SUMMER	AUTUMN	WINTER
foliage			
flowers			
bark			

Plant in a sunny spot to encourage a good stem colour. It is at its best when cut back to near ground level in late spring, every two years, to create a multistemmed plant whose rich **crimson-red** stems appear hot enough to warm the coldest winter garden. Cut back this way it will not grow more than 2m (6½ft) in height or spread. In autumn

the foliage turns a mixture of **reddish-purple** and **crimson**. For bright coral pink stems try the slightly smaller 'Sibirica', and if the idea of a white and green variegated leaf appeals to you, look at 'Sibirica Variegata'.

Hamamelis WITCH HAZEL

SPRING	SUMMER	AUTUMN	WINTER
foliage			
flowers			

H up to about 3.6m (12ft). In some, ultimate spread may be similar to height. A shaded spot is best for witch hazels, with a well-drained soil that is acid or neutral. These plants are very slow-growing and can also be grown in containers to great effect, but unless kept adequately watered throughout the year they die back. Many have good autumn colour – mainly bright **purples**, **reds** and **oranges**, which make them take on the appearance of a roaring fire. But their main attraction is that in mid- and late winter, when colour and warmth is harder to track down, witch hazels produce an Oriental-style display of extraordinary flowers, each resembling a frantically dancing spider frozen in mid-repertoire, and in most cases emitting a really spicy, sweet, sensuous perfume. Borne on bare branches, the flowers' looks and perfume are breathtaking. Some of my favourite witch hazels include *H.* x intermedia 'Jelena' (**yellow**

flowers with orange-red tints); 'Ruby Glow' and 'Diane' (**red** flowers); 'Pallida' (very strongly perfumed bright **yellow** flowers and bright yellow leaves in autumn) and *H. mollis* (lots of golden **yellow** very well-perfumed flowers and yellow leaves in autumn). There are several lovely varieties of *H. mollis*, including 'Goldcrest' and 'Brevipetala' (with golden **yellow** and strongly perfumed flowers and foliage that turn a good yellow colour in autumn).

ABOVE For me, a winter garden without one of the witch hazels is incomplete. Just when the air is at its coldest the bare stems are covered with wild, spidery flowers in hot shades of red, for example, this *Hamamelis* x *intermedia* 'Diane', orange or yellow, and many have a fantastic fragrance too.

Ilex HOLLY

SPRING	SUMMER	AUTUMN	WINTER
foliage			
berries			

Some hollies are probably better classed as shrubs than trees, but all can be kept to a reasonable size if cut back regularly. The evergreen spiky leaves are glossy and tough, being **dark green** or variegated with yellow, cream or near-white. The most widely grown are varieties of I. x *altaclerensis* (Highclere holly) and I. aquifolium (common holly). A potential added benefit is that, provided that you grow a female form and there is a suitable male near by,

you should get a good crop of berries each autumn. These are usually red.

I. x *altaclerensis* is particularly attractive, and useful varieties include 'Golden King' (despite its name, a female plant with gold-edged leaves), 'Lawsoniana' (dark green leaf edges whilst the central area of each leaf is wonderfully variegated with a mixture of pale green, yellow and green, but its berries are rather a dull red).

I. *aquifolium* 'Argentea Marginata' (H 5m/16½ft) has a rather conical shape, silver-edged leaves and red berries; 'Ferrox Argentea', also known as the silver hedgehog holly, has spiny hedgehog-like leaves edged in silver (a male); 'Golden Queen' (you've guessed it, a male plant) has green leaves with golden edges and a few leaves of pure gold; and 'Golden Milkboy' (also a male) with dark green leaves with a central golden blotch.

Juniperus JUNIPER

SPRING	SUMMER	AUTUMN	WINTER
foliage			

Several of the junipers make useful plants for a smallish garden and provide much-needed colour and texture in the winter and indeed for the entire year. They do well in sun or partial shade and prefer a slightly dry, miserable soil.

J. *chinensis* 'Plumosa Aurea', H 90cm

(36in), s 3m (10ft), has tightly packed yellowy-green foliage that turns a purple-brown colour over winter.

J. x *pfitzeriana* 'Sulphur Spray', H and s 2m (6½ft), has sulphur **yellow** foliage.

J. *squamata* 'Blue Star', H 60cm (24in), s 90cm (36in), extremely slow-growing, forms a really compact mound of **silvery-blue** foliage.

Pinus

SPRING	SUMMER	AUTUMN	WINTER
foliage			

P. *sylvestris* 'Gold Coin', H and s 2m (6½ft), slow-growing and with bright **yellow** foliage.

Prunus

SPRING	SUMMER	AUTUMN	WINTER
foliage			
flowers			
bark			

P. *serrula*, H 5m (16½ft), s 2.5m (8ft), does best in a well-drained and fertile soil in a sunny spot. This is probably my favourite tree when it comes to bark: in winter it stands out, inviting you to feel its brightly shiny **reddish-brown** trunk, which looks as if it has been polished. The bark is inclined to peel and is marked with horizontal, slightly raised buff-coloured bands. The peeling actually enhances the look of the trunk, as the skin-like tendrils of loose bark look honey-brown in the winter sunlight.

It does have flowers but these are small and really not of great significance. With *P.* x *subhirtella* 'Autumnalis', and the form of this with pink flowers, 'Autumnalis Rosea', **H** and **S** 8–9m (26–30ft), a sunny spot in almost any soil except one that is too wet or very dry seems to fit the bill. Keep this plant well fed. It will take a good few years for either of these forms of the so-called autumn-flowering cherry to reach their potential dimensions, and in the meantime they are both guaranteed to produce a fantastic display of tiny white or pink flowers respectively from early winter, often right through until spring. If you avoid flowering cherries because you find them too blowsy, these two should change your mind: they really are delicate-looking beasts and often turn a good yellow in autumn too.

Salix WILLOW

SPRING	SUMMER	AUTUMN	WINTER
flowers			
bark			

Not all willows need reach massive heights, and in winter some of the most striking splashes of colour can be produced from willows that have been cut back close to the ground every other year at the end of winter to create a plant more like a shrub than a tree. This will produce a truly flamboyant show of new, coloured

stems as well as a display of catkins. After two years it will reach a height of about 1.8m (6ft). Try *S. alba* subsp. *vitellina* (egg-yolk-**yellow** new growth) and the variety 'Britzensis' (**scarlet-orange** new shoots), or *S. acutifolia* 'Blue Streak' (rich **purple** shoots with a silvery-grey bloom and sharply contrasting silvery buds).

Thuja

SPRING	SUMMER	AUTUMN	WINTER
foliage			

There are many thujas that make a useful contribution to the garden at any time of year and that help greatly with form and colour over the winter months. When choosing thujas, as with other conifers, it is very important to ensure that you buy something that will fit in with your garden in the long term, or that you are prepared to remove swiftly once it gets too big. There are a number of good dwarf forms to fit the bill, including *T. orientalis* 'Aurea Nana', **H** and **S** 30–45cm (12–18in), which has a delightfully comfy near-spherical shape and a pretty almost **lime green** to **yellow** colour. *T. orientalis* 'Reingold' is more conical in shape and, because it is slow-growing, will rarely reach a height of more than 1.5m (5ft) in twenty years. It has a rich **golden** foliage with warm amber tints.

ABOVE Upright streaks of reddish-orange stand out especially well in a snow covered garden.

OPPOSITE Hollies have exciting, armed leaves but choose one like this *Ferox Argentea* and there is even more texture and colour, and in many cases there is that added extra, bright bunches of berries.

OTHER TREES WITH GOOD WINTER INTEREST

winterSHRUBS

Some of my favourite winter plants are shrubs, many of which bring texture and colour to your garden at this less colourful time of the year. Best of all are those whose winter flowers produce fantastic perfume too.

Aralia elata

SPRING	SUMMER	AUTUMN	WINTER
foliage			
stems			

H 5m (16½ft), **S** 1.2m (4ft). Grows best in a slightly sheltered spot with a moisture-retentive soil. It has evil-looking coarse thorns that are shown to best advantage in winter on the bare stems. The leaves are large and doubly divided and make a bold statement throughout the year, often developing good shades of **red** or **orange** during the autumn. This is definitely a plant that adds an unusual, slightly quirky element to the garden.

Chimonanthus praecox

SPRING	SUMMER	AUTUMN	WINTER
flowers			

H 3m (10ft), **S** 2m (6½ft). This shrub enjoys a sunny spot. It has lovely **yellow** flowers with an almost waxy

texture and a great perfume. Each has a purple centre and develops on the bare branches. For slightly larger flowers try 'Grandiflorus'.

Cornus stolonifera 'Flaviramea'

SPRING	SUMMER	AUTUMN	WINTER
stems/bark			

This can reach a height and spread of 2.5m (8ft) if allowed to grow unchecked. A moist, acid soil in a sunny site suits it best. With masses of upright, bright **yellow** stems this deciduous shrub looks fantastic during the winter months. To keep the stems bright, cut it back in late spring every second or third year. This will keep it to well within a height and spread of 1.5m (5ft). Grow it close to the **red**-stemmed *Cornus alba* 'Sibirica' for a truly fiery effect.

Daphne

SPRING	SUMMER	AUTUMN	WINTER
foliage			
flowers			

There are many daphnes meriting a place in your garden because of their perfumed and pretty flowers, which are produced in winter or early spring.

D. mezereum, **H** and **S** 1.2m (4ft), is a showy shrub. A moist soil that never becomes too wet and is free-draining in a sunny or partially shaded position will suit it best. From late winter into early spring the very straight, upright bare

OTHER SHRUBS WITH GOOD WINTER INTEREST

Cornus alba p. 57

Corylus avellana 'Contorta'

Cotoneaster dammeri

Cotoneaster horizontalis 'Variegatus' p. 52

Cotoneaster lacteus

Cotoneaster microphyllus

Euonymus fortunei 'Emerald Gaiety', 'Emerald 'n' Gold' and 'Silver Queen'

Gaultheria mucronata (also known as Pernettya mucronata)

Hebe 'Blue Clouds' p. 45

Salix matsudana 'Tortuosa'

Skimmia japonica

Stachyurus praecox p. 38

Symphoricarpos albus

Virburnum x burkwoodii p. 39

stems are studded with **reddish-pink** flowers, which have a strong perfume. In mid-summer you can then expect a showy display of bright **red** berries to develop in amongst the leaves.

D. odora 'Aureomarginata', **H** and **S** 1.8m (6ft), likes a moist soil that never dries out but which is also free-draining, in a sunny or partly shaded spot. I have found this shrub hardy even in tough winters but, in more exposed parts of Britain, a bit of winter protection is worthwhile in the form of some fleece – or better still, save yourself this hassle and plant the shrub close to a south- or west-facing wall. This evergreen daphne has bright green, leathery leaves edged with a **yellowy-cream** line. The pale **purple** flowers, grouped into a neat posy up to 2cm (¾in) wide on the shoot tip, produce a rich perfume. The flowers appear in mid-winter and often continue through until very early spring.

ABOVE The rich purple-red flowers of the mezereon help to bring warm colours to a garden in the cooler, less cheerful months of the year.

RIGHT The flowers of *Stachyurus praecox* look just like strings of pearls.

OPPOSITE *Chimonanthus praecox* is a real delight for the eyes and nose in any wintry garden.

Lonicera

SPRING	SUMMER	AUTUMN	WINTER
flowers			

L. fragrantissima, **H** and **S** 2.7m (9ft) and *L. x purpusii* 'Winter Beauty', **H** 2.5m (8ft), **S** 1.8m (6ft), have little, **pale-yellow** flowers held in small groups on the bare stems, which appear for much of the winter and into early spring, emitting a really sweet and slightly spicy fragrance. I find it impossible to pass either of these without stopping to enjoy the fragrance.

Mahonia

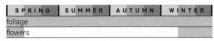

SPRING	SUMMER	AUTUMN	WINTER
foliage			
flowers			

H 3–4m (10–13ft), **S** 2m (6½ft) or so. Mahonias do pretty well in most situations and the majority thrive in part shade. These shrubs have almost holly-like, spiny-edged leaves that are dark green and glossy throughout the year, so they make a strong architectural statement in winter. Some, such as *M. aquifolium* (the Oregon grape), turn a **reddish-purple** in winter.

M. japonica is decked with clusters of pendulous **yellow**, sweetly scented flowers from the middle of winter right through until early spring.

The flowers of *M. x media* 'Charity' are also bright **yellow** and deliciously fragrant, but are held in upright clusters and turn the shrub into something very special from mid-autumn to mid-winter. The flower clusters of 'Winter Sun' are similarly erect but even more dense and usually somewhat longer.

Nandina domestica SACRED BAMBOO

SPRING	SUMMER	AUTUMN	WINTER
foliage			
flowers			
berries			

H 2m (6½ft), **S** 1.5m (5ft). Needs a sunny, sheltered spot with a well-drained but moisture-retentive soil. This glorious evergreen or semi-evergreen bamboo looks great in an autumn or winter garden. It is a plant well worth growing for its foliage alone: it holds fruits and has colour and texture for all seasons, the leaves starting off a **reddish-purple** colour, becoming green during the summer, and then in autumn and winter an even brighter **purple** colour. Towards the middle of summer it produces large sprays of **creamy-white** flowers, each flower about 1cm (½in) in diameter and star-shaped. Then, in hotter summers, the flowers are replaced by bright **red** berries. If you are short of space, try the smaller (**H** 1.2m/4ft, **S** 60cm /24in) variety 'Fire Power'.

Rubus cockburnianus GHOST BRAMBLE

SPRING	SUMMER	AUTUMN	WINTER
flowers			
stems			

H and **S** 2m (6½ft). Happy in any decent soil, in sun or shade. A real drama queen, with its ghostly **white** arching stems, this looks fantastic in a winter garden. In early summer it also produces sprays of small **purple** flowers.

Sarcococca

SPRING	SUMMER	AUTUMN	WINTER
foliage			
flowers			

S. confusa (Christmas box, sweet box), **H** and **S** 1.2m (4ft), likes a moist and yet well-drained soil in shade. This multi-stemmed evergreen shrub may not have huge impact for much of the year, but in winter, when it is adorned with numerous **white** flowers, your nose will notice it from the other end of the garden. The perfume is gorgeous; every year I never fail to be taken aback by its intensity. This species does not produce suckers, and so is not invasive, as many other sarcococcas are. If you are short of space, consider the similar but smaller plant *S. hookeriana* var. *humilis*, which only grows to a height and spread of about 60cm (24in).

Viburnum

SPRING	SUMMER	AUTUMN	WINTER
flowers			

V. farreri, **H** 2.5m (8ft), **S** 1.8m (6ft). Dappled shade suits this deciduous shrub well. The clusters of pale **pinkish-white** flowers are held in a slightly drooping fashion from late autumn right through until the beginning of spring. The flowers produce a delicious perfume that pervades the winter garden, especially if the plant is grown in a fairly protected spot. In spring the new leaves are a pretty bronze colour, turning bright green as they age.

Other viburnums to consider are *V.* x *bodnatense*, which has **pinkish-white** heavily scented flowers that are open from early winter to early spring, and the variety 'Dawn'.

ABOVE Warm pinks combined with a sumptuous perfume can be hard to find in winter, but take a look (and a sniff) at this *Viburnum* x *bodnantense* 'Dawn' and you need look no further. Planted in a sheltered spot it won't let you down.

OPPOSITE All the mahonias make great year-round shrubs with their spiky evergreen leaves, but in winter the yellow, often perfumed, flowers make them something very special indeed.

climbers

Shrubs and trees are often regarded as the plants that bring height and structure to a garden. Indeed they do, but climbers have an extremely important role to play too: although they may not create height on their own, they can ensure that existing objects such as sheds, structures such as arches and pergolas, or boundaries such as walls and fences, are brought to life and look their best. However you grow your climbers and whatever use you put them to, they should play an important part in creating your garden for all seasons, as they literally add another dimension to your gardening surfaces.

OPPOSITE There is an age-old elegance associated with wisterias. Any wall, be it of a garage or a modern or older house can be transformed in spring when this climber produces its flowers. It can also be grown over a pergola or as a standard in a half-barrel.

Choosing the right climbers is vital, akin to choosing a selection of good-quality and well-made paints and wallpaper for your house. To keep vertical surfaces looking great you will need different options for different positions and for the various seasons; so yes, you need to buy and plant more than one type of living 'wallpaper', but at least you will not need to keep replacing it! Some climbers have several seasons of interest, but most confine their displays to just one or sometimes two seasons. All of them will help to transform your garden into somewhere you love to be and, provided that you get the right combination, somewhere that looks good at any time of year.

It makes a lot of sense to use several different plants on any one surface, as long as space permits, as this should help to prolong the period over which it looks good. This may mean two plants that flower at different times – one that flowers in, say, spring, and another that produces good autumn colour. Evergreen climbers, including the ivies, can be used to great effect in combination with a flowering climber, the ivy helping to provide a year-round colourwash whilst the flowering climber brings in seasonal splashes of colour.

Climbing support

Whether you use a climber to hide or enhance, to clothe a house or garden wall, fence, trellis, arbour, arch, obelisk, shed, garage or simply a wire frame, you will need to consider a support system for it. To decide what type of additional support it will need, if any, it is essential that you know what sort of climber you are dealing with.

Those plants that have twining tendrils (for example sweet peas) or curling leaf stalks (clematis) are capable of getting a firm footing on a system of wires or trellis. Those that have adhesive pads or aerial roots that allow them to cling to a surface such as a wall or fence (parthenocissus and ivy) have no problems climbing and these do not even need a special support system to be erected. Others have no specialised mechanism, roses being the classic example, and these will therefore not only need a support system up which to clamber, but also need to be secured to this support. Some, such as honeysuckles, use much of their stem lengths to become twiners. The vast majority of all climbers, whatever method they do or do not have to adhere to your vertical surfaces, will need some initial help to get them up and on to the surface. Even the climbing hydrangea, which is a rampant climber once it gets established, may take several years of growth before it adheres properly to a wall.

With supports, I always suggest erring on the side of caution – if in doubt, build it stout! A fully grown climber in full leaf can be quite weighty and so sturdy supports are always better than something that may prove insufficient. Some climbers, for instance wisterias, need a

LEFT Instant architecture and colour are all yours when you grow the annual morning glory up a twiggy obelisk or other support. It will provide height and rich colour for much of the summer and in to early autumn and need not cost a fortune.

very strong or sturdy support to keep them upright. If you are growing two different climbers over a surface in an attempt to get a longer season of interest, you will of course need to ensure that the trellis or system of wires that you install is strong enough to carry the weight of both, and to provide a surface on to which they can both be attached. If climbers are to be grown over an arch or pergola, this too will need to be up to the job – it may look great at first, but there is no point growing a heavyweight climber over a delicate little arch that is destined to buckle, bend or break in a few years' time.

When choosing a timber support, always ensure that any softwood materials are pressure treated or tannalised, so that they last longer. The precise dimensions of the support will depend on several factors, including the potential size of the plant or plants, the location and whether or not you envisage carrying out regular pruning to keep the plant in check.

Planting next to a wall

When you are planting climbers it may be tempting to plant far too close to the wall because this will probably look better initially. But the area immediately adjacent to a house wall will tend to be very dry – the foundations and brickwork will pull moisture from the soil, and there will be a 'rain shadow' effect, because the wall, projecting roof tiles and guttering will between them drastically reduce the quantity of rain falling there. The dryness may lead to poor establishment of the plant, poor growth, lack of vigour and a huge increase in the likelihood that the plant will succumb to powdery mildew disease. So, however odd it may look for the first couple of years, I would recommend planting climbers a minimum of 45cm (18in) from the wall.

Good preparation of the soil in the planting area is also especially important for climbers to be grown close to walls, as the soil there tends to be drier and often poor. If the wall has a lot of loose mortar or is constructed using rock or stone with a high lime content, the soil close to the wall may have an unexpectedly high pH (be rather alkaline), which is something you will need to consider if you are planning to grow any lime-hating climbers on this area.

OPPOSITE Here a warm combination of colours comes from sweetpeas and nasturtiums grown close to a blue fence; you cannot get much bolder than that in one season can you? And it is a great way to cover a fence whilst longer-term climbers get established.

Climbers to prolong interest

Choosing climbers that not only flower but in addition produce either berries or attractive seedheads, or striking autumn colour, is another way of helping your wall, fences, pergolas and other structures look good for much of the year.

Annual climbers such as morning glories or sweet peas are useful, as these can easily be grown through existing established climbers and so help to bring some out-of-season colour or perfume into that part of the garden. Most grow rapidly, especially if planted out as small plants. Annual climbers are also a perfect way to produce quick yet fantastic colour on a support system that has not yet been filled by the longer-term climbers.

Some climbers can also be used to create a living structure, statue or feature in your garden, if trained on to a wire-mesh shape or wooden obelisk. Grown in this manner the plant takes on a whole new look and is often still very attractive even out of season.

Rambler roses and clematis do particularly well in association with trees. To increase the chances of both the rose or clematis and the tree performing to perfection, it is essential to do the following:

• Plant the new plant on the windward side of the tree – this ensures that when strong winds blow it will be blown towards the tree's trunk, not away from it. Planting in this position will also mean that once the plant is established, the new stems will be inclined to move towards the branch system of the tree.

• Dig a planting hole a minimum of 90cm (36in) away from the tree's trunk. This may look peculiar initially, but it is necessary if the new plant is to receive the rainfall it needs. As the soil may well be quite impoverished, dig a larger hole than you would normally, and incorporate plenty of good bulky organic matter into the hole, the surrounding soil and the mixture that you use to backfill the hole.

• Keep the plant well watered and fed, especially in the first few years as it establishes, because competition for both moisture and nutrients can be tight and the new addition is particularly likely to suffer without them. If the soil is particularly poor, it may be easier to get the rose or clematis established if you plant it in a large bucket – remove the base from the bucket first, to create a cylinder. This will enable you to direct water and nutrients to the new roots more easily. As the plant grows, its roots can venture out from their partial enclosure and tap the bigger area of soil that they will need in the long term.

• At planting, use bamboo canes to train the new, flexible stems towards the tree. You will need to use long canes, so that they can be positioned at an angle with the lower end inserted in the soil close to the rose and the upper end attached to the tree. Whilst the rose or clematis is still relatively small you may well need to help it along its way by tying in the new growth loosely, to prevent it from being dislodged during windy weather. Once it is established, this should no longer be a problem.

LEFT I am training this spring flowering *Clematis montana* 'Freda' and a perfumed summer-flowering honeysuckle up (and eventually over) my favourite garden sitting place, a wooden arbour. Persuading free-willed shoots to go where I need them is a regular task for the first few months.

spring CLIMBERS

The weather in spring is too cold for many climbers to perform, which makes those that do flower all the more valuable. Plant them in a protected position to reduce the risk of precious buds and blooms being damaged by frost.

Clematis

SPRING	SUMMER	AUTUMN	WINTER
foliage			
flowers			
seed heads			

C. alpina, **H** 2–2.7m (6½–9ft) forms a group of evergreen clematis usually in flower from mid- to late spring and it is surprisingly tough and versatile, even doing well on a north-facing wall or when grown in a pretty poor soil. The buds hang down slightly and are often somewhat pointed, but once they open, the flowers appear almost flat. Several of the named varieties including 'Frances Rivis' (a **violet-blue**), 'Rosy Pagoda' (**red** with a distinct white edging) and 'Ruby' (**pinky-purple**) are particularly well worth growing. Once the flowers have faded, attractive and very fluffy seedheads develop, further prolonging the decorative effect.

C. armandii, **H** 9m (30ft), is another evergreen climber and undoubtedly the most widely grown of the early-flowering clematis. In early spring an established plant should be covered in **creamy-white** flowers, each with a distinct vanilla perfume. The flowers, each resembling a six-pointed star, are held in clusters like loosely tied posies, and before each flower opens, the buds are attractively rounded, often with a slight hint of pink to the outside surface. Admittedly this has a potential to grow a bit too large for some gardens, but it is a truly lovely plant early in the year. Grow it somewhere where you can take full advantage of the delightful perfume and I am sure you will not regret planting it.

C. macropetala, **H** 2.5m (8ft), should help to brighten up gloomy walls or fences from the middle to the end of spring. *C. macropetala* itself has rich **blueish-violet** flowers, each about 10cm (4in) in diameter, and then, once these have all finally faded, produces really fantastic fluffy seedheads. There are several really good named varieties worth looking out for, including 'Markham's Pink' (**pinkish-mauve** flowers) and 'Snowbird' (**white** tinged with green).

The very last few weeks of spring can be enhanced by *C. montana*, height up to 10m (33ft), occasionally more, spread about 3m (10ft) or more. Although each of the white flowers is only about 4cm (1½in) in diameter, they are produced in such extraordinary quantities that it is not uncommon to see a *C. montana* so densely covered in flowers that it looks like a huge pile of only slightly off-white snow. I have seen them climbing on to telegraph poles and phone wires adjacent to houses – and then it must be said that the result was truly stunning. Especially interesting forms include 'Elizabeth' (**pale pink** with a very distinct vanilla-like perfume) and 'Broughton Star' (richer **pink** double flowers with prominent **golden-yellow** stamens). If your garden is relatively small and you don't fancy trying to cope with an excessively vigorous *C. montana*, the answer could be 'Freda', which is by far the least vigorous and has bright **pink** flowers and a wonderful **coppery-bronze** tinge to the foliage.

If you are looking for an evergreen clematis to help brighten up the late spring period, *C. paniculata*, **H** 4.5m (15ft), could fit the bill. With its bright **white** flowers and a central cluster of yellow stamens, this climber really looks pretty. I find that the only disadvantage with all these evergreen clematis is that the leaves often become marked and can look unsightly. If you want to minimise this, remember that the more sheltered the site, the less likely it is that there will be too much damage to the leaves.

ABOVE RIGHT These nodding, bell-shaped flowers of *Clematis macropetala* 'Markham's Pink' stay looking good on the plant for ages; their tightly packed petals make them particularly robust.

RIGHT This *Clematis montana* 'Elizabeth' may have simple flowers but their strong pink shade is offset perfectly by the backdrop of purple-tinted and attractively shaped leaves.

Lonicera x *tellmanniana* HONEYSUCKLE

SPRING	SUMMER	AUTUMN	WINTER
flowers			

H 3.6m (12ft). From the end of spring
and into the beginning of summer this
deciduous climber produces a good
quantity of **yellowy-copper**-coloured
flowers, often with a distinct red flush.
Like other honeysuckles this one will put
on its best show if grown in sun or
partial shade, but with its roots in more
dense shade, sheltered from the hot,
drying effects of bright sunshine. A soil
with plenty of organic matter and which
does not dry out at any stage will also
produce the best results. (See also p. 76.)

Wisteria

SPRING	SUMMER	AUTUMN	WINTER
foliage			
flowers			

H 9–15m (30–50ft), depending on
which one you choose. Wisterias are
beautiful, but it has to be said that their
flowering period is pretty short and
indeed the flowers are often damaged
extensively by late frosts, with the result
that they certainly don't provide colour

ABOVE RIGHT Whether you choose pale purple,
violet, pink or a white *Wisteria floribunda*
'Alba' it puts on an albeit short-lived,
unsurpassable display. Definitely well worth
the wait and great if you want to introduce
an oriental charm or cottage-garden feel.

for much of the year. However, the
impact given by an established wisteria
heavily draped with **purple**, **pink**, **white**
or **violet-blue** flower trusses is a sight
capable of taking your breath away,
and as an added bonus many wisterias
also have a good perfume. Trained over
a wall or sturdy fence with a strong
support system or over an archway,
pergola or even through a large established tree, a wisteria in full bloom is
something you will never forget.

One of the earliest to flower is
W. floribunda (Japanese wisteria), which
has **blue-violet**, slightly fragrant flower

trusses, anything up to about 30cm
(12in) in length. There is a **white** form,
'Alba' and, if you want even longer
flower trusses, try 'Multijuga' (often still
known as 'Macrobotrys'), as this
purple, near-violet variety will produce
trusses up to 60cm (24in) in length.

W. sinensis (Chinese wisteria)
produces its flowers just before the
leaves open. The flowers are a **violet-
blue** colour with only a slight fragrance.
The Chinese wisteria is by far the most
rapid-growing and vigorous of the
wisterias, reaching a height of 15m
(50ft) or sometimes even more.

Slightly later flowering are *W.* x
formosa (**violet** flower trusses up to 30cm
/12in with a strong fragrance) and its
variety 'Black Dragon' with deeper **purple**
flowers, but be warned: I have found the
latter to be distinctly shyer to flower.

Because of the risk of the buds or
flowers being damaged by frosts, it is
best to plant wisterias in a spot
sheltered from the coldest winds or
early-morning spring sunshine.

OTHER CLIMBERS WITH GOOD SPRING INTEREST

summerCLIMBERS

It is easy to find a climber to produce a mass of colour in summer, and a garden without a perfumed climber has a gap that needs to be filled. Plant favourites to enjoy in the months when you are most likely to sit outside.

Actinidia kolomikta

SPRING	SUMMER	AUTUMN	WINTER
foliage

H 5m (16½ft), S 3m (10ft). This is without a doubt one of the most peculiar climbers I know and I will confess that the first time I saw it growing I thought that a particularly infuriating painter and decorator had gone berserk rather too close to its foliage. The near heart-shaped leaves are **green** when they first appear, but then become distinctly marked with bright **pink** and **white**. The foliage looks like this throughout the summer and at this time of year it also produces small and, in comparison with the foliage, rather boring, white flowers, each up to 2cm (¾in) in diameter. A sunny or at most partially shaded site is essential, as the wacky leaf colouring does not develop if the plants are grown in too much shade. If you plant one of these, it is worth bearing in mind that when they are very young they rarely colour up properly; it will take several years for the colour to start to develop, so a little patience is necessary.

ABOVE Probably the craziest-looking climber I know, *Actinidia kolomikta* may not colour up well in the first few years after planting, but then there will be no stopping it.

Clematis

SPRING	SUMMER	AUTUMN	WINTER
flowers			

From the end of spring through until mid-summer there is a whole range of clematis that produce an abundance of flowers, and in many cases this display is followed by another flush of blooms towards the end of summer or the beginning of autumn. There are numerous different, quite large-flowered clematis available for this time of year, in pretty well every shade of **pink**, **purple**, **red** and **blue** you can imagine, plus of course white and occasionally **yellow**. The best way to find precisely what you want is to check through the catalogue of a specialist clematis nursery, or failing this, to go along to your garden centre in early summer – you are likely to find a good selection there. Some of my favourites for this time of year include 'Bees' Jubilee' (flowers **mauve-pink** with a strong carmine stripe and rich maroon-colour stamens – very similar to those of 'Nelly Moser' but a good deal bigger); 'Doctor Ruppel' (**red** with a bright carmine stripe and a cluster of central gold stamens); 'Fireworks' (**pale purple** with a wide maroon stripe and dark red stamens); 'Lasurstern' (strong **blueish-mauve** with a slightly wavy edge and bright white stamens); 'Marie Boisselot' (**white** with yellow stamens and flowers from the mid-spring through until early autumn, often without much of a break); 'Niobe' (velvety-looking rich **dark red** with gold stamens, flowering from the middle of spring until early autumn), and 'Vyvyan Pennell' (a fantastic **purple**, violet and blue multipetalled flower that resembles a peony, often producing a later flush of single flowers).

Hydrangea anomala subsp. *petiolaris*

SPRING	SUMMER	AUTUMN	WINTER
foliage			
flowers			

H 3.6–6m (12–20ft). For much of the summer this deciduous climber is covered in 25cm- (10in-) wide **creamy-white** flattened flowerheads. I must confess to not being much of a fan of shrubby hydrangeas, but this is a rather more delicate-looking creature than some and is very useful if you have a shady wall that you would like to cover. I used one to great effect on a previous house to cover up some really nasty mismatching brickwork. It is a self-clinging climber, so you do not even need to erect a support. Bear in mind that it often takes three or more years to get it clinging successfully but, once it is firmly attached, it will romp away.

Lonicera HONEYSUCKLE

SPRING	SUMMER	AUTUMN	WINTER
flowers			
berries			

If you want a climber that performs well in the summer and in some cases through into autumn, the honeysuckles are worth considering, particularly if you wish to create a cottage garden feel or simply ensure that the structure you are aiming to cover with foliage and flowers has a truly informal laid-back look. Being natural twiners and scramblers, the honeysuckles are incapable of looking regimented and perhaps this is one of the reasons why I love them so much. But it is not just their untidy good looks that have so much appeal: so too does the fantastically sweet, often slightly lemony or spicy perfume that pervades the air when one is growing near by. There are a few honeysuckles that are not fragrant, but the majority have a perfume that would make the plants worthy of inclusion even if they didn't look so pretty. Individual honeysuckle flowers are usually tubular, but they are often fused together to create a floral chandelier. Then, once the flowers have finished, quite fleshy, often bright **red** berries are produced, which encourage birds and hedgehogs into the garden as they regard these as an appealing source of food. Honeysuckles look fantastic grown over an arch, arbour, pergola, wall or sturdy fence, or even allowed to

scramble up through the crown of a tree.

L. x *americana*, H 3m (10ft), is evergreen and covered in really fragrant **cream** and **pink** flowers from the middle of summer through to mid-autumn.

L. x *brownii* 'Dropmore Scarlet', H 3.6m (12ft), is a deciduous honeysuckle, and from early summer through until early autumn produces spikes of bright **scarlet-orange** flowers.

L. *etrusca*, H 2.5m (8ft), has **creamy-yellow** fragrant flowers, sometimes with an orangey-red tint; these appear on this deciduous or sometimes semi-evergreen climber from the beginning of summer through until early autumn.

L. x *italica*, H 4m (13ft), has maroon-coloured buds that are really beautiful on this deciduous climber and from late spring through until mid-summer the buds open to produce **yellow** and **pink** flowers with probably the strongest perfume of all the honeysuckles. Then towards the end of summer, and often through into early autumn, **orangey-red** berries are formed.

L. *japonica* 'Halliana', H 4—4.5m (13—15ft), is semi-evergreen, retaining a good number of leaves most years. From mid-summer until early autumn it is decked with **white** and **yellow** flowers, all with a strong perfume.

L. *periclymenum* (native woodbine), H 3.6m (12ft), is a deciduous and decidedly vigorous climber that has

wonderfully perfumed **whitish-cream** and purple flowers throughout the summer and into early autumn. There are several varieties of it that are well worth considering. These include 'Graham Thomas', which from mid-summer to early autumn produces large quantities of beautifully perfumed, **creamy-white** flowers, followed by **reddish-orange** berries. The flowering season of 'Belgica' is somewhat shorter because the flowers are really only at their best in mid-summer, but they are a delightful combination of **pink** and **red** and again have a wonderful perfume; then towards the end of summer orange berries are produced, which gradually turn quite a rich shade of **red** by the autumn. 'Serotina' (also known as the Late Dutch Honeysuckle) has white, purple and red flowers from the middle of summer until early autumn; in the autumn it produces **reddish-purple** berries — at the same time the foliage develops more of a bronzish tint.

Most of these climbing honeysuckles prefer to be grown with their roots in a cool position and their twining stems in the sun or partial shade.

ABOVE The easy, ambling air given off by the twining stems of an established honeysuckle help to bring a relaxed feel to this shaded garden corner. But the knock-out perfume from the flowers will soon wake you up.

Jasminum officinale
COMMON WHITE JASMINE

SPRING	SUMMER	AUTUMN	WINTER
foliage			
flowers			

H 9m (30ft). Easily kept in check should you wish to restrict its height. From mid-summer until early autumn, this twining climber should be covered in small white and deliciously fragrant flowers. Some support will obviously be necessary, but it is a relatively lightweight beast and so there is no need for anything too sturdy. There are several variegated foliage forms, including 'Argenteovariegatum' and 'Aureum', although I must admit that these don't seem to be anything like as vigorous as the common white jasmine.

OTHER CLIMBERS WITH GOOD SUMMER INTEREST

Campsis

Clematis alpina p. 72

Clematis orientalis p. 80

Cobaea scandens

Hedera p. 83

Humulus lupulus 'Aureus' p. 80

Ipomoea p. 130

Lathyrus p. 130

Lonicera x tellmanniana p. 74

Parthenocissus henryana p. 80

Tropaeolum p. 139

Vitis p. 81

Rosa ROSE

SPRING	SUMMER	AUTUMN	WINTER
flowers			

The climbing and rambling roses must be one of the most widely grown flowers for summer interest. (Both are climbing plants, but ramblers are often much more vigorous and so less suitable for small gardens.) Many are perfumed and the flower colours include **white**, **cream**, **red**, **pink**, **yellow**, **orange** and **apricot** in every imaginable shade.

Most of the climbing roses have fairly large flowers, often held in small groups, and they tend to produce a flush of flowers and are repeat-flowering. The second flush of flowers is often produced in late summer or sometimes even early autumn. To encourage plenty of flowers, it helps if you can train the shoots as close as possible into a horizontal position and, if you are tying them to a pillar or similar structure, bend them gently into a spiral shape. Climbers have flowers that may be single, semi-double or double. The vast majority have a wonderful perfume.

Rambler roses have stems that are somewhat more flexible than those of climbers, and so would often be my choice for growing over a structure where you will need to bend the stems

quite a lot. However, they only flower once, usually in early or mid-summer. The flowers tend to be small compared with those of climbers, but they are held in bigger clusters, so still have a great deal of impact. The flowers are invariably semi-double or double and have a reasonable, but often slightly lighter perfume than climbers.

ABOVE A rambling or climbing rose such as this *Rosa* 'Veilchenblau' looks perfect when trained over a doorway or gate in a wall; a perfect way to transform an ugly shed or garage too.

autumnCLIMBERS

Once autumn arrives, there are some fantastic opportunities to clothe walls in rich reds, oranges and purples as the leaves prepare to fall, and also several flowering climbers that you can use to great effect.

Celastrus orbiculatus
ORIENTAL BITTERSWEET

SPRING	SUMMER	AUTUMN	WINTER
flowers			
fruits			

H 12m (40ft). During the summer small greenish-white clusters of flowers appear on this twining climber and these are followed by not particularly exciting-looking yellow to buff-coloured fruits in the autumn. It is only once the fruits are ripe and rupture that they produce a lovely display, as the inside of each of the fruits is a much brighter, more cheerful **yellow**, and within the fruit is a bright **scarlet** seed. This is a useful climber for growing up a support or even into a tree in a shady or partially shaded position. Do make sure that the celastrus you buy is one of the Hermaphrodite Group as these are self-fertile and so you only need one plant in order to get a good display of fruits. Those that are not in this group have the male and female flowers on separate plants and so you will need two to get the berries – and frankly without the berries, there is not much point in growing this plant.

ABOVE RIGHT Summer just would not be summer without a handful of your favourite clematis. I think this *Clematis* 'Rouge Cardinal' is stunning, but the potential range of colours clematis can provide at this time of year is almost unending, so take your pick.

Clematis

SPRING	SUMMER	AUTUMN	WINTER
flowers			

The late-flowering large-flowered clematis, H 1.8–6m (6–20ft) depending on the one you choose, flower from the end of summer and into early autumn, and can not only help to prolong the display of flowers in your garden but also invariably bring bright, almost summery colours into your autumn garden. There are plenty of lovely varieties to choose from, including 'Comtesse de Bouchaud' (a plentiful supply of satiny **pink** flowers with yellow stamens); 'Gipsy Queen' (**purple** flowers with a hint of blue and dark red, near-purple stamens); 'Hagley Hybrid' (pale **pink** flowers with brown-tipped stamens); 'Rouge Cardinal' (**purplish-red**, producing flowers from early summer through until early autumn), and 'Warszawska Nike' (strong **purple** flowers, each measuring anything up to 25cm/10in in diameter, with a central cluster of prominent yellow stamens).

C. orientalis and varieties, **H** up to 3.6m (12ft), come into their own at the end of summer and into the beginning of autumn, producing pendulous, lantern-like, **yellow** flowers, which are then followed by wonderfully fluffy seedheads.

Humulus lupulus 'Aureus' GOLDEN HOP

SPRING	SUMMER	AUTUMN	WINTER
foliage			
flowers			

H 3–6m (10–20ft). The **golden-yellow** leaves have an almost metallic look to them and look especially fantastic when caught in bright sunshine. This is a herbaceous perennial climber, so expect it to die back towards the end of each year and then reappear in the spring. The foliage is fantastic throughout the summer and can look lovely over an arbour or arch, or even if allowed to scramble through an otherwise rather dull and uninteresting length of hedge. In mid- and late summer the plants carry small cone-like flowers. If this particular variety is to produce top-quality golden colour as it should, a position in full sunshine is essential.

Parthenocissus henryana

SPRING	SUMMER	AUTUMN	WINTER
foliage			

H 10m (33ft), **S** 6m (20ft). Much as I love the sight of *Parthenocissus quinquefolia* (Virginia creeper) on somebody else's wall in the autumn, it is so incredibly vigorous – and I would even go so far as to say rampant – that it can be a bit of a nightmare in most gardens. I had one once on the wall of a house and it seemed to spend all its time trying to find its way beneath the roof tiles and also played host to a huge colony of sparrows, which meant that our front path was constantly covered in bird droppings. With this in mind I am more inclined to recommend *P. henryana*. I am also fonder of this because it has much

more interesting leaves throughout the year – a good **dark green** but with strongly marked silvery-white veins on each leaflet and often a slight tinge of pink, not only on the stems but also on the leaf stalks. This means that the foliage is very attractive from spring, through summer and into autumn. Then, once autumn arrives, it turns a bright **red** colour, admittedly not quite as fantastic as the Virginia creeper, but it is a wonderful plant anyway – certainly better value for the rest of the year and a good deal easier to control. Like the Virginia creeper, *P. henryana* is self-clinging and so you can allow it to grow up a wall without any support system. If you want the best autumn coloration, try to choose a north- or east-facing wall for it.

Passiflora caerulea
COMMON PASSION FLOWER

SPRING	SUMMER	AUTUMN	WINTER
flowers			
fruits			

H 10m (33ft). If you want to introduce a touch of the exotic to your garden, growing this passion flower or one of its named forms is a good way to do it, as it is without doubt the hardiest passion flower you are likely to find. It is in

ABOVE Grapes may make great eating (and drinking), but never forget that many, including this *Vitis coignetiae*, also have prettily shaped leaves and tremendous autumn colour.

OPPOSITE The arrangement, colour and shape of the leaves of this *Parthenocissus henryana* are great throughout the year, but this self-clinging climber develops fiery shades in autumn.

flower for a good part of the summer, but often looks particularly splendid in early autumn, when it is covered with large numbers of **pale pink** or **pale purple** flowers, often with a slight fragrance. These really are extraordinary to look at, each resembling a spacecraft, perhaps, more than a typical flower. As an added bonus the striking flowers are often followed by egg-like **orange** or sometimes **yellow** fruits, which add further interest. It is worth remembering that the foliage is attractive too. Although the plant will certainly need winter protection in a cold garden, it usually survives quite well in most situations.

Vitis GRAPE

SPRING	SUMMER	AUTUMN	WINTER
foliage			

There is certainly nothing to stop you growing *V. vinifera*, the fruiting grape, as a climber in your garden, and if you do you will have the sizeable benefit of a reasonable crop of good-tasting fruits in early autumn. However, in many gardens grape vines are not that easily persuaded to crop really well and, although the autumn colour is quite good, if you want something truly spectacular you would be better off choosing one of the more ornamental forms.

V. coignetiae (crimson glory vine),

H 25m (80ft) – but there is no need to panic because it is quite easy to keep under control and is also relatively slow-growing – has large, somewhat rounded and slightly lobed leaves, each measuring up to 30cm (12in) in length, which for much of the year form a fairly attractive covering to a wall, sturdy pergola or other support system. In the autumn the leaves come into their own as they develop extremely striking tints of **orange**, **red**, **purple**, **yellow** and **crimson**. It can also be used to great effect if it is allowed to scramble through a large tree, bringing extra interest to the tree as well.

V. 'Brant', **H** 9m (30ft), has rather more lobed leaves, which turn richer shades of **pink**, **bronze**, **orange** and **red** during the autumn, and curiously the leaf veins remain green, so producing a lovely design on the surface of the autumn foliage.

OTHER CLIMBERS WITH GOOD AUTUMN INTEREST

Clematis – some, including 'Marie Boisselot', 'Niobe', 'Vyvyan Pennell'
Hedera p. 83
Jasminum nudiflorum p. 83
Jasminum officinale p. 78
Lonicera – some, including *L. etrusca*, *L. periclymenum* 'Serotina', *L.* x *americana* and *L.* x *brownii* 'Dropmore Scarlet' p. 76
Rosa – some climbers p. 78

winterCLIMBERS

By now many climbers are bare, but there are a few vital ones that either retain their leaves or, better still, produce small and yet very striking flowers. They can be grown on their own or with climbers that peak earlier in the year.

Clematis cirrhosa

SPRING	SUMMER	AUTUMN	WINTER
foliage			
flowers			

H 6m (20ft). It never ceases to amaze me when this extraordinarily delicate-looking climber produces its pale **yellow** to **white** bell-shaped flowers. They usually develop in early winter and then last through until the spring. Get close enough and you will notice an almost lemony perfume. Peek inside and you will see a distinct red to brown freckling. These are truly pretty flowers, which look all the more demure for being set against finely divided green foliage. Come the winter this often puts on a splendid show, developing a slight bronze tinting. There are several really good forms, including 'Freckles', which has a very strong reddish-purple freckling.

ABOVE In winter why not enjoy these cheekily freckled flowers of *Clematis cirrhosa balearica* 'Freckles' as they appear, come rain or shine, right through until the spring.

OPPOSITE The arrangement of the attractively shaped leaves on an ivy beats many fabric designs hands down; what better way to cover an upright garden surface?

Hedera IVY

SPRING	SUMMER	AUTUMN	WINTER
foliage			

Despite the fact that they are often branded as boring green climbers of little interest, the ivies are truly useful plants. With their evergreen foliage on self-clinging stems they can be a great boon throughout the year, but particularly over the winter months. Allow them to climb up walls, pergolas, arches or fences and you can have a near-permanent backdrop of colour.

H. helix (common ivy) will grow to a height of 10m (33ft) or more and has attractively lobed leaves. There are also plenty of named varieties that have wonderful leaf variegation in shades of **silver** and **pale yellow**. Some of these produce plants that are a lot smaller than the species, so even easier to control. Other varieties such as 'Dragon Claw' have a delightful wavy edge to the leaves.

Although garden centres often sell a reasonable range of ivies, it is best to try to contact a specialist nursery and believe me you will be amazed by what a wide range of ivies there are to be had and just how variable and delightful they can be. Don't forget that, if you use these plants as a backdrop to cover an ugly or boring wall or fence, there is no earthly reason why you cannot grow another climber in the area as well, to bring colour and perhaps perfume at other times of the year. Treat ivy as an entity on its own or as the most fantastic wallpaper design you could ever come across and you will be well rewarded.

Jasminum nudiflorum WINTER JASMINE

SPRING	SUMMER	AUTUMN	WINTER
foliage			
flowers			

H 4.5m (15ft). This is really more of a scrambler than a climber. It is very easy to train against a wall, but you will need a system of wires or some other structure on to which you can attach the stems. Throughout the winter, indeed from the end of autumn right through until the beginning of spring, the bare stems are covered with bright **yellow** star-like flowers, each up to 2.5cm (1in) in diameter. Then, come the beginning of spring, a good mass of dark green leaves develops. If you prefer golden foliage, try the slightly more temperamental 'Aureum', which has yellow blotches on the leaves. It will thrive in just about any position in the garden and will help to bring a warm glow to a chilly winter's morning.

flowers

A garden without flowers would be like, well, apple pie without the cream – somehow incomplete and certainly not reaching its potential. In most gardens flowers play a major role, albeit smaller than those all-important trees and shrubs. But all too often gardens are crammed full of fabulous flowers from late spring until mid-summer, only to crash into a miserable, drab heap at summer's end. True, trees and shrubs can keep the garden looking interesting throughout the year, but a garden needs a well-planned planting of floral jewels too, to prevent it from being lacklustre.

OPPOSITE 'Come on Baby, Light my Fire'! This radiant, hot display may at first glance bring about thoughts of warm summer days but, believe me, this is pure autumn, and not difficult to achieve.

Apart from the many trees, shrubs and climbers that produce attractive flowers, you can use all sorts of other flowers to bring colour, shape, texture and sometimes even perfume to your garden at various times of the year. In this chapter I shall look at how those smaller, non-woody plants, which are grown largely or wholly for their blooms, can be used to best effect. These include: annuals (flowers which come up or are planted and die within one year); biennials (those which produce a plant in their first year and then in their second and final year produce flowers); perennials (the majority of these are herbaceous – that is, they come up each spring, flower at some stage and then die back in the late autumn, repeating this cycle for many years); and bulbous plants (including bulbs, corms, tubers and rhizomatous plants which each year produce foliage and flowers from a bulbous under-ground structure, and then die back, ready to reappear in the following years). Although these flowering plants are not the largest of garden residents, the majority of gardens incorporate many different varieties of them in large numbers and so help to make the seasonal changes all the more obvious, without necessarily making one season less interesting than the next.

Rather than seeking year-round interest, if you use your garden infrequently except during the summer months, you may decide that you just want to prolong the summer display slightly, so that the garden looks good from late spring through until early autumn. This way you can be sure that there are flowers to enjoy at the times when you are most likely to venture outside. Or you may be like me and realise that the better-looking the garden is at any time of the year, the more inclined you will be to go out there and tend it, enjoy and appreciate it, and soak up its relaxing atmosphere, whatever the weather. If this is the case you will need to do more strategic planning, as there is no doubt that in the 'extreme' seasons of winter and most of autumn it is less easy to fill the garden with flowers.

As you plan you will need to consider the sort of style you want your garden to take on, as the annuals, biennials, herbaceous perennials and bulbs that you choose will have great influence on the garden's style at any time of year. For instance, lupins and aquilegia spell out 'cottage garden' loud and clear – but then again they can also be used in other types of garden to great effect.

OPPOSITE There is a time-tested charm about the delicate yet striking flowers of aquilegia or columbine and for a lightly shaded spot in the garden they fit the bill perfectly. Great self-seeders, you will soon have a lot more than you bargained for!

Foliage appeal

Although there is a much wider selection of flowering plants for the spring and early summer months than there is for the remainder of the year, always bear in mind that some plants are attractive even when not in flower. Foliage plays a vital role if you want to choose garden plants that look good for as much of the year as possible. Take the luxuriant whorl of foliage formed by a heuchera; the mound shape it creates is often semi-evergreen and, even though in cooler gardens it dies back over winter, the plant still looks good in spring, summer and autumn, the flower spikes being an added bonus rather than the plant's primary appeal.

Most pulmonarias (or lungworts) also have attractively marked leaves, blotched, spotted or edged in silver or white and often evergreen; provided that you tidy up any mildewed or scruffy leaves in the autumn, they too are plants with year-round interest. Add to this their bright-blue, pink, red or white flowers (or sometimes a mixture of colours on one plant), and you'll understand why I cannot resist them.

Also useful in this way are the bugles (*Ajuga reptans*). There are many forms of this plant and they all rapidly create a dense mat of purple, red, brown or variegated foliage. Then, from spring into early summer, purple or bright blue flower spikes appear.

Generally considered more of a rock garden plant (but also great planted in walls, through cracks in paving or in amongst gravel), the houseleeks (*Sempervivum* spp.) create spreading and ever-expanding 'families' of rosettes of fleshy, pointed leaves, sometimes flushed or tipped purple; then in the summer fleshy pink flower spikes top the older rosettes as an added bonus, but it is the foliage of these plants that makes them so worthwhile in a garden.

Even those herbaceous plants whose foliage is not inclined to stay around throughout the year are well worth including in a garden if the foliage itself is attractive – after all, not many plants produce good-looking flowers from spring right through until autumn either. Lady's mantle (*Alchemilla mollis*), hostas, tiarella and ornamental deadnettles or the lamiums are perfect examples of this. Many of the herbaceous geraniums also have attractively cut and sometimes purple-patterned leaves. In a few

ABOVE Hostas may produce pretty flower spikes but it is those bold, often variegated, leaves which make them so popular provided, of course, you can keep the slugs at bay.

OPPOSITE Grasses, especially once adorned with their flower- or seed-heads, provide texture, colour and movement in a garden. Grown in amongst herbaceous perennials it seems that both partners look even better for the presence of their neighbours.

plants both the flower and the foliage are fantastic – the hardy cyclamen
with their cerise, lilac or white flowers and their neat, marbled silver and
grey-green leaves, for instance, earn bonus points.

Take a closer look at the leaves of many widely grown plants such as
aquilegias, corydalis and euphorbia and you may start to see them in an
even more favourable light. The silvery foliage created by a dense covering
of fine hairs on leaves such as *Cineraria maritima* or *Stachys lanata* will
also help to provide interest for much or all of the year, bringing colour
and a tempting texture to any flower bed or container. All these are plants
for several seasons' enjoyment.

Added interest

Some flowers grown mainly for their spring or summer blooms also have
great appeal when that rush of colour is over and the seedhead develops.
I always leave the seedheads of plants such as the hollyhocks, eryngium,
alliums, Chinese lanterns and teasels in the flower borders in my garden.
Being made of tougher, more resilient material, they remain in good

condition throughout autumn and often through the winter, and they not only add useful colour and texture but also look exceptionally beautiful when decorated with a hoar frost. I must confess that I often leave a few flower stems of hollyhocks too. I suspect that visiting neighbours and the postman probably think it is because I have forgotten to cut them back but, no, I enjoy the way they look. You can of course sacrifice a few of these plants and use them as indoor decorations, creating a wonderful and unusual selection of dried flowers to enjoy throughout the year.

Many of the ornamental grasses, which have become so much more popular in recent years, also retain a good form, texture and colour over the winter months and will provide a useful backdrop for spring flowers as they start to emerge. In the popular 'prairie' style planting, which includes many grasses of various heights, they help to ensure that, even if a relatively small area is planted up, the season of interest is prolonged.

Most of us grow annuals, biennials, perennials or bulbs primarily for their wonderful flowers, or sometimes for their fantastic foliage. Choose a few flowers that also have a perfume and you will add yet another dimension. True, this may not prolong the season of interest, but it will certainly heighten the pleasure you get when you are in the garden. Plant fragrant flowers close to a terrace, patio or even a house window and you will be able to enjoy everything they have to offer at every possible opportunity. Some flowers, such as those of many of the narcissus including 'Geranium', have a wonderful fragrance that can pervade the air over a good few metres. Others such as *Iris reticulata* may be far more subtle, but plant a few somewhere that your nose can reach easily and you'll understand why they are such favourites of mine: subtle but seriously sensual!

Brightening the duller seasons

Bulbs, in particular those that have a relatively small quantity of foliage, or miniature forms, perhaps miniature narcissus or crocus, can also be used to great effect in a flowerbed. Obviously if they have too much leaf growth, this can become a nuisance, especially since the foliage needs to be allowed to continue growing, allowing the bulbs to flower well the

OPPOSITE The sturdy-looking, often spherical flowerheads of the alliums look stunning when in bloom, but refrain from plucking them from the border when flowering is over and the space-age seed heads will develop and look good for much of the winter.

following year. But use your bulbs wisely and you need not have this problem. Small clumps of inexpensive miniature bulbs such as the narcissus 'Tête-à-Tête' look fabulous, and although their foliage still needs to be left in place for a minimum of six weeks after flowering is over, because it is shorter it is soon masked by nearby herbaceous plant foliage, which starts to grow rapidly in early and mid-spring. I love to include clusters of autumn-flowering crocus in sunny spots in a flower border, just as the foliage of the herbaceous plants is starting to flop and long after most have ceased flowering. Dizzily pretty clumps of lilac *Crocus kotschyanus* subsp. *kotschyanus* or *C. speciosus* pop up and help to cheer me up, and to detract from the deteriorating foliage near by.

If you are determined to brighten borders with bulbs at any time of year but are put off by the prospect of later having to watch all the foliage of larger varieties yellow and die back, you can always plant the bulbs in pond baskets. Any mesh basket will do, as long as it allows you to plant the bulbs deep enough. Once the flowers have faded you can simply lift the basket and fill in the gap with some new-season colour. The basket of bulbs can then be allowed to grow undisturbed in an out-of-the-way spot in the garden. Come the autumn they can be plunged again, ready to put on a pretty display in the spring.

The so-called tender perennials and annuals can help to bring areas of the garden to life when they would otherwise have been a bit quiet: planting any of these in bare patches of soil close to shrubs or climbers, for instance, will ensure splashes of colour when those larger woody plants are themselves not in flower. Provided that these temporary flowers are not put in too shady a spot, they will perform well. Include winter or early spring flowers, such as winter-flowering pansies, winter bellis or pom-pom daisies, primulas and polyanthus, and even these less colourful times of year can suddenly come to life. If the roots of trees or shrubs make it difficult to carry out any short-term planting such as this, an alternative is to plant up a selection of seasonal containers of flowers and use these to 'decorate' sparse areas. Containers can easily be replaced as the months progress, so keeping colour and interest there constantly.

Planting for effect

I am a great believer in cramming in lots of flowering plants. Not for me
the sparse over-ordered and excessively organised look; I like a more
cheery, abundant flowerbed style. This means that at every opportunity I
use plants that look good for more than one season, and I also include
those that have a relatively short performance time, but then have the
good grace to fade quickly and quietly in to insignificance, so allowing
that prime space they took up to be occupied by the next star performer.
For this reason, the dicentras (bleeding hearts), especially *Dicentra
spectabilis*, are great if space is limited. Their elegantly arching stems,
positively dripping with heart-shaped jewel-like flowers, bring welcome
colour to borders in late spring and early summer but then shortly
afterwards the whole plant dies back, making plenty of space for the
summer-flowering herbaceous perennials.

ABOVE Everyone adores daffodils, but that
floppy green and later yellowing foliage does
not rate so highly. Grow the bulbs in pond
baskets so they can be lifted when the
flowers are over, and the foliage can die
back in a less prominent position. Meanwhile
fill the gap with a seasonal favourite and
replant the bulb basket in autumn.

Whether you are using bulbs, herbaceous perennials, annuals or biennials, or a combination of several types of flower, it can be difficult to decide how many of each to plant. If space is really short you will need to be sure that you have chosen what you really need and want. If space is at less of a premium, you may decide to be a bit more adventurous. I always prefer to see bulbs in groups. A group, of upwards of three, looks better than one on its own, which manages to appear lonely, whatever other plants surround it. If a plant is likely to grow particularly large or to have a very strong architectural shape, it may look good planted singly, but most prefer a few companions. I am a great fan of odd numbers of bulbs, herbaceous, biennial and annual flowers and so would always suggest planting in, say, ones, threes or fives. The quantity you choose will probably largely depend on the type of plant and its potential spread and height, and of course the size of your garden and the space you have to fill. When they are grown in uneven numbers you will find that these plants all look more natural and give a decidedly more relaxed feel than an even-number planting, which grows somewhat erratically and ends up looking a bit of a mess. Some people love straight lines, but as far as I am concerned the only place I want to see plants in straight lines is in a kitchen garden – vegetables or fruit look great like this, but flowers look as if they have been conscripted into a floral army that they would prefer not to have joined.

Choose wisely

By choosing a wide range of different flowers you should be able to prolong the flowering season and have something gorgeous in the garden throughout the year, even if there are peaks and troughs as the seasons progress. By taking a look at some of my favourites, which I describe in the following seasonal sections, you will be able to get some good ideas. Remember that there is also a lot to be learned from a well-stocked nursery or garden centre. A visit at any one time of year will reveal those flowers that are looking at their most attractive at that moment. These are usually in a prominent position and displayed in such a way that it is extremely hard to resist buying them. By all means

OPPOSITE The fantastic and slightly furry foliage and delicate yellow flower spikes of *Alchemilla mollis* are perfect companions for the rich-purple flowers and interestingly shaped foliage of herbaceous *Geranium magnificum*. Cramming in suits these both well.

invest in a few of the most flower-laden plants of the month, but if you want to have flowers at every season you will need to return regularly, as those seasonal spectaculars change frequently.

If you have fallen for one particular flower, whatever it may be, it is worth investigating its close relatives, its various varieties or cultivars. By choosing several different forms of a single plant you may well be able to hugely extend the period of time over which you can enjoy its flowers, as each variety will have a slightly different flowering season. Combine the late starters with the early starters and you can have the best of both worlds.

Maintenance for best performance

Any flowering plant will tend to perform better and for a longer period if it is well looked after and happy in the position in which it is growing. This means that it is essential to choose plants that really are suited to the spot you have to offer, to plant them carefully and then, once they are growing well, to maintain them to the best of your ability. Precise requirements will vary from plant to plant, so you will need to check these: for instance, some may require staking, some pinching out, some have very specific feeding requirements. All will do better with an adequate supply of water, and a suitable feeding regime as well as regular deadheading, which will ensure that energy is not wasted on seed production but is instead used to produce more, larger flowers over a longer period (see also p. 177). Some flowers respond well to a bit of relatively rough treatment: the herbaceous geraniums are a classic example of plants that will often put on two good displays of flowers if as soon as the first flowers have faded (usually fairly early in the summer) you cut the plants back hard – a pair of shears is perfect for a sizeable clump. A drastic haircut will not only help to keep such a plant looking attractively neat and compact (no need to fear, though, that it will look clipped or over-groomed), but will also encourage a second flush of flowers towards the very end of summer or in early autumn. If the plant is kept well fed, it will perform like this each year with no problem.

OPPOSITE A carpet of spring flowering anemone *(Anemone blanda)* with their dizzily pretty white and purple flowers and divided leaves looks much better than a bark mulch, and also does a good job at swamping out weeds.

spring PERENNIALS

After the cool, often dark, months of winter we all need cheering up, and what better way than by seeing the garden move into a more vivacious stage, as day length and light levels start to increase and spring-blooming flowers bring it to life.

Ajuga BUGLE

SPRING	SUMMER	AUTUMN	WINTER
foliage			
flowers			

A. reptans (common bugle) and its numerous cultivars are widely grown, largely because they are useful as low-growing evergreen plants and make excellent ground cover. Precise heights and spreads vary from one cultivar to another, but they are usually about 10cm (4in) high with a spread of 30cm (12in). In spring and early summer fairly short, bright **blue** spikes of flowers are formed on *A. reptans* and these contrast beautifully with the dark green glossy leaves. If you are after more colourful foliage, take a look at 'Braunherz' (**purply-brown**), 'Burgundy Glow' (variegated leaves including **green**, **reddish**, **purple** and **white**), 'Variegata' (**cream** and **greyish-green** variegation) and 'Atropurpurea' (rich **purple** leaves with a hint of bronze-brown). Some cultivars are also well worth considering for their flowers, in particular those of 'Purple Torch' (rich green leaves and **pink** flowers), 'Alba' (dark green leaves and **white** flowers) and 'Pink Surprise' (rich **pink** flowers and purply-brown foliage).

A. pyramidalis (pyramid bugle) has one particularly attractively cultivar known as 'Metallica Crispa', **H** 10cm (4in), **S** about 45cm (18in). This has leaves of

a slightly bronzed colour, with crinkled edges and rich **blue** flowers. Grow this and you will add a touch of lacy elegance to your ground-cover planting.

All bugles do best in a fairly moist soil and perform brilliantly in either sun or shade, although *A.reptans* 'Variegata' tends to look a lot more colourful in shade and conversely the colour of *A. reptans* 'Atropurpurea' is at its richest if grown in a sunny spot.

Arabis ROCKCRESS

SPRING	SUMMER	AUTUMN	WINTER
foliage			
flowers			

H 7–25cm (3–10in), **S** 30–60cm (12–24in), depending on the variety. The various rockcresses are great ground-cover or mat-forming plants, which between spring and summer are covered with small but pretty flowers. Those with evergreen foliage are particularly useful. All of them tend to be very tough and easy to grow, so can help to bring a lovely bit of texture and colour to even a fairly miserable site in a flowerbed, or to a gap in paving or a planting hole in a wall. The flowers are either **white** (for example *A. alpina* subsp. *caucasica* 'Schneehaube' and 'Snow White'), **pink** (for example *A.* x *arendsii* 'Rosabella') or **red** (for example *A. blepharophylla* 'Frühlingszauber').

Although the display of flowers is quite long lasting, to make these plants even better value, try growing one of the *Arabis ferdinandi-coburgi* varieties, such as the variegated form 'Aureovariegata' (with yellow leaf edges), or 'Old Gold' (green and rich yellow variegation). On both these plants the flowers are **white** and produced in spring.

All arabis plants perform best in a sunny spot and on a well-drained soil. If you want to prevent some of the more rampant forms from becoming too straggly, as soon as the flowers have finished, trim them over lightly, which will help to keep them relatively compact and bushy.

Armeria THRIFT

SPRING	SUMMER	AUTUMN	WINTER
foliage			
flowers			

H 20–25cm (8–10in), **S** 25–50cm (10–20in). I am immensely fond of these extraordinary plants and one of the reasons is that they have something to offer throughout the year. They are very hardy, tough little souls with evergreen foliage that always reminds me of an overexcited, green porcupine. The foliage is held in a compact and dense tuft or mound, which in itself is attractive and brings texture and the desire to touch and feel into the garden. They are really adaptable plants and, although they always need a well-drained soil and plenty of sun if they are to perform to perfection, you can use them in a variety of situations, including flowerbeds, as border edging, in rock gardens or even in sizeable containers. In theory these plants produce their delightful near-spherical flower clusters between spring and summer, but I have often had them flowering in late autumn too. There are numerous different varieties to choose from, which between them provide delightful pompoms in **white** or various shades of **pink**, through to near **red**. These include *A. maritima* 'Alba' (**white** flowers), *A. juniperifolia* 'Bevan's Variety' (rich **rose-pink**), *A. maritima*

'Bloodstone' (very **dark pink** to **red**) and *A. alpina* 'Bee's Ruby' (ruby **red**). These plants don't take up too much space, although some have a tendency to spread after a while. They are such a delight that I would recommend cramming some in anywhere you can.

ABOVE The almost papery pompom flowers of thrift make a striking display and look partic-ularly at home growing amongst or close to rock or stone. The rich green, spiky foliage looks great for much of the year, a real bonus.
OPPOSITE All the ajugas make good ground cover because of their carpet-forming foliage, but when topped with masses of pretty flower spikes, like this *Ajuga braunherz*, the effect is quite stunning and brings in the bees for an early supply of nectar.

Diascia

SPRING	SUMMER	AUTUMN	WINTER
flowers			

H 45cm (18in), **S** 40cm (16in), with
some variation depending on which
type you choose. There are several
different species and varieties of diascia
that are well worth including in the
garden. Admittedly they are not the
hardiest of plants and should ideally be
given protection or brought into a
protected spot over the winter months.
If you are prepared to do this, their
delicate flower spikes covered in
seriously pretty **pink**, near **red** or
sometimes **apricot**-coloured flowers are
well worth the effort. They flower at any
time from late spring through to early
autumn, depending on which one you
choose, and if you give a plant a slight
haircut at the beginning of summer
once the main flush of flowers is over,
you invariably get a later flush towards
the end of the season. To flower well
they need plenty of sun, but at the same
time it is essential to ensure that the soil
in which they grow does not become too
dry – otherwise they will look thin,
miserable and flower only sparsely.

D. barberae 'Blackthorn Apricot' has
delicious **apricot**- and -coloured flowers.

D. rigescens is a bushy plant with
crimson to **pink** flowers from late
spring until early autumn.

D. vigilis is probably the hardiest species with a clear, quite delicate **pink** flower; it is larger than most with a height of about 50cm (20in) and a spread of 50cm (20in).

Other particularly lovely varieties include 'Ruby Field' (**ruby-red** flowers), 'Rupert Lambert' (pink), and 'Twinkle' and 'Lilac Mist' (both a **pinky-purple** colour).

Dicentra

SPRING	SUMMER	AUTUMN	WINTER
foliage			
flowers			

H 60cm (24in), **S** 45cm (18in). This is a truly delightful plant, with curious heart-shaped flowers and quite often a very attractive leaf shape.

D. spectabilis (bleeding heart or Dutchman's breeches) has wonderfully ferny **pale-green** foliage, held on elegantly arching stems and then slightly taller flower stems decked with the heart-shaped flowers. This common form has a **dark-red** flower with inner white petals – hence the name bleeding heart. For something even more elegant choose the variety 'Alba' with **pure-**

white flowers.

D. formosa has more delicate grey-green very ferny foliage and a plentiful supply of dangling, somewhat smaller flowers in various colours including **white**, **yellow** and a **pinky-purple**. These are produced from the end of spring and into early summer.

There are also lots of different varieties, including my favourite 'Luxuriant', which is about 30cm (12in) tall and has particularly prolific ferny, bright green leaves and larger than average **pink** flowers. 'Snowflakes' has **white** flowers and brighter-green foliage, and 'Pearl Drops' has **white** flowers with a slight pink tinge. 'Bacchanal' has **crimson-red** flowers.

For best results grow all dicentras in a fairly moist soil with a plentiful supply of organic matter in it and ideally position them in a spot with sunshine or dappled shade.

Doronicum LEOPARD'S BANE

SPRING	SUMMER	AUTUMN	WINTER
flowers			

H 30–90cm (12–36in), **S** 40–45cm (16–18in). I am a great fan of leopard's banes. They are especially useful if you want to bring some splashes of bright **yellow** into a relatively shady spot, although they also do well in sun. It is probably gardening

heresy to suggest this, but from a distance the flowers always remind me of particularly vigorous and healthy-looking dandelions. Bright golden yellow, they can bring a real glow to a gloomy corner. I have grown them with great success in a wide range of soils, from fairly free-draining sandy sites to heavy clay. There are several different types to look out for, including *D.* 'Frühlingspracht' (also sometimes labelled as 'Spring Beauty'), with double golden-yellow flowers, and *D.* x *excelsum* 'Harpur Crewe', with really large single golden-yellow flowers.

Epimedium

SPRING	SUMMER	AUTUMN	WINTER
foliage			
flowers			

The epimediums are variable flowers: some are herbaceous, whilst others are evergreen and so put on a good show of leaves for twelve months of the year. In the springtime, when the new leaves are produced, many types of epimedium look particularly fantastic because this young foliage is richly tinted with **red**, **coppery-brown** or **pink**. Once the leaves mature, they turn pure green. But, come the autumn, the foliage of some varieties takes on delicious autumn tints of bronze-brown, yellow or red. As if this isn't enough, in the spring these clump-forming plants produce

unbelievably delicate sprays of flowers. There is a wide range of plants to choose from, with flowers that may be **white**, **yellow**, **reddish** or **orange**, and the majority of them have extraordinary shapes, most of which have an almost space-age quality, looking more like something out of a *Dr Who* movie than a flowerbed. Garden centres usually have a few different epimediums in stock, but if you want to investigate these plants further and find a much wider range of varieties and species, a good nursery is your best source. Size varies with the variety, but most are 25–50cm (10–20in) high and 30–60cm (12–24in) in spread. Epimediums are great plants if you have one of those often rather difficult-to-fill shady spots in your garden, as they tend to look rather miserable if planted in full sun – instead choose a fairly moist but well-drained spot in full

or part shade, and ensure that you incorporate some extra leaf mould or other bulky organic matter.

Eremurus FOXTAIL LILY

SPRING	SUMMER	AUTUMN	WINTER
flowers			

The individual flowers on these extraordinary plants are really quite small and delicately star-shaped, but they are grouped together into huge towering spikes, which create serious impact from late spring right through to the beginning of summer. There are several different types readily available, with sizes varying from **H** 1–2m (3½–6½ft), **S** 60–90cm (24–36in). Flower colour includes **white** (*E. himalaicus*), **yellow** (*E. stenophyllus* subsp. *stenophyllus*) and **pink** (*E. robustus*). You can also buy several good hybrids, including the Shelford and Ruiter hybrids, which come in a range of colours, including **pink**, **orange**, **yellow** and **white**. To get these magnificent plants to give you their best possible display (and they're guaranteed to bring a smile to your face because there really is something quite amusing about them), it is essential that you plant them in a sunny spot with a well-drained soil. Although they are basically regarded as hardy, it is also well worthwhile mulching the crowns of the plants, particularly early

in the year, as this should decrease the risk of frost damage. As with many bulbous plants, their deteriorating foliage looks a bit of a mess, and so it is often best to plant foxtail lilies amongst shrubs, where their yellowing leaves can be masked to a good extent.

Euphorbia SPURGE

SPRING	SUMMER	AUTUMN	WINTER
foliage			
flowers			

Most of the spurges flower towards the end of spring and into early summer. Although the flowers certainly add to the appearance of these extraordinary plants, it is their fantastic foliage that makes them such good value in a garden. There are many different euphorbias to choose from, including evergreen and herbaceous perennials

Paeonia PEONY

SPRING	SUMMER	AUTUMN	WINTER
foliage			
flowers			

From late spring through until early summer an established herbaceous peony guarantees a truly luxurious and breathtaking display. The flowers can be single, semi-double or double and, in the former two cases, an added bonus is a prominent cluster of stamens which are often a rich gold-yellow colour. Peonies may not have the longest display of flowers, but when they appear, they are so striking that they are still something I would try to include in an herbaceous border, even in a fairly small garden. The size usually varies: **H** 60cm (24in) and **s** 60–75cm (24–30in). Flower colours include **white** (for example *P. lactiflora*, single white, and *P. lactiflora* 'Festiva Maxima' with double white flowers with a crimson blotch at the base of the central petals and a distinct perfume); **cream** or **yellow** (for example *P. lactiflora* 'Laura Dessert', which is perfumed and double); **pink** (for example *P. lactiflora* 'Sarah Bernhardt', which is double, with **pale-pink** ruffled petals and scented flowers); and *P. officinalis* 'Anemoniflora Rosea' (**deep-pink** foliage), and **red** (for example *P. officinalis* 'Rubra Plena'). There are many other cultivars that perform beautifully and have the same wonderfully silky petals forming the

that, to my mind, make most exciting garden plants. Once a clump of euphorbias has become established, it makes a truly eyecatching and wacky sight! They are variable in size, most having a height and spread of 45cm–1m (18in–3½ft). Many of them are a combination of bright and **lime green** with **yellow**, for example

E. polychroma. Others such as *E. dulcis* 'Chameleon' have dark **purple** foliage and bracts, while others such as *E. griffithii* and its varieties tend to have bright **red** or **orange** flower clusters towards the end of spring. Euphorbias are another type of plant that never ceases to bring a smile to my face, as you really get the feeling they are doing things just to suit themselves, but nevertheless they make a fantastic garden plant. The vast majority prefer a sunny spot with a well-drained soil. I have only one word of warning about them: their milky white sap may bring you out in an unpleasant rash if it touches your skin, particularly during periods of bright sunlight.

ABOVE Resembling huge, silken roses, peonies spell luxury and opulence. The bright yellow bunches of stamens set off the shiny petals to perfection.

OPPOSITE The foliage of *pulmonarias* is often strikingly marked with white or silver and, arranged in a neat mound, it provides good ground cover or border edging. This *Pumonaria officinalis* 'Sissinghurst White' has white flowers, but others may be pink, blue or violet.

attention-grabbing blooms. All peonies do best in a well-drained soil in a sunny spot and benefit from regular feeding.

Pulmonaria LUNGWORT

SPRING	SUMMER	AUTUMN	WINTER
foliage			
flowers			

The lungworts are classic spring-flowering plants, brightening any partially or even fully shaded spot. The great thing about these herbaceous perennials Is that, pretty as their numerous funnel-shaped flowers are, they are truly plants for all seasons as in most gardens they retain much of their foliage throughout the year – believe me the leaves are something really spectacular. Most are basically a medium green and covered in dense, bristly hairs, but the fantastic thing about them is the markings. Only a few have plain green leaves; the vast majority are excitingly decorated, enough to leave any fabric designer in awe! The patterns include **silvery-white** blotches, such as those seen on *P. saccharata* and its varieties, such as 'Mrs Moon' (**violet** to **pale-pink** flowers too), 'Frühlingshimmel' (**pale-blue** flowers) and 'Alba' (**white** flowers, produced from prettily pink-coloured buds). The foliage of *P. argentea* are an almost completely **silvery-white** colour with a mottled green edge. Many *P. officinalis* have also got both gorgeous flowers and fantastic foliage, including

'Sissinghurst White' (**white** flowers and silver-spotted foliage), 'Bowles' Blue' (**pale-blue** flowers, and white and pale green markings on the leaves). The lungworts are easy to please and seem to thrive in every soil in which I have ever tried to grow them, including chalky, acidic, heavy and light, and they thrive in those tricky-to-fill, shady places.

Pulsatilla PASQUEFLOWER

SPRING	SUMMER	AUTUMN	WINTER
flowers			
seed heads			

P. vulgaris is probably one of the easiest to grow of the pasqueflowers, and although its spring flowers may not be particularly long-lasting, the display they put on is delightful and once the flowers have faded they leave behind extraordinary tufted seedheads, which

remain on the plant well into winter. In addition, the foliage brings interest to the border, as its texture is rather special, the leaves being finely divided and covered in a very dense silky layer of hair, which also makes them appear silvery. The flowers of the various cultivars come in shades of **white**, **pink**, **red** and a **purple** that is so dark that it is nearly black. For pasqueflowers to do well, it is essential that they are grown in an extremely well-drained soil, as any sogginess around the roots will cause them to die rapidly. A neutral or chalky soil in full sun suits them best.

OTHER PERENNIALS WITH GOOD SPRING INTEREST

Alchemilla mollis p. 36

Anemone hupehensis p. 134

Anemone x *hybrida* p. 134

Argyranthemum p. 135

Cimicifuga p. 136

Helenium p. 137

Helleborus argutifolius p. 148

Helleborus foetidus p. 148

Helleborus orientalis p. 149

Hemerocallis p. 137

Kniphofia p. 137

Lupinus p. 120

Rudbeckia p. 138

Tiarella p. 123

Tropaeolum speciosum p. 139

Tropaeolum tuberosum p. 139

spring BULBOUS PLANTS

Spring without a good number of flowering bulbs is an impossible concept. Whether in beds, borders or containers, or naturalised in grass, bulbs allow you to bring masses of colour to your garden with relatively little cost.

Anemone WIND FLOWER

SPRING	SUMMER	AUTUMN	WINTER
flowers			

A. blanda, **H** 20cm (8in) and **s** 30cm (12in), produces a reliable display of starlike flowers between early and mid-spring. Each of the flowers measures up to about 4cm (1½in) in diameter and because they grow well in a fairly dry, shady position they are an extremely useful way of brightening up this often difficult-to-fill area of a garden. Flowers are available in a range of colours, including **blue** (for instance 'Blue'); **white** ('White Splendour'); **pink** ('Pink Star', 'Charmer') and rich **reddish-pink** to **purple** ('Radar', 'Violet Star'). Although their flowering period is not particularly long, they fit in well in small spaces and because they tend to form mats they can be used rather like small-scale ground colour.

A. coronaria (crown anemone), **H** 30–60cm (12–24in), **s** 15cm (6in). I sometimes think that the flowers on these plants are so unbelievably bright that it is almost as if someone has daubed them with paint from a child's paint box. There is a wide range of colours available, including **mauve**, **white**, **blue**, **red** and a gorgeous screaming cerise-**pink**, and, as if to make the flowers all the more striking, each has a black central cluster of

stamens. They are truly beautiful in a wickedly tempting sort of way and, because they are in flower from spring into early summer, they are one of the best ways to add rich colours to a border and yet allow space for similar colours coming from other plants to be used for the remainder of the summer or into autumn. There are two main groups: the Saint Brigid Group with semi-double flowers and the De Caen Group with single flowers; and there are several varieties in each of these. It is essential that these anemones have a moist yet well-drained soil, ideally in partial shade, or failing this in full sun.

Chionodoxa

SPRING	SUMMER	AUTUMN	WINTER
flowers			

H 10–25cm (4–10in), **s** 7–10cm (3–4in). To make a real impact with these relatively small bulbs, it is essential to plant them in good quantities, towards the front of a border, amongst shrubs, in good-sized containers or in a rock garden. They come into bloom in early spring, just when I for one really need cheering up, and their **pink**, **lilac**-coloured or rich **purple-blue** flowers are enough to cheer up the most miserable of early spring days. The flowers are a strange mixture of delicate yet sturdy, as each individual is well constructed and has no problem coping with poor weather early in the year, yet the overall effect is one of dizzy feminine prettiness. Because they flower relatively early in the year you can even plant them amongst herbaceous perennials; the flowering of the chionodoxa is usually well over before the newly emerging foliage of the herbaceous perennials gets to any decent size. Chionodoxa do best in sun or part shade in a moist, yet well-drained soil.

Crocus

SPRING	SUMMER	AUTUMN	WINTER
flowers			

The spring-flowering crocuses are plants that, to my mind, are essential if you want your garden to be a cheery and inviting place early in the year. I add them to flowerbeds and borders, rock gardens, grassy areas (where I allow them to naturalise) and containers. Most are 7–10cm (3–4in) tall and a visit to any good garden centre or a look at any decent bulb catalogue will reveal a whole host of varieties. My only word of warning is that seeing all these will probably tempt you into buying more than you really need – but then these truly delightful silken-petalled heralds of spring are so small that you can pack plenty of them in to even a tiny garden. The main flower colours include **white**, **cream**, **purple**, **yellow**,

lilac as well as several which are striped or blotched. I adore them all, but I now avoid the bargain mixed packs and varieties that have purely yellow flowers as I find that the local sparrow population rips them to shreds in no time at all. Crocuses need a well-drained soil and plenty of sun, and definitely look most appealing when planted in groups, or better still drifts.

ABOVE I try to plant crocuses in as many places as possible; they are one of the true heralds of spring and look great in grass, borders or containers. This *Crocus tommasinianus* is a great reminder of all that the garden will have in store in the year ahead.

Cyclamen coum

SPRING	SUMMER	AUTUMN	WINTER
foliage			
flowers			

From the middle of winter, right through until mid-spring, this cyclamen produces breathtakingly beautiful **pale-pink**, **dark-pink**, **magenta** or **white** flowers, all with petals that are swept elegantly upwards and held at the top of a reddish-brown shepherd's crook-shaped flower stalk. The base of each petal is marked with either a magenta or purple splotch. This is the sort of flower that really draws you in close to have a better look, and the great thing is that, even if these plants did not bear flowers, I would still grow them for their foliage alone.

Although on occasion the lobed leaves are a plain rich green, the majority of those on the cyclamen available have extraordinary, clearly defined grey, silver or pale-green patterns on them, often resembling an elaborate and intricately structured piece of marble.

Fritillaria FRITILLARY

SPRING	SUMMER	AUTUMN	WINTER
flowers			

Fritillaries range in height from about 20cm (8in) to 1.5m (5ft) and their appearance varies pretty well as dramatically too, from *F. imperialis* (crown imperial) with its extraordinarily striking flowers to the much more delicate *F. meleagris* (snake's head fritillary) with its delicate chequerboard **pinky-purple** and **white** or **pale-pink** chequered flowers. Fritillaries tend to flower between mid- and late spring, and because their flowerheads, particularly those of the bell-shaped ones such as snake's head fritillary and *F. michailovskyi*, nod in the breeze, they look fantastic planted somewhere where there is a bit of a breeze and where they can be allowed to naturalise. Plenty of sun and a well-drained spot are essential. If you are short of space, provided that you use a compost enriched with extra grit for drainage, most of the fritillaries do well in containers. *F. michailovskyi* hates getting the slightest bit soggy around the base and so is generally best grown in a shallow well-drained container.

Hyacinthoides non-scripta BLUEBELL

SPRING	SUMMER	AUTUMN	WINTER
flowers			

H 20–25cm (8–10in). Bluebells may not be the longest-lasting flowering bulb you could choose to plant, but the display they put on when planted *en masse* is something to make even a non-gardener wilt with pleasure. Grow the English or wild type of bluebells in preference to the Spanish ones (which although larger, to my mind look almost too sturdy and certainly out of place if you are attempting to create a woodland feel) underneath trees or shrubs. Admittedly they can become almost invasive once established, but in the meantime the display they put on in late spring is truly fantastic and you may even notice a delicate perfume being produced from their nodding **blue** flowers. If you want to create a woodland effect, plant a mass of bluebells beneath trees and allow them to naturalise, and towards the end of each spring you will have something magical. Their deteriorating foliage is not the prettiest of sights so, lovely as the flowers are, these bulbs are best planted in relatively out-of-the-way places.

Iris

SPRING	SUMMER	AUTUMN	WINTER
foliage			
flowers			

There is an iris to suit pretty well every taste in colour, but all share an amazing combination of elegance and striking style. Their flowering season is prolonged, provided that you use a wide range of varieties; indeed you could have irises in flower from mid-winter right through to the middle of summer. The majority of larger iris put on a fantastic display in the spring. Some such as *I. pseudacorus* (yellow water flag) can be grown to great effect in a pond, or around its margins. The majority of irises, however, are bulbous or rhizomatous and do best in a well-drained soil, preferably with a good amount of sun. Even so, most perform quite well in a fairly heavy soil, provided that it is not actually wet or waterlogged, but if in doubt add plenty of grit. Lots of irises are readily available from garden centres or nurseries, so take a look at the shelves or catalogues to see precisely which you prefer. Irises are great in open ground, but the smaller ones in particular make excellent additions to long- or short-term container plantings, helping to bring a bit of off-season colour.

Leucojum SNOWFLAKE

SPRING	SUMMER	AUTUMN	WINTER
flowers			

Both *L. vernum* (spring snowflake) and *L. aestivum* (summer snowflake), H 75cm (30in), flower in spring, with *L. vernum* starting as early as the end of winter and finishing in early spring and *L. aestivum* flowering through to the end of spring. *L. aestivum* produces quite chunky-looking **white** bell-shaped flowers with delicate green edging. There are several flowers on each head which nod delicately in the spring breezes. Although the flowers themselves are not long-lived, the plant certainly helps to bring interest during the spring months and its deteriorating foliage is not too unsightly, especially if the bulbs are planted close to herbaceous perennials. For best results choose a soil with plenty of bulky organic matter in it and ensure that the ground is not allowed to dry out too much.

OPPOSITE Snake's head fritillaries look fantastic planted in erratic drifts beneath trees or shrubs or in grass, but plant somewhere you can see them close up too, their intricately checked flowers are a real delight.

Narcissus DAFFODILS AND OTHER NARCISSUS

SPRING	SUMMER	AUTUMN	WINTER
flowers			

Choose a selection of these glorious flowers and you should be able to have blooms from the end of winter right through early spring. Some of the smallest such as *N. bulbocodium* (hoop petticoat daffodil) is a mere 10–20cm (4–8in) tall, as are some of the common miniature forms such as 'Tête-à-tête', H 15cm (6in), and so are readily grown in containers or flowerbeds, or even naturalised in fairly short grass beneath shrubs. Others, such as the most widely grown forms of trumpet daffodils, range from 30–60cm (12–24in) in height. They have flowers in various combinations of **yellow**, **orange**, **salmon**, **white** and **cream**. For me daffodils are a vital ingredient of spring. Many not only look delightfully pretty, but also have a good perfume. Larger forms can obviously be grown in borders, but because their deteriorating foliage needs to be left in place for at least six weeks (if the bulbs are to continue to perform well), it is often

easier either to plant them in temporary baskets (see p. 92) or simply to put something else in a prominent position in a border and plant daffodils somewhere where their yellowing foliage need not become an eyesore. With the exception of a seriously wet or waterlogged soil, daffodils seem to thrive almost anywhere and do well in a partially shaded or sunny spot. If you are gardening in a fairly windy place, it is best to choose the shorter stems or more miniature forms as these are rarely blown to the ground by winds.

Scilla

SPRING	SUMMER	AUTUMN	WINTER
flowers			

The tallest of the hardy scillas is only about 25cm (10in) high and many such as *S. bifolia* only reach a height of about

15cm (6in), but all deserve a place in the garden, where they help to bring delightful spots of colour in springtime.

S. siberica (Siberian squill) has a good dense flowerhead composed of numerous tiny, bell-shaped, rich **azure-blue** flowers and those of 'Spring Beauty' are an even darker colour.

The flowers of some of the other scillas such as *S. bifolia* are star-shaped and carried on the plant from the end of winter right through into early spring. They have a delicate perfume and work well in containers or open ground. Most perform best in a well-drained soil that contains quite a lot of organic matter and is in dappled shade.

Tulipa TULIP

SPRING	SUMMER	AUTUMN	WINTER
flowers			

A high proportion of spring-flowering plants seem to have blooms that are yellow or blue, but not so tulips. Although there are some delightful yellow forms, these bulbs produce flowers in a wide range of colours including **purple**, **lilac**, **red**, **pink**, **orange**, **yellow**, **cream** and **white**. The majority of them produce goblet-shaped flowers, but some open into an almost star-like cup shape. Once again the flowering period may not be particularly long, but as they are a means of bringing a range of glorious colours into your garden at this time, it would be impossible to miss out on tulips. Once flowering is over you may be left with the leaves, but they do not seem to be quite as long-lasting as those of the daffodils, so pose little problem. There is a wide range of heights and forms of tulip available. Most have single flowers, but a few such as 'Peach Blossom' have double flowers. All have petals resembling pieces of neatly cut silk, sometimes marked with a completely contrasting colour towards the base, so making the view of the inner surface of a tulip's petals as delightful from above as the whole flower is from the side. Take a glance inside the tulip: the combination of the stamens and the bases of the petals is truly breathtaking. Most do best if lifted annually and then replanted in the autumn. However, if you find that time is short, you could consider naturalising some of the more vigorous or species types of tulip. *T. sprengeri* is very tough and self-seeds regularly, but needs a well-drained soil. Tulips are great in beds, borders or containers and the smaller types could also be grown in a rock garden.

OTHER BULBOUS PLANTS WITH GOOD SPRING INTEREST

Crocus tommasinianus p. 146

Iris reticulata p. 80

Leucojum vernum p. 150

spring ANNUALS&BIENNIALS

If you make good use of spring-flowering annuals and biennials, a garden can be almost as colourful in spring as it is in summer. Whether you grow your own or buy them in, you'll not regret planting them.

Bellis perennis POMPOM DAISY

SPRING	SUMMER	AUTUMN	WINTER
flowers			

H and **S** 15–20cm (6–8in). There is something immensely cheerful about these **pink**, **red**, **white** or occasionally **purple** daisy-like flowers. The single forms remind me of a chimney sweep's brushes and the double forms resemble pompoms. The flowers often start up in the autumn and then subside slightly over the winter months before coming into their own with a burst of triumph in the spring. They add a touch of informal charm to a bedding plant display in a flowerbed or container and seem to act like a magnet for small children too.

Erysimum cheiri WALLFLOWER

SPRING	SUMMER	AUTUMN	WINTER
flowers			

H 20–60cm (8–24in), **S** 20–45cm (8–18in). There may be something decidedly old-fashioned about wall-flowers, but at the same time they have immense charm and appeal with their rounded perfumed heads of good-sized flowers in shades of **bronzish-brown**, **red**, **orange**, **yellow** and **cream**. These biennials make an excellent addition to any spring bedding plant display. That said, although it is easy to associate them with the fairly formal parks-department planting, wallflowers have a cottage garden air about them and look great dotted in amongst pretty well any

plant that will give them space to fill out and perform to perfection. It is possible to buy bare-root wallflowers ready for planting towards the end of summer or early autumn, and this is the best way to grow them if you are short of space. However, if you want to raise your own from seed, there is a fantastic

ABOVE Bright they may be, but these *Erysimum* 'Scarlet Bedder' wallflowers provide a necessary warm glow to a spring flowerbed, and look great with their traditional partners, forget-me-nots.
OPPOSITE The pompom daisies are a family favourite of ours. Adored by children and adults alike, their lollipop-like flowers are remarkably tough and have even been known to flower at Christmas time.

array available from any good garden centre. Wallflowers thrive in most soils; however, if conditions are either too wet or excessively fertile the plants tend to flower less. As with some perennials, if you give your wallflowers a slight haircut once the flowers are over, you often get a second slightly later flush of flowers on both the biennials and also on perennial forms.

Myosotis FORGET-ME-NOT

SPRING	SUMMER	AUTUMN	WINTER
flowers			

H 15–25cm (6–10in), **S** 25cm (10in). Tiny they might be but the forget-me-not's perfectly symmetrical **pale-blue** flowers, often with a whitish and yellow central eye, are grouped together in flat-topped clusters, which abound on the gloriously delicate plants. They create a dense blue mist of colour that floats like a blue cloud in the spring flowerbed. White and pale pink forms are also available. Although these plants are generally regarded as biennials, they can sometimes last for several years but are best removed after they have flowered and set seed. Tap the plants sharply before pulling them up to scatter the seed and you can be sure of an even bigger drift of blue when these seeds germinate and the plants mature to flowering stage. Light shade suits

forget-me-nots best, but I have seen them growing in pretty well every conceivable situation including crevices in paving, so don't let not having exactly the right spot put you off.

Primula PRIMROSE AND POLYANTHUS

SPRING	SUMMER	AUTUMN	WINTER
flowers			

Between them these charming flowers cover almost every shade of **yellow**, **cream**, **purple**, **lilac**, **red**, **orange** and **pink**, and bring some true poster-paint colours to a spring garden. Use the paler colours such as the various creams and true primrose yellow to create a more subtle, almost woodland effect in sun or dappled shade. Primroses, primulas and polyanthus are all striking plants despite their small size – most are 10–20cm (4–8in) high – often holding their flowers into the plant quite closely, so making each plant resemble a posy when in full bloom. They flower early to mid-spring and some will even produce blooms towards the end of winter. The rosettes of tight green foliage even look attractive before the flowers appear and once they have faded.

OTHER ANNUALS AND BIENNIALS WITH GOOD SPRING INTEREST

Senecio cineraria 'Silver dust' p. 151
Viola x *wittrockiana* p. 133

summerPERENNIALS

Summer brings with it warmer temperatures and brighter days and your garden can have its own brighter look, right through to the end of the season – largely provided by the rich, warm colours of summer-blooming flowers.

Acanthus BEAR'S BREECHES

SPRING	SUMMER	AUTUMN	WINTER
foliage			
flowers			

The two most widely grown species are *A. mollis*, **H** 1.2m (4ft), **S** 90cm (36in), and *A. spinosus*, **H** 1.2m (4ft), **S** 60cm (24in). The Latin name of the latter lets you into a secret – it has long spines on the tips of the leaves. However, although this may mean that you decide to grow it towards the back of a border and well away from paths, it is an extremely worthwhile plant, producing **white** and pale **purplish** flowers in abundance towards the end of summer, just at that time when most flowerbeds could do with an extra splash of interest.

The softer-leaved *A. mollis* produces its **white** and **mauve** flower spikes at the beginning of summer and has relatively soft spines at the leaf tips. The 60cm (24in) long leaves are very attractive – so much so that this plant is perhaps one you will decide to put towards the front of the border so that you can enjoy the foliage even when the plant is not in flower.

Plenty of sun and a well-drained soil are essential if you want your bear's breeches to perform to capacity, but they do fairly well in slight shade.

Alcea rosea HOLLYHOCK

SPRING	SUMMER	AUTUMN	WINTER
flowers			

H 60cm–2.2m (24in–7ft), s 60–75cm (24–30in). I have a passion for these wonderfully tall plants, which seem to have a mind of their own, unless you are really good about ensuring that they are kept well and firmly staked from early on in the season. Perhaps one of the archetypal cottage garden plants, the hollyhock produces hugely long, tall flower spikes decked with either single or double flowers, the flower spikes opening from the base upwards often over a period of many weeks during the summer. Double forms such as 'Powder Puff' and Chater's Double Group are sometimes slightly shorter than the singles, and there is also a short form known as Majorette Group, which only grows to 60–90cm (24–36in) and has semi-double flowers. Hollyhocks are generally treated as biennials, although

OPPOSITE Striking and somehow somewhat wicked looking, the tall flower spikes of *Acanthus* help to bring height and impact to the border, but the foliage too provides welcome texture.

ABOVE RIGHT Definitely larger than life, hollyhocks look equally at home in a cottage garden or more modern surroundings as they stand like rows of sometimes errant soldiers.

in some cases they perform quite well for several years. Sadly, because they are very prone to the debilitating disease known as hollyhock rust, you should be prepared to replace them at regular intervals. My particular favourites are the single forms, which, like the doubles, come in various shades of **red**, **pink**, **white**, **purple**, **cream** and **yellow**; there is also a lovely very dark-purple to **near-black** variety known as 'Nigra'. For best results grow hollyhocks in a sunny spot, and bear in mind that the more shade they have, the more inclined they are to grow even taller, therefore needing even firmer staking if they are to stay in line. Alternatively let them do their own thing and flop

about a bit. Such 'escapees' are even more fun and have a definite appeal as far as I am concerned.

Alchemilla mollis LADY'S MANTLE

SPRING	SUMMER	AUTUMN	WINTER
foliage			
flowers			

H 50cm (20in), s 75cm (30in). Lady's mantle should be in flower for much of the summer and, although each **yellowy-green** star-shaped flower is fairly small (about 5mm/¼in diameter), it is held in good-sized flowerheads that are a real delight. The great thing about this plant is that its foliage is special too, each leaf being near-circular but slightly lobed with clearly serrated edges. The leaves are light green and covered in short hairs, which gives them a velvety look and feel. If you need a plant to cheer you up after it has been raining, this is the one, as the droplets of rain on lady's mantle foliage are truly stunning, looking like sparkling diamonds (they are probably the most photographed form of rain you will ever find). This plant will grow in pretty well every soil unless it is waterlogged, and indeed you are likely to find that it seeds itself really freely, putting on a wonderful display in cracks in paving, walls and so forth, but having the potential to sometimes become almost weed-like in its ability to spread.

Anchusa azurea ALKANET

SPRING	SUMMER	AUTUMN	WINTER
flowers			

H 50cm–1.5m (20in–5ft), **S** 30–60cm
(12–24in). *A. azurea* itself is really
quite a size, reaching up to 1.5m (5ft)
in height, so you need to have the
space to accommodate it. It has tall
spikes of beautifully **bright-blue**
flowers, often with a yellow or white
eye, which are produced from the end
of spring right through to early or
sometimes even mid-summer. There are
several varieties that are particularly
attractive and also somewhat smaller,
including 'Loddon Royalist', a bushy
plant reaching about 90cm (36in) in
height and with **royal-blue** flowers.
Whether you choose this or one of the
other varieties, an anchusa will bring
some really good strong blues into your
garden, and stand up straight and tall –
anchusas are very proud! A well-fed and
well-drained soil is best for them; with
the taller varieties remember that you
will need to do some staking.

Aquilegia COLUMBINE, GRANNY'S BONNET

SPRING	SUMMER	AUTUMN	WINTER
foliage			
flowers			

There are several different varieties of
columbine. Those most commonly
grown have a height of about 60cm
(24in) and a spread of about 45cm

(18in). Some of the named varieties
are particularly attractive and many can
easily be raised from seed. Their flowers
are unbelievably elaborate in shape and
when you look at them from the right
angle, you can see why they have the
common name of columbine, which is
taken from the Latin word meaning a
dove. Flowers vary in colour depending
on the variety; those most common are
red, **yellow**, **purple**, **blue** and **white**,
often with more than one colour on
each flowerhead. There are lots of
lovely varieties including the McKana
Group hybrids (particularly strong-
growing plants with very bright and
quite large flowers). 'Nora Barlow' has
extraordinary flowers in **pink**, **lime
green** and **white**. Sun or dappled
shade suits columbines best and I have
always found they perform well in all
but the heaviest of clay soils.

Digitalis FOXGLOVE

SPRING	SUMMER	AUTUMN	WINTER
foliage			
flowers			

Perhaps the most commonly grown
foxglove is *D. purpurea* (common
foxglove), **H** 1.2–1.5m (4–5ft), **S** 60cm
(24in), and its numerous garden
varieties. The flowers of the common
foxglove may be various shades of
pink or **purple**, with prominent rich-
purple spotting on the lower internal

surface of each of the tubular flowers
in the spike. The blooms are produced
for much of the summer, with timing
varying with the variety grown. *D.
purpurea* f. *albiflora* has delightful
pure-white flowers and grows to a
maximum height of about 1.5m (5ft).
If you need something even smaller,
consider the Foxy Group, which reach
a mere 75cm (30in) and have flowers
in a range of colours including **pink**,
white, **cream** and **purply-red**. To my
mind foxgloves look best in a very
informal situation, be it a cottage
garden or a natural-looking semi-
shaded part of the garden; but I have
also seen them grown to perfection in a
more regimented fashion, so try this if
that's what suits your gardening style.

There are many other species
of foxglove that are also worth
investigating, including *D. ferruginea*
(rusty foxglove) (**H** 1.2m/4ft, **S**
60cm/24in), which has beautiful pale
browny-orange or almost **buff-**
coloured flowers, again held on a
flower spike during the summer
months.

The flowers of *D. lanata* (**H** 75cm/
30in, **S** 45cm/18in) have a delicate
caramel-colour flower, intricately
marked with brown veins. Grow these
and they will grace your garden from
mid- to late summer and you can

enjoy the really downy greyish-green leaves for even longer.

D. lutea (straw foxglove), **H** 60cm (24in), **S** 45cm (18in), is a truly perennial species that flowers from the middle to the end of summer, sometimes even into early autumn, producing **pale-yellow** flower spikes. All foxgloves do well in either sun or part shade, and certainly perform better in a fairly moist but also well-drained site.

Although foxgloves are perennial, it is worth bearing in mind that many are not particularly long-lived, so they are often grown as biennials. Some, however, in particular the common foxglove and the straw foxglove, are rampant self-seeders and provided that you are careful what you remove when you do your weeding, you will find that you soon have lovely colonies of them on a regular basis.

LEFT Combine the lofty foxgloves with cottagey columbines and you can almost hear the bees buzz. If grown in sun, foxgloves remain shorter but still show above the columbines.

Echinops GLOBE THISTLE

SPRING	SUMMER	AUTUMN	WINTER
foliage			
flowers			

There are several really attractive forms of this unusual, spiky and truly architectural plant. The biggest is *E. sphaerocephalus*, with an ultimate height of up to 2m (6½ft). Each of the **whitish-grey** flowerheads are up to 6cm (2½in) in diameter. For a smaller space and a particularly rich **purply-blue**, try growing *E. ritro* 'Veitch's Blue', whose spherical pompom flowers look fantastic in any garden and attract bees in huge quantities, but are likely to fall victim to flower arrangers!

A sunny spot, preferably with a well-drained soil, will produce the best results with echinops, but I have known these plants to do well, sometimes even producing a few flowers towards the base of the plant into the middle of autumn. Even before the blooms are produced, the silvery, divided, almost thistle-like foliage mound is really attractive and may make a stunning backdrop for other brighter ingredients of the border earlier in the season.

Eryngium ERYNGO

SPRING	SUMMER	AUTUMN	WINTER
foliage			
flowers			

Most of these have a height of 60–90cm (24–36in) and a spread of 50–75cm (20–30in). They are great value during the summer months when they produce their extraordinary flowers, which are often tinged with metallic **blue**, and rather uncannily give the feeling that they are a strange hybrid of a thistle and a spacecraft. They attract enormous numbers of bees and butterflies from mid- through to late summer, when they are at their best.

E. alpinum (alpine eryngo) forms a good clump and has really glossy, almost heart-shaped basal leaves, **blueish-purple** flowerheads and feathery bracts.

E. bourgatii has a steely blue tinge, not only to the flowerheads but also to the stem, which is made to look all the more attractive by quite prominent silver veining. The form 'Oxford Blue' has flowerheads that are a particularly rich silvery-blue colour.

If you have got quite a bit of space to spare, try growing *E. giganteum*, also known as 'Miss Willmott's Ghost'. Unlike the others, this eryngo is a biennial. It has truly stunning **blue** flowerheads with a surround of prominent, silver, rather spiny bracts around each. Do beware because it will reach a height of 1.2m (4ft) with a spread of 75cm (30in) and is very much inclined to throw seed about with gay abandon, so before you know it you may have more plants than you had bargained for – and perhaps more than fit the space you have to offer.

A sunny, well-drained spot is what you need if you are to get these fascinating plants to perform to perfection. If you leave them in the border you will often find that the remains of the flowerheads, although perhaps losing some of their wild blue colours, still look very attractive, so providing some winter interest too.

ABOVE LEFT This *Eryngium bourgatii* (Sea Holly) is perfect when it comes to introducing an almost man made colour and space-age shape and again will act like a magnet for bees.
OPPOSITE Hardy herbaceous geraniums are some of the most easy-going plants and most thrive in sun or shade, reliably producing a good show of colour with little effort on your part.

Geranium GERANIUM

SPRING	SUMMER	AUTUMN	WINTER
foliage			
flowers			

The hardy herbaceous geraniums have got to be some of the most useful plants for gardeners. Many perform remarkably well in some of the much-harder-to-fill spots that are likely to crop up in pretty well any garden, including quite dense shade and dry shade. The vast majority of those geraniums readily available are completely hardy and with their fantastic flowers, mostly in shades

of **pink**, **purple**, **lilac** or **white**, they are truly stunning for much of the summer. Those that flower relatively early can often be persuaded to put on a second, if slightly less flamboyant show towards the end of the summer or into autumn if you give them a short sharp haircut straight after the first flowering. The foliage is often finely divided and sometimes attractively marked with purple blotches and so although the flowering season may be largely restricted to summer, these can be

plants for several seasons.

One of my favourites is *G. psilostemon*, **H** 1.2m (4ft), **S** 90cm–1.2m (3–4ft), which has lovely bright **magenta** flowers, each with a central black eye and prominent veining. This is a particularly good variety as it flowers throughout the summer and into autumn, and then, come the autumn, the foliage takes on some good tints too.

There are many smaller forms, including *G. clarkei* x *collinum* 'Kashmir Pink' with **bright-pink**, very delicate flowers and *G. clarkei* x *collinum* 'Kashmir Purple' with rich **purplish** flowers. *G.* 'Johnson's Blue' has **clear-blue**, very open flowers that are produced from the end of spring right through until autumn. Because this is a relatively compact plant and has a tendency to form a mound (**H** and **S** 30cm/12in) with its finely cut leaves it is great for a relatively small garden or can even be used to edge a large border.

If you are happy to put up with smaller flowers, but want some more unusual colours, take a look at the dusky cranesbills, including *G. phaeum*, which has near **black**, **purplish-red** flowers, again likely to appear from the end of spring through into autumn. The foliage of this particular plant is evergreen and it does particularly well in dry shade.

Heuchera CORAL BELLS

SPRING	SUMMER	AUTUMN	WINTER
foliage			
flowers			

H 45–60cm (18–24in), s 30cm (12in). To be honest these gorgeous plants are really grown more for their foliage than for their flowers. Each leaf is slightly lobed and has deep patterns on it marked out by the veins. The leaves are held in a really attractive mound shape and in most cases they are evergreen, or at least partially so, which means that they will provide colour, interest and form in a flowerbed throughout the year. Quite often with all heucheras there is a second, later and somewhat smaller flush of flowers towards the end of summer. But their attractiveness does not stop there, as they tend to be beautifully patterned and marbled with different colours, depending on which you choose. Probably the best known is *H. micrantha* var. *diversifolia* 'Palace Purple', which has broad **purple** to **copper**-coloured leaves which have an almost metallic sheen. Then, in early summer, spikes of tiny **off-white** flowers pop out in amongst the leaves. 'Pewter Moon' is another favourite of mine; again with **purple** leaves, but this time richly covered with a silvery-grey marbling. **Pale-pink** flowers top the display during the summer.

It is worth looking out for other heucheras. Many of those with purplish leaf colour have a really bright pinky-purple under surface to the leaf, providing yet another dimension of interest. They do well in sun or light shade and love to be given an annual mulch of leaf mould or well-rotted garden compost.

It is also worth looking out for the even more delicate plants of x *Heucherella*. These are hybrids between *Heuchera* and *Tiarella*, somewhat larger than heuchera. Their foliage is less attractive, but it turns a good bronzish-brown colour in the autumn and tends to remain on the plant, so prolonging the plant's season of interest. In addition the flowers are slightly more showy.

Lupinus LUPIN

SPRING	SUMMER	AUTUMN	WINTER
foliage			
flowers			

With really striking flower spikes held high above wonderful bright-green hand-like leaves, lupins are plants I would be loath to do without. Whether it is grown as a classic cottage garden flower or in a more formal situation, once a lupin is in flower you certainly cannot ignore it. You will find that there is a flower colour to suit pretty well every situation. These include **white**, **cream**, **yellow**, **pink**, **red**, **purple** and **orange**, either alone or in combination. The great thing about lupins is that, although their flowers are certainly well worth having during the summer, the bright-green leaves tend to be held in quite a neat clump at least until flowering is under way and they themselves make a beautiful addition to any garden border. Most of the hybrids grown in gardens provide useful colour in the early part of the summer when many other flowers have not really started to put on much of a performance. Lupins vary in size, most being about 90cm (36in) tall and having a spread of about 45cm (18in); but there are smaller varieties available too. Lupins do best in sun or partial shade in a neutral or even slightly acid soil. If like me you have a passion for these plants and garden on chalk, you may find that, using a process of elimination, you are still able to grow a few. I found that the wonderfully rich **red** 'My Castle' did well on a heavy and extremely alkaline soil, whereas many others failed completely.

Lychnis CATCHFLY

SPRING	SUMMER	AUTUMN	WINTER
foliage			
flowers			

This is a classic cottage garden flower. The most widely grown form is *L. chalcedonica*, H 90cm (36in), s 40cm (16in), which has bright **scarlet** flowers in early and mid-summer. There are also **white**, **pink** and double **red** forms that are worth looking out for.

L. coronaria (also known as Dusty Miller) is somewhat larger, **H** 60cm (24in), **S** 45cm (18in), has richer **purply-red** flowers and tends to flower throughout the summer. An added bonus is that it has striking densely hairy leaves, which appear almost silvery-grey, and the basal rosette of leaves makes a feature in its own right. Again there are plenty of named varieties available to provide you with **white** or **pink** flowers.

They all do well in either sun or part

ABOVE Lychnis, like this *Lychnis chaledonica*, can look a bit untidy, but plant with plenty of other more structured flowers nearby and you will enjoy their bright flowerheads.

ABOVE RIGHT With their tissue-paper thin petals, poppies such as this *Papaver commutatum*, look too delicate to survive outside, but do not be fooled, they are tough little souls and never fail to please.

shade. It is essential to ensure that *L. chalcedonica* and its varieties are not allowed to get too dry or their flowering and general vigour is likely to suffer.

Nicotiana alata FLOWERING TOBACCO PLANT

SPRING	SUMMER	AUTUMN	WINTER
flowers			

There are numerous varieties of this plant available, with heights from 25–90cm (10–36in) and a spread of anything up to 30–40cm (12–16in). One of the most popular is the Domino Series, which includes **salmon pink**, **white**, **red** and **lime green**, all of which are available either as a mixture or separately. The variety 'Lime Green' has **yellowish-green** flowers and certainly helps to add a touch of the extraordinary to any summer planting. Although in theory herbaceous perennials, the flowering tobaccos are invariably grown as annuals in the UK and produce a wonderful display for much of the summer and often well into autumn. The species *N. alata* has white flowers from mid-summer throughout much of autumn and these have a gorgeous perfume, but only open in the evening. Sadly the numerous named varieties rarely have a significant perfume, but at least their flowers are open throughout the day. The plants perform best in full sun, but in partial shade they still put on a fairly

good show. It is easy to be put off by the strange sticky nature of many of the flowering tobaccos, but the stickiness is entirely natural and nothing to be concerned about.

Papaver POPPY

SPRING	SUMMER	AUTUMN	WINTER
flowers			

If you want some seriously bright colour and eyecatching glamour, there is bound to be a poppy to suit you, but the poppies are a very variable group of flowers, including herbaceous and evergreen perennials and annuals. Most are not particularly sturdy plants, but are a wonderful way to fill in the odd thin planting or gap in a herbaceous border.

Take a look at any you like, but

probably those best suited to growing in a garden are *P. commutatum*, **H** and **S** 45cm (18in). The screaming **scarlet** flowers of this wonderful annual are pure delight in the middle of summer. The base of each petal is marked with a black blotch, adding a definite touch of drama to their appearance. Once the flowers are over, the plants are decorated with near-spherical and yet quite attractive seed capsules, which prolong their interest.

P. nudicaule (Iceland poppy) is quite different in appearance, having **yellow**, **orange** or **red** flowers that are much smaller and make a fantastic display from the end of spring right through to the beginning of summer, or the end of summer if grown from later sowings. The Iceland poppies are really best grown as annuals and love full sunshine. There are lots of lovely cultivars that are well worth looking out for and can all be grown from seed with ease.

P. orientale (Oriental poppy) is at its best from early to mid-spring and is the sturdiest of poppies, being an herbaceous perennial and forming really good-sized clumps. There are a number of very worthwhile cultivars including 'Mrs Perry' (strong **salmon pink** flowers with a black blotch at the base of each petal), 'Perry's White' (**pure-white** flowers with a dark centre) and 'Allegro' (**scarlet** petals with strong black blotches).

Probably the best-known and widest-grown variety is 'Ladybird', which has especially big, very **bright-red** flowers and is worth fitting in anywhere you can.

Penstemon

SPRING	SUMMER	AUTUMN	WINTER
flowers			

Penstemon is one of those plants that has become trendy in recent years, and in this case the plant deserves the popularity it has gained. The majority of the full-sized (non-alpine) penstemons are at their most colourful between the beginning of summer and early autumn, when they are decked with tubular flowers held proudly on showy spikes. The majority of them have a height of 50–80cm (20–32in) and a spread of 20–30cm (8–12in). A visit to any decent garden centre will provide you with a host of different varieties, but if you can search the beds of a specialist nursery you will find even more. Most of the flowers are in shades of **red**, **pink**, **purple** or **white** and there are lots of varieties well worth growing, including: 'Apple Blossom' (**pale pink**), 'Sour Grapes' (**purple to blue**), 'Stapleford Gem' (**pale blue to purple**) and 'Port Wine' (**rich purply-red**). The majority of penstemons are not fully hardy. In order to increase their chances of surviving from year to year, it is essential to dig in

large quantities of grit to the soil before planting, as winter wet is their biggest downfall. However, in all but warmer more protected gardens you may need either to take cuttings to ensure that you have plants for the following year, or to lift them carefully and take them into a more protected spot. Mounding loose material such as chipped bark or

ABOVE Penstemons like this *Penstemon* 'Stapleford Gem' look good in a border, but try to plant a few in a spot where you look up into the throats of the flowers so you can enjoy their fine markings as you pass.

OPPOSITE It may not be flamboyant but tiarella is stunningly pretty; its spikes of star-like flowers seem to hover like a mist over the rosettes of foliage.

dry leaves over the crowns may also help to give penstemons that little bit of much needed protection if they are to stay out in the borders over the winter.

Tiarella FOAM FLOWER

SPRING	SUMMER	AUTUMN	WINTER
foliage			
flowers			

Most tiarella plants flower from the end of spring into early summer and so can be a great way to help bring colour when things are often still a bit sparse. The great thing about them is that their mound-like foliage tends to be evergreen and often quite attractively patterned, so making them a really useful addition to the garden. The flower spikes are extremely delicate; often on dark flower stems the tiny flowers are **white** or **pale pink**, often darker pink in the bud and opening in succession, starting from the base of the flower spike, and forming tiny dizzily pretty white stars as they do so.

T. cordifolia produces **white** flower spikes, and the pale-green leaves become distinctly bronze-tinted as the colder temperatures of winter arrive.

T. wherryi is my favourite (**H** 15cm /6in, **S** 30cm/12in) with its flowers in shades of **white** and **pink**, and a fantastic rich red wine-coloured mottling on the foliage. If you fancy completely **pink** flowers, try 'Pink Foam'.

A fairly moist and humus-rich soil is essential for tiarellas, and they do particularly well in a shady spot.

OTHER PERENNIALS WITH GOOD SUMMER INTEREST

Ajuga p. 98

Arabis p. 98

Armeria p. 99

Diascia p. 100

Eremurus p. 103

Euphorbia p. 103

Paeonia p. 104

Pulmonaria p. 105

summerBULBOUSPLANTS

The great thing about bulbs is that they delight you just when you had forgotten that they were there hiding beneath the soil. Forget the concept that spring is the only month for bulbs and check out those that bloom in summer too.

Agapanthus

	SPRING	SUMMER	AUTUMN	WINTER
foliage				
flowers				

If you like the idea of tall flower spikes topped with bell- or trumpet-shaped flowers, often held in a good-sized pompom, you certainly need to consider growing agapanthus. To make life easier it is essential to choose those agapanthus that are relatively hardy, as some are so tender that they need to be moved into a protected spot each year. If you do decide to choose these more tender ones, however, remember that it is easiest to grow them in a good-sized container which you can move into a protected position for the winter.

Some of the hardiest are the Headbourne hybrids, **H** 90cm (36in), with good **blue** flowers; and 'Bressingham White', **H** 90cm (3ft), with **pure-white** flowers. *A. campanulatus* 'Isis', **H** 75cm (30in), with really rich, relatively **dark-blue** flowers, should be hardy in all but the coldest areas.

Allium ORNAMENTAL ONION

	SPRING	SUMMER	AUTUMN	WINTER
flowers				
seed heads				

The flowerheads of the alliums are often held in tight or loose globes and in some cases can be many inches across. All do well in beds and borders and can also be grown to great effect in containers.

Some of the smaller ones include *A. moly* (also known as the golden garlic), which reaches a height of 10–30cm (4–12in) and is in flower from early to mid-summer.

One of the biggest is *A. cristophii* (star of Persia), with a height of up to 1.2m (4ft) and flowerheads that seem to be unbelievably big, each reaching up to 20cm (8in) in diameter and composed of numerous tightly packed star-shaped **silvery-purple** flowers. This is one of those plants that look particularly good not only when in flower but also once the flowers have faded and the wonderfully architectural, dried flowerhead remains in the border.

A. giganteum grows even taller,

reaching nearly 2m (6½ft) in height. In most areas it is hardy, but if in doubt it is worth providing some insulation over the bulbs for the winter months. These **light-violet** flowerheads are slightly smaller, up to 12cm (5in), and produced at the beginning of summer.

There are lots more alliums worth considering, so do take a look on your local garden centre shelves or browse through the bulb catalogues to find out what else is available.

ABOVE Fiery colours are the hallmark of the montbretias as they produce their arching flower spikes, but the pale green sword-like leaves look very good too.

OPPOSITE Alliums like this *Allium giganteum* are the floral equivalent of exclamation marks in a summer border.

Crocosmia MONTBRETIA

SPRING	SUMMER	AUTUMN	WINTER
foliage			
flowers			

H 45cm–1.2m (18in–4ft). With their fiery **red**, **orange** or **yellow** trumpet-shaped blooms splayed out along the length of each arching flower spike, montbretias can create a miniature firework display all on their own. Once established they grow strongly and before you know it you will have a good-sized clump. They flower towards the end of summer and in early autumn and so help to fill that tricky late-summer gap. Even when the plant is not in flower the mass of really bright-green, delicate yet also sword-like foliage creates a good-looking mound shape, rather resembling a furious green porcupine. There is a plentiful supply of good garden varieties, including 'Lucifer' (a rich glowing **red**), 'Canary Bird' (smaller **orangey-yellow** flowers), 'Spitfire' (**bright orange-red**) and 'Severn Sunrise' (**orangey-pink**). Whichever one you choose, it is essential to provide the corms with sun (or at worst part shade) and a soil that does not dry out. One of the best-performing clumps of montbretia I have ever known was in the garden where I lived as a child: it was positioned next to a south-facing garage wall but directly under a garden tap which never quite ceased dripping.

Dahlia

SPRING	SUMMER	AUTUMN	WINTER
foliage			
flowers			

I am the first to admit that I am not really much of a woman for dahlias – but in the same breath, I also have to confess that these are useful plants, as they flower right through from mid-summer until the autumn frosts arrive. You can get spiky-flowered dahlias, singles, those which resemble pom-poms or water lilies, and some are even described as cacti and anemones – which gives you a pretty clear insight into the range available and also the extraordinary guises that the flowers take on. In only a few gardens in the UK are you likely to find that dahlias are adequately hardy to be left out in the ground and perhaps this is part of the reason they are not as widely grown as they might be. In order to ensure that they survive you need to lift them in the autumn, keep them under frost-free conditions over the winter and then plant them out again in the spring. All this aside, if you want flowers in a wide range of forms and shapes in colours varying from **red** and **pink** through **lilac**, **orange**, **yellow**, **purple** and **white**, dahlias could fit the bill. A few such as 'Bishop of Llandaff' have the added appeal of really rich-red foliage.

Dierama pulcherrimum
ANGEL'S FISHING RODS

SPRING	SUMMER	AUTUMN	WINTER
foliage			
flowers			

This is a plant with a mind of its own and some serious wacky tendencies! Masses of green, almost grass-like foliage make an attractive evergreen clump up to 1.5m (5ft) in height, and then during the summer long arching stems burst out and put on a wonderful display as **pink** funnel-shaped flowers dangle gracefully along the upper reaches of each of the 'fishing rods'. In any sunny spot with a fairly rich soil, this plant will do well, but add a little bit of air movement (even that provided by a seaside garden) and those fishing rods will dance a jig that will bring great excitement and life to your garden and a smile to your face!

Galtonia SUMMER HYACINTH

SPRING	SUMMER	AUTUMN	WINTER
foliage			
flowers			

Towards the end of summer the attractive clumps of the glossy green leaves of summer hyacinths suddenly take on a new lease of life as tall flower spikes adorned with **white** bell-shaped flowers burst forth.

G. candicans is about 90cm (36in) high with each flower spike often carrying twenty-five to thirty **white** flowers.

G. viridiflora is only about 60cm (24in) tall and although the flowers are somewhat less showy, up to thirty will be produced on each flower stem.

In most gardens, unless they are exceedingly wet or cold, it is quite safe to leave the bulbs in the ground, perhaps covering the clump with a bulky mulch to give them some protection, but in colder

ABOVE Constant movement is guaranteed with the dizzily arching flowerstems of *Dierama pulcherrimum* but its delicate prettiness belies the fact that this is a very tough plant, even performing to perfection when regularly knocked to the ground by salt-laden winds.

wetter areas it may be advisable to lift them and store them over winter before replanting them in the spring.

Iris

SPRING	SUMMER	AUTUMN	WINTER
foliage			
flowers			

I am a proud fan of irises, whatever their size and colour. Named after the Greek goddess of the rainbow, these fantastic flowers have an intricate patterning and mixture of colours that you will only truly appreciate when you have had a long, hard and very close look at them. Enjoy them at a distance and they will provide you with strong architectural shape and some wonderful colours too. The reticulata irises are in flower as early as winter (see p. 149) and through to spring or very early summer (see p. 109); get up close to them and you will be able to enjoy the delicate perfume of many of them. The majority of the irises are larger and flower during the summer months, often starting towards the end of spring and putting on a lovely show on top of 70cm–1.5m (28in–5ft) tall flower stems.

Send off for a few catalogues listing irises and feast your eyes before taking the plunge and planting them wherever you can find the space.

Lilium LILY

SPRING	SUMMER	AUTUMN	WINTER
flowers			

Many of the lilies have flowers that are not only stunningly beautiful but also have a strong and extremely seductive perfume, with heights ranging from about 30cm (12in) to 2m (6½ft). You can make them fulfil

---

OTHER BULBOUS PLANTS WITH GOOD SUMMER INTEREST

Anchusa azurea p. 116

Anemone coronaria

Cyclamen purpurascens p. 142

Several other Lilium, including *L. regale* and *L. superbum* p. 142

Schizostylis coccinea p. 143

---

plenty of different roles, whether in borders or pots and other containers. Most of them are perfectly hardy, but if in doubt it wouldn't harm to move those in containers into a more sheltered position over the winter months.

Sadly one of my favourites, *L. longiflorum* (Easter lily), is not really fully hardy. However, if you have ever grown it and enjoyed the mass of large white trumpet-shaped flowers, which are produced from a single bulb from mid- to late summer, each producing a truly gorgeous perfume, something tells me that you might at least consider growing a few in a pot and providing them with some winter protection.

Many lilies have trumpet- or star-shaped flowers. *L. martagon* (Martagon or Turk's cap lily) has a rather different flower shape with the petals curled to resemble a Turk's cap. Many widely grown lilies such as 'Star Gazer' (**pink** and **white** star-shaped fragrant flowers with rich carmine spotting, produced in later summer) can be bought from garden centres and again look good in beds or containers.

If you grow these or any other of the wide varieties of the lilies in pots, make sure that you use a John Innes No. 2 compost and a deep layer of crocks or stones at the base of the pot to ensure that drainage is good. Lilies

like to have good drainage and most should be kept well fed with a high-potash liquid feed throughout the growing period. The foliage tends to remain a fairly shiny attractive green colour for a reasonable length of time before it starts to yellow and deteriorate, so although not particularly attractive they are not the eyesore that some other bulbous plants can be once their display of flowers is over.

Zantedeschia ARUM LILY, CALLA LILY

SPRING	SUMMER	AUTUMN	WINTER
foliage			
flowers			

Arum lilies tend to do their best in a damp or even wet soil.

Try growing *Z. aethiopica* in water or right at the edge of your pond and it should put on a good display of **white** spathes, each with a yellow central stick-like spadix for many years. This particular arum is one of the hardiest and so should not need any particular care over winter unless the water in which it is growing freezes. If your garden is a colder region or you simply don't want to take any risks, grow 'Crowborough', which is even hardier.

The other species of arum lily are not hardy, and pretty as they may look are really not something I would advise you to include in your garden.

summerANNUALS&BIENNIALS

For near-instant summer colour annuals are the answer. Raised from seed they are inexpensive; many can also be purchased as 'bedding plants'. I have not suggested specific varieties - choose whatever takes your fancy.

Centaurea cyanus CORNFLOWER

SPRING	SUMMER	AUTUMN	WINTER
flowers			

H 30–90cm (12–36in), **s** 20–30cm (8–12in), depending on the variety. From the beginning of summer right through to the onset of autumn, cornflowers produce a constant supply of **blue**, **white**, **purple**, **pink** or **red** flowers. All are easy to grow from seed and there are lots available, including many dwarf varieties which are particularly suitable for smaller spaces and growing in containers. The flowers resemble multi-legged colourful spiders and look delightful in any informal planting. They thrive in poor situations, including chalky soils. Like most annuals they perform best in a sunny spot and good drainage is essential.

Convolvulus tricolor

SPRING	SUMMER	AUTUMN	WINTER
flowers

H 30–60cm (12–24in), **S** 30–40cm (12–16in). I know it is breaking all gardening protocol to say this, but I am actually rather fond of bindweed. Admittedly it can be a menace if it is really deeply entrenched in your soil and entwines itself around all your shrubs, but there is no denying that the flowers are very beautiful. So what better than growing an annual that has flowers similar in many ways to those of bindweed and yet poses no threat of becoming invasive? *C. tricolor* and its various varieties are readily grown from seed, or can be purchased as small plants in garden centres. The flowers are a vibrant rich **blue** with yellow and white centres and cover the plant profusely from mid- to late summer. This plant looks great in beds and borders and also thrives in containers. With its paint-box colours, it is bound to make a bold statement.

OPPOSITE Relaxed, informal and delightfully pretty but also incredibly inexpensive – a drift of cornflowers can be achieved for the price of a packet of seeds.

RIGHT Sunflowers need not just be bright yellow, but are now available in numerous shades of orange, brown and gold, and from giant through to child-high.

Eschscholzia californica CALIFORNIA POPPY

SPRING	SUMMER	AUTUMN	WINTER
flowers

H mostly about 30cm (12in), **S** about 20cm (8in), but variable with variety. Throughout the summer and often into early autumn *E. californica* will produce a plentiful supply of vibrant **orange** and **yellow** flowers. If you grow one of the many varieties available from seed, this colour range will be increased to include **white**, **pink** and **cream**; you will also find that there are semi-double and double varieties available and even some flowers with slightly frilled petals. This hardy annual is very easy to raise from seed and is best sown directly into its flowering position. It is a delicate-looking plant and both the

greenish-blue, finely divided foliage and the silky petalled flowers are truly elegant. A few weeks before the first flowers appear, the foliage is quite a delight. It is essential that California poppies have plenty of sun and preferably a really well-drained and low-nutrient soil – if they are too well fed or watered, flowering suffers and you are likely to see more of the foliage than you had intended.

Helianthus SUNFLOWER

SPRING	SUMMER	AUTUMN	WINTER
flowers

Make a statement and make it bold, that's what I say. Daisy-like flowers have a habit of cheering up even the most miserable. Grow these in your garden on a gigantic scale, perhaps even on huge tall stems, in the form of sunflowers and you won't be able to resist smiling – and they will also bring a smile to your neighbour's face, almost regardless of how grumpy they have a tendency to be! There are now numerous varieties of *H. annuus* (common sunflower), whose blooms come in various shades of **yellow**, **orange** and **bronze**, with heights varying from about 60cm (24in) to the sort of thing that will tower right over your fence, perhaps reaching 2.5m (8ft) or more. Although direct sowing of the seed is usually recommended, I find that if I do this far too many are lost to the local slug and snail population, so I am more inclined to grow them in cells or small pots and then plant them out once they are a few inches tall.

Sunflowers do well in a very sunny spot, but partial shade seems to do little if anything to set them back. It is always worth bearing in mind that it really is true that they will turn their flowerheads in order to follow the sun, so whatever you do make sure that you don't end up with your sunflowers pointing their cheerful faces away from your garden. Some of the shorter varieties are quite branched and sturdy and do not require staking, but most of those that produce a single large flower stem with perhaps just a few side branches need a rigid stake from quite early on. A good bamboo cane is usually sufficient.

Ipomoea MORNING GLORY

SPRING	SUMMER	AUTUMN	WINTER
foliage			
flowers			

H 2.5–3m (8–10ft), **S** 60–90cm (24–36in). These half-hardy annual climbers grow at an amazing rate once they have got going.

I. purpurea, the common morning glory, is a truly delightful plant – sow a packet of seeds and you will be rewarded with beautiful trumpet-shaped flowers in brilliant bold shades of **pink**, **red**, **purple** and **white**, sometimes even striped, set off by near heart-shaped leaves.

I. coccinea produces much smaller flowers, each measuring only about 2cm (¾in) in diameter, but these are a really good rich **scarlet** colour and distinctly fragrant. Because they form in clusters the overall impact they make is quite something to see.

If you want a really bright electric **blue**, take a look at *I. tricolor* 'Heavenly Blue'.

Much as I love morning glories and enjoy growing them up trellis, through shrubs, over obelisks or simply on any sort of support, I am the first to admit that they can occasionally be tricky, especially if you sow the seed too early on. The slightest bit of cold on the young foliage will cause the plants to become bleached and miserable and set them back quite badly, so it is better to wait a little longer before sowing seeds of this particular annual.

Lathyrus

SPRING	SUMMER	AUTUMN	WINTER
foliage			
flowers			

L. odoratus (sweet pea), **H** 1.8–3m (6–10ft), depending on the variety. There are probably hundreds of different named varieties of sweet pea, most of which have incredibly delicate, almost butterfly-like flowers, often with a rich perfume. Sweet peas produce a good show throughout the summer months and in milder years may even be found flowering, if somewhat sparsely, into autumn. There are now also some dwarf varieties available, which are particularly suitable for growing in containers or in beds and borders. Sweet peas are another flower that I find hard to resist and they can so easily be combined with other garden plantings. Grow them up a new piece of trellis to take up some of those vacant spaces before a woody climber gets established, incorporate them into runner bean or climbing French bean wigwams to add extra colour and interest, or simply grow them up a support such as an obelisk or wire frame.

There are also worthwhile forms of *L. latifolius* (perennial pea). This naturally **pink**-flowered climber reaches a height of about 3m (10ft), but forms open up other opportunities – for instance 'Red Pearl' (bright **red**) and 'Albus' (**creamy-white**).

OPPOSITE This relative newcomer on the bedding plant scene is one of my favourites, flowering reliably and often in to autumn, this mound-shaped laurentia is attractive even when not in flower and is perfect for containers.

Laurentia axillaries

SPRING	SUMMER	AUTUMN	WINTER
foliage			
flowers			

H 30–40cm (12–16in), S 25cm (10in). From the beginning of summer, right through until early autumn, this extraordinary plant produces masses of **lavender-blue** star-like flowers, often with a gentle fragrance. Although in truth a half-hardy herbaceous perennial, it is something I would really only consider using as an annual. You can be sure that it will provide welcome colour and interest in hanging baskets, tubs, windowboxes or borders. Sometimes the flowers may be a bit slow in coming, but in the meantime you can enjoy a very compact mound-shaped mass of slim dark-green leaves. If purple is not your colour, choose from the other varieties available, which include the **white** 'Shooting Stars' and 'Blue Stars', which tends, needless to say, towards a richer **blue** colour. The more sun these plants get, the better they are likely to perform.

Lavatera trimestris

SPRING	SUMMER	AUTUMN	WINTER
flowers			

H 90cm (36in), S 45cm (18in). From the middle of summer through until early autumn, this surprisingly bushy-looking annual is well decorated with 7–10cm (3–4in) diameter flowers. There are a number of different varieties readily available, including 'Pink Beauty' (pale **pink** with prominent dark veins), 'Silver Cup' (an almost silvery pale **pink** with darker veins) and 'Mont Blanc' (**white** flowers). The seeds are best sown direct where you need them to flower.

Nigella damascena LOVE-IN-A-MIST

SPRING	SUMMER	AUTUMN	WINTER
flowers			
seed heads			

H 50cm (20in), S 25cm (10in), but there are also numerous really good garden cultivars that are much smaller and more compact and so probably more suitable to the majority of gardens. For much of the summer these hardy annuals produce a plentiful supply of unbelievably delicate-looking flowers in shades of **lilac**, **blueish-purple**, **pink** and **white** – all laid out against a truly dainty backdrop of feathery, rich-green leaves. Whether you choose one of the single-coloured forms or go for a mixed variety, such as one in the Persian Jewels series, you can't fail to be delighted by the flowers and, once these have faded, extraordinary almost manmade-looking large, inflated seedheads develop and carry the interest on into early autumn.

Pelargonium TENDER GERANIUM

SPRING	SUMMER	AUTUMN	WINTER
foliage			
flowers			

H and **S** 20–45cm (8–18in). The zonal pelargoniums in particular are great if you want to bring some bright showy colours into your garden over the summer months. They are so called because the near circular and noticeably hairy leaves are clearly marked with a purplish-red banding or zoning. Available in numerous shades of **red**, **pink**, near **purple** and **white**, zonal pelargoniums are not hardy and so need to be either brought into a completely frost-free area over winter or replaced annually. Provided that they are given plenty of sun and kept adequately fed with a high potash fertilizer, they should flower profusely for much of the summer and sometimes into early autumn. Plant them in either a formal bedding display or better still in pots, tubs, hanging baskets, windowboxes and other containers, and they will look fantastic. A wide range is usually available from good garden centres and nurseries, and many can be readily grown from seed. It is also worth looking out for some of the Angel varieties of pelargonium (which have smaller flowers with two colour tones) and also the Stellar varieties (with starlike flowers). Some pelargoniums, including 'Flower of Spring', have variegation on the foliage such as the silver leaf edges seen on this variety, and obviously any leaf marking, whether reddish-purple or white or yellow, will help to ensure that the plants earn their space in your garden.

Petunia

SPRING	SUMMER	AUTUMN	WINTER
flowers			

H 15–30cm (6–12in). The majority of petunias are fairly compact, but there are some extremely useful trailing or spreading forms too. To be absolutely honest I am not sure that I like petunias, but I have to admit that they make an impact as summer bedding plants and provide an immense amount of colour with relatively little effort. You can choose single or even some double-flowered forms in a wide range of colours, including every imaginable shade of **pink**, **lilac**, **yellow**, **red** and **white**. Many petunias are not strictly a single colour because although their base colour may be just, say, pink, there is often a deeper flush towards the centre of the flower, which is largely composed of prominently marked veins.

Occasionally grown as border edging or added to flowerbeds, petunias are generally used in hanging baskets, window boxes and other summer containers, but the trailing forms can equally well be used as groundcover plants. Many can be raised from seed and a few are best propagated using cuttings or simply bought as plants from your local garden centre. There are lots to look out for, including the trailing forms such as the Surfinia Series, the Carillion Series and Million Bells Series and the 'Purple Wave' petunia. There are numerous upright forms, including the Mirage Series, 'Pink Lady' and 'Lavender Storm'.

Viola x wittrockiana PANSY

SPRING	SUMMER	AUTUMN	WINTER
flowers

H 15cm (6in), **S** 20cm (8in). Like many other people I have a long-term weakness for pansies. With their bright flowers like smiling faces they add a

cheerful, light-hearted air to any garden from the beginning of summer right through to the start of autumn, or in some cases winter (see p. 151). There is a huge range of colours, including **purple**, **yellow**, **cream**, **red** and **white**, often with several colours combined on any single flower. Even single-colour flowers often have subtle additions of colour in the form of prominent guidelines, which help to direct bees to the central area for pollination. There are lots of different varieties that are readily available either as plants or from seed, including the Joker Series. With pansies, as with other plants often grown as annuals, it is essential to

deadhead them regularly if you want to ensure a good supply of flowers. They perform best in a sunny site, but do fairly well in partial shade too. I am a great believer in using pansies in a wide range of situations, not only in containers but also as border edging or perhaps even simply as 'gap fillers' to provide long-lasting colour in relatively bare areas in a newly planted border.

OPPOSITE Petunias are one of the most widely used bedding plants in beds and containers; in subtle and not so subtle shades they are available in virtually all the colours of the rainbow.

ABOVE RIGHT Cheekily grinning pansies will turn their faces to the sun and their charm is quite irresistible.

OTHER ANNUALS AND BIENNIALS WITH GOOD SUMMER INTEREST

Callistephus chinensis p. 144

Cosmos p. 144

Gazania p. 144

Senecio cineraria 'Silver Dust' p. 151

autumnPERENNIALS

The infamous late summer and autumn gap is not as difficult to fill as you might think: there is plenty of potential. Select perennials carefully and you can have a floral and foliage display that positively glows with rich, autumn colours.

Anemone

SPRING	SUMMER	AUTUMN	WINTER
foliage			
flowers			

From the end of summer and through into the middle of autumn, the late-flowering *Anemone* x *hybrida* and *A. hupehensis* (Japanese anemones) are a wonderful addition to any herbaceous or mixed border. Provided that they have a small amount of shade, they will grow in pretty well any situation. They tolerate full sun as long as the soil is kept really moist.

A. hupehensis (**H** 75cm/30in, **S** 45cm/18in) and its varieties are available in a range of colours, including **dark pink**, **pale pink** and **white**. Whatever colour you choose, you can always enjoy the shell-like, slightly cupped petals forming a simple but extremely pleasing flower shape that has in the centre a

prominent central circle of stamens. There are several really good garden varieties, including 'Hadspen Abundance' (**near-purple** flowers) and *A. hupehensis* var. *japonica* 'Prinz Heinrich' (**dark-pink** flowers).

The varieties of *A.* x *hybrida* flower at a similar time, but the plants themselves tend to be somewhat taller, anything up to 1.5m (5ft) in height and 60cm (24in) spread. Their flowers come in an identical range of colours. Some of the best-known and extremely worthwhile varieties are 'Königin Charlotte' (semi-double, **pale-purple**, almost frilly flowers), 'Géante des Blanches' (semi-double **white** flowers), 'Honorine Joubert' (single **white** flowers) and 'Whirlwind' (noticeably twisted **white** petals forming a semi-double flower). These plants rarely take up much space in the border until they reach full size, usually some time towards the end of summer, at which stage they are also likely to be starting to flower, which means that earlier on in the season the space they do not take up can be used by other ingredients of your border.

Argyranthemum MARGUERITE

SPRING	SUMMER	AUTUMN	WINTER
foliage			
flowers			

H 30–50cm (12–20in), **S** 90cm (36in). From early summer right through until the middle of autumn, marguerites are a pure delight in any sunny spot. Whether grown in containers, trained as a standard or incorporated into a summer bedding display, their cheerful daisy-like flowers and good green feathery foliage look fantastic.

Most have **white** flowers, but there are many hybrid varieties that provide variation to the theme. One of the most popular is 'Jamaica Primrose' (**pale-yellow** flowers and dark-green foliage). It is also worth looking out for 'Vancouver' (**rich-pink** flowers with centres like anemones), 'Powder Puff' (double form with **pale-pink** flowers) and 'Edelweiss' (semi-double **white** flowers). Although it is possible to persuade marguerites to overwinter successfully in very mild areas, if you are prepared to give them a good

bulky mulch of straw or similar material for protection over the winter, it is best not to take any risks and to bring them into a cool greenhouse over the winter months.

Aster

SPRING	SUMMER	AUTUMN	WINTER
flowers			

Aster novae-angliae, *A. novi-belgii*, *A. amellus* (Michaelmas daisies) vary immensely in their heights and spreads, but you should be able to find plenty of really good-looking varieties of each that are not too tall and provide an immense amount of autumn colour without taking over the border. The plants are covered in daisy-like flowers in a range of shades of **purple**, **violet**, **pink**, **red**,

blue and **white**, often with a central golden mound of stamens. Many form a fairly woody structure but, as these are herbaceous perennials, they die back at the end of the year. These are flowers with a complete air of informality, never quite growing into a neat shape and certainly looking as if they are having a good time regardless of what the rest of

ABOVE These daisy-shaped *Argyranthemum* 'Jamaica Primrose' and A. 'Peach Cheeks' flowers are always cheering

OPPOSITE With flowers looking as if sculpted from seashells this *Anemone* x *hybrida* 'Honorine Robert' also has attractively cut foliage deserved of a place in the border and perfect for late summer and early autumn.

the world thinks! There are lots of cultivars to look out for, including *A. amellus* 'King George' (**bluish-violet** flowers and resistant to mildew), *A. amellus* 'Pink Zenith' (**bright-pink** flowers and resistant to mildew), *A. amellus* 'Veilchenkönigin' (**purply-violet** flowers and resistant to mildew), *A. novae-angliae* 'Herbstschnee' (**white** flowers on mildew-resistant, fairly woody plants, reaching a height of up to 90cm (36in), *A. novae-angliae* 'Marie Ballard' (large **lavender-blue** double flowers on 90cm/36in-tall plants) and *A. novae-angliae* 'Helen Ballard' (**reddish-purple** double flowers on 90cm/36in-tall plants).

Cimicifuga BUGBANE

SPRING	SUMMER	AUTUMN	WINTER
foliage			
flowers			

If you have a fairly damp spot and want to grow something tall (perhaps at the back of a border), the bugbanes are something you can't afford to miss. Most flower in late summer and into early autumn, and their foliage tends to change colour once autumn arrives. They produce unmissable flower spikes, each composed of numerous tiny star-shaped flowers. The most widely grown forms are probably *C. racemosa* (black snake root), which has **white** flower spikes and grows to a height of up to 2m (6½ft), and *C. simplex*, which is

slightly shorter, reaching a height of only about 1.2m (4ft) and again produces **white** flower spikes towards the end of summer and into autumn. The variety *C. simplex* var. *matsumurae* 'Elstead' has a distinct purple tinge to the stem and the buds are an attractive brown colour, later opening to produce **creamy-white** star-shaped flowers. If you grow *C. simplex* var. *matsumurae* 'White Pearl' you can enjoy not only the **white** flowers, which are so well set off against the very pale green leaves, but also later on the attractive lime-green seedheads that are formed.

Echinacea CONEFLOWER

SPRING	SUMMER	AUTUMN	WINTER
flowers			

If like me you love daisy-shaped flowers, and also have a weakness for pinks and purples and slightly unnatural-looking colours, the echinacea will be extremely hard to resist. Echinaceas flower from late summer into early autumn.

The most widely grown is *E. purpurea*, whose **purplish**, **pinky-purple** or **white** flowers are made to look all the more startling by the brownish-orange raised centre. On a plant that grows to a height of 1.5m (5ft) with a spread of 50cm

(20in), the flowers make a lot of impact. They have a tendency to be rather variable, so it is often best to go for one of the cultivars. Wonderful **white** flowers are yours for the enjoying if you grow 'White Lustre' (with an extraordinary greenish centre) or 'White Swan' (**white** with a hint of green and then a golden-coloured centre), but if you like an unusual shade of **pinky-purple**, try 'Magnus', which has a beautiful rich orange centre. Full sun is essential for these plants and they will definitely do best if kept well fed.

Helenium SNEEZEWEED

SPRING	SUMMER	AUTUMN	WINTER
flowers			

Introducing the classic autumn colours into your flowerbeds and borders is easy with the heleniums as they are available in almost every imaginable shade of **brown**, **orange**, **bronze**, **burgundy**, **gold** and **yellow**. It is best to stick to the garden hybrids as these are generally the most reliable and the ones likely to provide you with the most flamboyant display from late summer right through to mid-autumn. The majority of them have a height of about 90cm (36in) and a spread of about 30cm (12in). Particularly exciting hybrids include 'Coppelia' (**reddish-copper** and **orange**), 'Bruno' (a **reddish-mahogany**) and 'The Bishop'

(**bright-yellow** flowers from the end of summer to early autumn). A sunny spot and fertile soil is essential if you want these plants to do well. Also, in order to encourage a reasonable second flush of flowers, remove the faded flowerheads and stem tips as soon as the first flush of flowers has finished.

Hemerocallis DAY LILY

SPRING	SUMMER	AUTUMN	WINTER
flowers			

H 50–75cm (20–30in). The name day lily explains clearly enough the fact that each individual flower lasts for only one day, sometimes not even that, so you would be forgiven for wondering why I have included them here. But while each bloom is out it is a truly fantastic and very appealing sight, and so many flowers are produced that there will be a good stream of colour from each plant. The herbaceous types of day lily are the best ones to grow in gardens, as the evergreen forms tend to be somewhat tender. Most flower from the end of summer through into early autumn and most make good flowers in herbaceous or mixed borders, but if space is limited look out for the dwarf forms, which are more suited to a smaller garden and also look good in containers. There are lots of different varieties to choose from, their flowers

resembling lilies or brightly coloured stars in shades of **yellow**, **orange**, **pink**, **bronze** and **red**, often with several colours on each bloom. Some are also fragrant and, provided that you grow them in a fairly moist site in full sun, they should flower really well. To be honest day lilies sometimes have colour combinations that would make you put your hands over your eyes if they were on an article of clothing. Nevertheless, as is invariably the case in the plant world, somehow day lilies manage to get away with it.

Kniphofia RED HOT POKER, TORCH LILY

SPRING	SUMMER	AUTUMN	WINTER
flowers			

Most have a height of 60–90cm (24–36in) and a spread of 50–60cm (20–24in). One of the easiest ways to add warmth to your garden at the back end of summer and into early autumn is to plant some of the red hot pokers. As their name suggests, they come in a range of colours, including **orange**,

OPPOSITE There is a real richness to the colours of the echinacea flowers. Many, including this *E. purpurea* 'Robert Bloom', have an almost metallic sheen to them as their cheery and elegant flowers pop up towards the end of summer.

red, **golden yellow**, **pale yellow** and **cream**. The flower spikes are topped with a mass of small tubular flowers, each up to 4cm (1½in) long, and these not only look good but also seem to attract bees and other pollinating insects in great numbers. If space is short, look out for the smaller varieties such as 'Little Maid' (**ivory** and **pale yellow** and reaching a height of up to 50cm/20in). Plenty of sun is essential for these hot little numbers, as is a well-drained soil and, if conditions are rather poor, so much the better.

Monarda SWEET BERGAMOT

SPRING	SUMMER	AUTUMN	WINTER
flowers			

H 1–1.2m (3½–4ft), **s** 45cm (18in). There are several different species of monarda that are worth growing in the garden, but on the whole the garden cultivars are likely to give best results. From mid-summer through until early autumn the bergamot produces its extraordinary blooms. Each consists of narrow tubular flowers, held in whorls, and underneath the cluster of these tiny flowers are often coloured bracts helping to create the image of a much bigger individual bloom and creating a slightly unexpected and space-age shape. The flower colours include various shades of **pink**, **red**, **purple-pink** and **white**. Although these plants are herbaceous perennials, while they are not in flower they have the added benefit of being decidedly aromatic and so help introduce yet another dimension to your garden for much of the year. Bergamots prefer a moist soil and indeed you can even grow them close to the edge of a pond or bog garden. If you can provide sun or part shade, so much the better.

ABOVE If you like the unusual, then take a closer look at the monardas, all have intricate and complex flowers with real autumn impact and are distinctly aromatic. A great way to bring in lots of bees too.

Rudbeckia CONEFLOWER

SPRING	SUMMER	AUTUMN	WINTER
flowers			

Quite irresistible as far as I am concerned, these flowers (**H** 60cm–1.8m/ 24in–6ft, **s** 45–60cm/18–24in) are something you should always try to include, particularly if you are attempting to fill that rather tricky late summer to early autumn gap. The majority are herbaceous perennials, but it is also worth remembering that there are several good annual varieties that are readily available as well. Whatever you choose, you will find that the striking daisy-like flowers come in a range of shades of **orange** and **yellow**, and that each has a sharply contrasting raised cone-like centre. All the widely grown varieties are treated as herbaceous perennials, except for *R. herta*, which is often so short-lived that it tends to be grown as an annual. As well as the traditional single forms there are now plenty of semi-double and doubles to choose from, including *R.* 'Goldquelle' (**yellow** petals around green centres), 'Marmalade' (strong **gold** with a truly black centre) and 'Goldilocks' (strong **gold** with a more prominent black centre).

Sedum STONECROPS AND ICEPLANTS

SPRING	SUMMER	AUTUMN	WINTER
foliage			
flowers			

There are several stonecrops that are worth including in the garden, especially for their autumn contribution. Their greyish-green succulent foliage acts as a useful backdrop to the masses of tiny star-shaped flowers which are held together in tight flowerheads. Some of my favourites include *S. spectabile*, which is itself attractive, but other forms such as 'Iceberg' and 'Brilliant' (rich **rose pink**) are even better and *S. cauticola* 'Bertram Anderson', which has the added attraction of blueish-purple foliage and looks positively crazy, yet very attractive against the **red** flowers. The sedum known as 'Herbstfreude' or 'Autumn Joy' has pretty **pink** flowers and should be in bloom right through until the middle of autumn. The attractive foliage on the sedum is an additional reason for including it in your garden, and I also find that it tends to appear relatively late in the year, so ensuring that there is plenty of space by the plant earlier on when other plants need it. Although in theory you should remove all the faded flowerheads, I leave them on the plant when they are dry and brown, as they look attractive, and, if you are naughty enough to leave them throughout the winter, a dusting of frost makes them look even more exciting. Sedums do well in all but very heavy, wet soils and perform best if given plenty of sun.

Tropaeolum NASTURTIUM

SPRING	SUMMER	AUTUMN	WINTER
foliage			
flowers			

If like me you are a fan of nasturtiums, you won't be able to resist *T. speciosum* (flame creeper), **H** 3m (10ft), **S** 60cm (24in), a hardy herbaceous climbing version with bright **flame-red** flowers, each up to 2.5cm (1in) in diameter. From the middle of summer right through into early autumn, this nasturtium produces a mass of flowers that are a perfect way to introduce off-season colour into a shrub that has already produced its own show earlier on in the year. Later in the autumn, the faded flowers are replaced by bright-blue berries, each of which is surrounded by a purply-red scale. The fantastic flowers are reason enough to grow the flame creeper, but the plant has as well a mass of bright-green lobed leaves that are a beautiful sight in their own right – I am sure you will understand why this is another plant that you should try to include, albeit as a 'decoration' on another larger woodier plant in your garden.

Less flamboyant and also only a half-hardy herbaceous perennial is *T. tuberosum*, **H** 3m (10ft), **S** 60cm (24in).

This has more tubular **orangey-red** flowers, which decorate this climber from mid-summer right through until early or sometimes mid-autumn. A sunny site is essential for good growth of these show-stealing flowers, as is a well-drained soil. It is worth remembering that they often do well – provided that they have a good amount of sun – once they have climbed up their support plant. This means that you can plant them in a semi-shaded spot, as long as the middle and upper parts of the shrub or tree, up which they are to clamber, are in full sun. The tubers of *T. tuberosum* need to be lifted in the winter and stored in dry sawdust or a peat substitute in a cool and frost-free shed before they are replanted the following spring.

OTHER PERENNIALS WITH GOOD AUTUMN INTEREST

Ajuga p. 98

Armeria p. 99

Diascia p. 100

Echinops p. 118

Epimedium (some) p. 101

Euphorbia p. 103

Geranium – some herbaceous p. 119

Heuchera p. 120

Heucherella p. 120

Penstemon p. 122

Pulmonaria p. 105

Tiarella p. 123

autumnBULBOUSPLANTS

The rich colours of autumn foliage can be made to look all the prettier if well underplanted, and autumn-flowering bulbs can do a great job. Treat them as jewels in that golden autumnal crown.

Amaryllis belladonna

JERSEY LILY OR BELLADONNA LILY

SPRING	SUMMER	AUTUMN	WINTER
flowers			

H 60cm (24in). Although it is not fully hardy, I can't resist including the belladonna lily as it is such a breathtaking sight when in full flower between the end of summer and early autumn. Each plant bears a cluster of six large trumpet-shaped **pink** blooms carried on a deep purple flower stem. You can grow it either in a container, which is then easily moved into a protected position over the winter, or in a flower border. Provided that temperatures do not drop below about -5°C (23°F), the bulbs generally survive, but planting the bulbs close to a south- or west-facing wall will help to increase their chances of survival, as will regular mulching with light material to ensure that they are well protected over the winter. Plenty of sun is essential or else amaryllis will be very shy in flowering.

Colchicum

SPRING	SUMMER	AUTUMN	WINTER
flowers			

C. autumnale (naked ladies or meadow saffron), **H** 15cm (6in), at the beginning of autumn, produces an extraordinary miniature bunch of anything up to six **lilac**, crocus-shaped flowers; then it is not until much later in the year that the leaves appear. It is a truly fantastic plant, but do bear in mind that the leaves are quite a size, each measuring up to 30cm (12in), and so you need to allow some space for them in your border.

C. speciosum, **H** 23cm (9in), is almost like a larger version of the meadow saffron but each plant

produces up to three much more flamboyant pale to **dark-pink** flowers at some stage during the autumn period.

There are also several widely grown garden varieties, including C. 'Water Lily' (**pinkish-purple** and fully double) and 'Lilac Wonder' (**lilac** with very faint white markings).

Crocus AUTUMN-FLOWERING CROCUSES

SPRING	SUMMER	AUTUMN	WINTER
flowers			

There are several types of crocus, which, although looking very similar to their spring counterparts, actually produce their flowers during the autumn months. The following are probably among the most reliable and certainly some of the best value.

C. kotschyanus subsp. *kotschyanus* (also known as *C. zonatus*) has a

delicate pale **lilac**-coloured flower with prominent purple veins and a central ring of yellow colour inside. Flowers are produced in the middle of autumn. Plenty of sun and preferably a really dry summer preceding the autumn are essential if they are to perform well.

C. speciosus will grace your garden right through the autumn period, producing flowers in a range of colours, including **lilac**, **purple** and **white**. The great thing about this one is that not only has it a very long flowering period but it is also extremely vigorous and will reproduce itself readily both by seed and as offsets, making it particularly useful for naturalising in short grass.

C. sativus (saffron crocus) has a

darker **purple** flower with even darker veins and a really prominent bright scarlet stigma (from which culinary saffron is produced). The main flowering period is mid-autumn and plenty of sun is necessary for it to flower well.

Cyclamen

SPRING	SUMMER	AUTUMN	WINTER
foliage			
flowers			

C. hederifolium (also known as *C. neapolitanum* or the hardy autumn cyclamen), **H** 15cm (6in), **S** 20cm (8in), is pure delight with its wonderful winged typical cyclamen-shaped **pink** flowers forming for many weeks from late summer right through much of the autumn. Even when not in flower

C. hederofolium is a useful plant, as the clusters of dark greyish-green, near heart-shaped leaves are intricately marked with patterns in various shades of silver, grey or sometimes even cream. There is also a **white** form, 'Album', which for me is perhaps even more attractive, as the flowers set off the marbled leaf markings so well.

Far less obviously marked are the more rounded leaves of *C. purpurascens*, **H** and **S** 10cm (4in), but the really strongly coloured **carmine** flowers that are produced from the middle of summer right through into early autumn have the added bonus that they are quite strongly fragrant.

Provided that the soil is well drained, cyclamen perform to perfection in a variety of spots. One of my favourite places to see these little charmers growing is beneath trees or shrubs.

Leucojum autumnale AUTUMN SNOWFLAKE

SPRING	SUMMER	AUTUMN	WINTER
flowers			

H 15cm (6in), **S** 10cm (4in). Throughout early and mid-autumn these hardy bulbs produce elegant stems from which hang numerous small **white** bell-shaped flowers, which move gently in the autumn breeze. Plenty of sun and a well-drained soil are essential, whether the plant is in a flower border or rock garden.

Lilium LILY

SPRING	SUMMER	AUTUMN	WINTER
flowers			

Several of the lilies (see p. 127) concentrate their flowering in the earlier parts of autumn.

These include *L. lancifolium* (tiger lily), **H** 90cm (36in), which has up to forty individual **bright-orange**, spotted purple turk's cap flowers clustered up the flower spike.

L. regale (regal lily), although mainly flowering towards the end of summer, is often still in bloom in early autumn, producing large, funnel-shaped, very fragrant **white** flowers with up to twenty on each flower stem and a wonderful purply-pink outer petal colour.

L. superbum (swamp lily), **H** 2m (6½ft), is truly a superb and very imposing sight as each flower stem supports anything up to forty gently nodding **orange** to **red** turk's cap flowers from the end of summer right through into early autumn. As its common name implies, this plant prefers a moist soil.

Nerine bowdenii

SPRING	SUMMER	AUTUMN	WINTER
flowers			

H 45cm (18in). The rich **pink**, strangely spiky flowers always remind me of a windswept umbrella which has been turned inside out and then lost its fabric, leaving just the spokes behind. But far from being a miserable sight, in the autumn the flowers are one of the best ways to bring rich pink to your border. There is a risk that wet soils or

ABOVE Lively foliage topped with strident flower spikes ensure that schizostylis, here S. coccinea, never escape without comment.

OPPOSITE Nerine bowdenii look fantastic in a warm, sheltered spot, their pink flowers adding to the garden's palette of colour each autumn.

particularly cold conditions will kill off this gorgeous bulb, so if possible plant it near a sheltered south- or west-facing wall and ensure that the area is well mulched over the winter.

Schizostylis coccinea KAFFIR LILY

SPRING	SUMMER	AUTUMN	WINTER
foliage			
flowers			

H 60cm (24in), S 25cm (10in). From the end of summer right through into early or sometimes mid-autumn the Kaffir lily produces elegant stems of startlingly pretty flowers, which often open to become almost star-shaped. This species has rich flowers that seem to glow in their brightness, but there are several really good named varieties that are also worth considering, including 'Sunrise' (**pale pink**), 'Jennifer' (fairly large and

slightly **darker pink**) and S. coccinea S. alba (which flowers, but sadly is not as hardy as the others). Although this plant is generally regarded as adequately hardy, if you are in any doubt or if you simply want to further increase your chances of these plants surviving, make sure that the crowns are well mulched with free-draining light material over the winter months.

Sternbergia lutea

SPRING	SUMMER	AUTUMN	WINTER
flowers			

H 15cm (6in). I always find that the bright **yellow** flowers are almost out of proportion with the size of the rest of the plant. Each measures up to 5cm (2in) in length and resembles a cross between a crocus and a tulip. These plants do best in a well-drained soil with a sunny site. Again planting these close to a south- or west-facing wall will increase their chances of performing well and lasting a reasonable length of time.

OTHER BULBOUS PLANTS WITH GOOD AUTUMN INTEREST

Allium cristophii p.124

Allium giganteum p. 124

Crocosmia p. 125

Dahlia p. 125

Iris foetidissima p. 149

Iris unguicularis p. 150

autumnANNUALS&BIENNIALS

Autumn-flowering annuals and biennials make useful additions to all areas of the garden, even containers, helping to ensure that the late summer and autumn gap is not just filled but positively overflowing.

Callistephus chinensis CHINA ASTER

SPRING	SUMMER	AUTUMN	WINTER
flowers			

H 40–80cm (16–32in), **S** 30–40cm (12–16in). From the end of summer until early autumn, it is possible to bring a truly summer bedding-like display to your beds and borders by planting up with China asters. Whether you grow them as a display like this or put them into a mixed border or container, their brightly coloured flowers in all shades of **pink**, **blue**, **red**, **cream**, **lavender**, **purple**, **violet** and **white** are guaranteed to charm you. There are numerous readily available varieties, most of which have double flowers that always remind me of a delicate version of the chrysanthemum. All can be easily grown from seed. The best way to find the variety that suits you in terms of colour and size is to check the seed packets, but reliable favourites include 'Ostrich Plume' (with particularly long and slightly wavy petals) and 'Pompom Mixed' (with relatively small, almost button-like blooms) and 'Milady'. With a height of only 30cm (12in) these relatively compact plants are extremely useful.

OPPOSITE You could call them gaudy or garish but I think that China asters are gorgeous and immensely cheerful with their unstoppable and unmissably bright flowers.

Cosmos bipinnatus

SPRING	SUMMER	AUTUMN	WINTER
flowers			

H 1–1.5m (3½–5ft), **S** 60cm (24in). Check the seed catalogues to see precisely which varieties are available and you will find a lovely selection of these pretty daisy-like bushy annuals with flowers in shades of **pink**, **crimson** and occasionally **white**. They are in flower from the middle of summer through into much of autumn and tend to have a quite prominent golden-yellow centre, with the variety 'Sea Shells' having **pink**, **white** or **red** strangely fluted flowers.

Gazania rigens

SPRING	SUMMER	AUTUMN	WINTER
foliage			
flowers			

Although I am including these wonderfully bright flowers in the annuals section, in theory they are perennial and, although in many gardens they are definitely best removed and replaced each year, if you do as I have done and grow them in a container placed in a fairly protected spot, they often last for several years. Huge numbers of large, very bright **yellow**, **red**, **orange** or **brown** flowers are produced from the middle of summer through until the middle of autumn, sometimes even later. The foliage itself is also attractive,

often densely covered in felty hairs and so appearing soft yet silver, making the brightness of their flowers appear all the more splendid. Plenty of sun is essential or else you will find that the flowers simply close up and hide away until bright enough sunshine prevails and they feel inclined to grace you with their stunning good looks. Most have a height of about 30cm (12in) and a spread of about 25cm (10in).

Gazanias are easily raised by seed and any current seed catalogue will provide you with plenty of choices to brighten up your garden in the autumn. As well as sun, a well-drained soil is essential and, for best results, it is advisable to underfeed slightly – so avoid using too much garden compost, manure or high nitrogen feed anywhere near these plants.

OTHER ANNUALS AND BIENNIALS WITH GOOD AUTUMN INTEREST

Alcea rosea p. 115

Bellis perennis p. 112

Centaurea cyanus p. 128

Helianthus p. 129

Ipomoea p. 130

Laurentia p. 131

Lavatera trimestris p. 131

Nicotiana alata p. 121

Senecio cineraria 'Silverdust' p. 151

Viola x *wittrockiana* p. 133

winterFLOWERS

In the bleaker months of winter even a single flower makes a welcome sight. It never ceases to amaze me that those blooms that have the courage to appear do so with style and impact. They may not be large or showy, but each is a real jewel.

Crocus tommasinianus

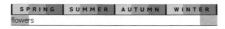

SPRING	SUMMER	AUTUMN	WINTER
flowers			

H 10cm (4in). The **lilac**-coloured flowers of this crocus are some of the earliest to appear, often popping up above ground in late winter and then continuing to put on a good display at the beginning of spring. At the first hint of sunshine, the flowers open out wide, becoming star-shaped. There are several good garden varieties, including 'Whitewell Purple' (rich **purple** flowers) and 'Ruby Giant' (rich **purple** flowers), which flowers usually slightly later than the other variety, but is also a little bit larger. 'Ruby Giant' looks particularly good if allowed to naturalise in short grass.

Cyclamen coum

SPRING	SUMMER	AUTUMN	WINTER
foliage			
flowers			

H 6cm (2½in), **S** 15cm (6in). From the middle of winter until early spring you can be sure of a good display of **pink** or **magenta** flowers from this delightful and totally hardy cyclamen. Like many other garden cyclamen, the leaves are rounded, almost kidney-shaped and quite often intricately marked with beautiful grey, silver or light-green patterns. On some the extent of the leaf markings is such that the entire leaf may appear silvered. There is also a wonderful white form, *C. coum* f. *album*, whose white flowers are marked with a magenta blotch at the base of each petal. A well-drained soil that is also fairly rich in organic matter proves best for this cyclamen and regular applications of leaf mould to the area in which they are growing should help them to thrive.

Eranthis hyemalis WINTER ACONITE

SPRING	SUMMER	AUTUMN	WINTER
flowers			

H and **S** 15cm (6in). Buttercups may be the plant that many gardeners love to hate, but I must confess that I find their shiny almost glowing flowers a pure delight, admittedly looking all the better if in a bit of grassland rather than in my flowerbeds or borders. If you too like buttercups, the winter aconites are something you should not miss. Towards the end of winter and into early spring, bright **lemon-yellow** flowers appear, each up to 2.5cm (1in) in diameter and obviously closely related to buttercups, sometimes even pushing their way up through a light dusting of snow. Each has its own ruff-like circle of divided leaves which form just below the base of each flower. Plant the tubers beneath trees or shrubs and you will have a truly heart-warming sight the following winter and for many winters to come. Well-drained soil is essential, as dryness over the summer months ensures that they flower well. The tubers are usually planted during the summer but, if you find that the plants do not seem to grow as you had hoped, buy them 'in the green' – that is, in leaf – and plant them in early spring.

Erica WINTER HEATHS AND HEATHERS

SPRING	SUMMER	AUTUMN	WINTER
foliage			
flowers			

H 15–30cm (6–12in), S anything up to 45cm (18in). There are various types of *E. carnea* that are particularly good for winter colour. The flowers put on a good display from the middle of winter until the middle of spring. The best way to find out what is available is simply to visit several good nurseries or garden centres, but look out for the following: 'Foxhollow' (**yellowish** foliage with a hint of bronze, which then turns an orangey-red as temperatures drop); 'Myretoun Ruby' (rich **reddish-crimson** flowers); 'Pink Spangles' (**pale-pink** flowers, the colour darkening as they age on a trailing plant with a spread of up to 30cm/12in), and 'Springwood White' (bright-green leaves and **white** flowers on a plant with a spread of up to 60cm/24in).

There are also several forms of *E. x darleyensis*, H 45cm (18in), S 60cm (24in). This is a winter-flowering

heather whose tiny flowers usually last from mid-winter to mid-spring, but sometimes it will start to flower towards the end of autumn. Again there are plenty to look out for, including 'Furzey' (**pinky-lilac** flowers which darken as they age), 'J. W. Porter' (**pinky-mauve** flowers and dark green foliage which during the spring becomes tipped with cream and red) and 'White Perfection' (**white** flowers with bright green foliage).

ABOVE You may not have the space for quite this quantity of winter flowering heathers, but an equally stunning effect can easily be achieved in a small flower bed or if a few are used in a winter container.

Galanthus

SPRING	SUMMER	AUTUMN	WINTER
flowers			

G. nivalis (common snowdrop),
H 8–25cm (3–10in). It is as if these
much-loved flowers have a mind of their
own, for as soon as there is the
slightest late winter breeze they tend to
dance and prance in an almost cheeky
fashion; they even manage to appear
through a light fall of snow, and stand
looking proud and yet still breathtakingly beautiful, regardless of the
weather. They are probably best
allowed to naturalise in grass, and
given time you can create a small
snowdrop drift all of your own. Dappled
shade under trees is what seems to suit
them best. If you like double flowers,
which I must confess I rarely do, there

are double forms including 'Flore Pleno'.

G. elwesii, which produces flowers
from the middle to the end of winter,
has broader leaves and two distinct
green marks on the inner petals.
Although sometimes harder to establish
than the common snowdrop, if you
have a fairly dry limey soil, this may be
the one for you.

There are other named forms
well worth looking out for, including
G. 'S. Arnott', which is particularly
vigorous and has slightly larger flowers
with a delicate, almost almond-like
perfume towards the end of winter. This
particular one seems to naturalise
especially well.

Helleborus HELLEBORE

SPRING	SUMMER	AUTUMN	WINTER
flowers			

If you grow the right combination of
hellebores you can guarantee plenty of
colour in your garden from mid-winter
right through until the end of spring.
There are several different species and
varieties that are excellent for winter
colour including *H. argutifolius*, **H**
75–90cm (30–36in), **s** 60cm (24in),
certainly something rather unusual as
the flowers are a typical hellebore
shape, being almost cup-shaped with
prominent stamens; however, instead of
being the sort of colour one would

normally associate with flowers, they
are green. The great thing is that they
are almost indestructible and so persist
on the plant from the middle of winter,
often until mid-spring, seemingly
completely unfazed by any unpleasant
weather that is thrown at them.

Another green-flowered hellebore is
H. foetidus (stinking hellebore), **H** 75cm
(30in), **s** 60cm (24in), which has
somewhat nodding **green** flowers, but
often with a particularly evil-looking
purple flush to them. These appear
towards the end of winter and last until
the beginning of spring. Although they
certainly add a bit of drama to your
border, it is worth bearing in mind that
this evergreen has a rather peculiar,
somewhat unpleasant smell and is also
known to cause skin irritations. I must
admit that I don't find the smell too
bad, but I have run into trouble and
received an unpleasant rash.

H. niger (Christmas rose), **H** 30cm
(12in), **s** 45cm (18in), has **white**
flowers that often develop a pinkish
tinge as they age and each has a
prominent cluster of golden-yellow
stamens. Despite its name this
hellebore is almost never in flower at
Christmas but is more inclined to put on
a good display in the middle of winter,
somewhat after the festive season.
There are also several named varieties of

the Christmas rose that are well worth looking out for, including 'Potter's Wheel', which has particularly large flowers each measuring up to 10cm (4in) in diameter.

H. orientalis (Lenten rose), **H** and **S** 45cm (18in), is one of my real favourites, not only because it is fantastically good-looking, but also because it is so useful when it comes to filling that

ABOVE Hellebores may not always flower at the time their common name suggests, but they can be guaranteed to look delightful, whatever the weather.

ABOVE RIGHT Make sure you plant some *Iris reticulata* at eye and nose level to enjoy all aspects of their silken flowers.

OPPOSITE Snowdrops are great naturalised in drifts, in pots or in amongst other winter favourites in a border.

difficult gap between the latter part of winter and the earliest part of spring. The flowers are up to 7cm (3in) in diameter and are very wide-ranging in colour, from **white** to **pink** or **purple**, and there are some particularly good named types: Ballard's Group (really rich **blackish-purple** flowers) and the Kochii Group (with **greeny-yellow** flowers turning a brighter yellow as they open). Many of the forms of *H. orientalis* are particularly attractive because they have intense, clearly defined, tiny freckles or spots in patterns on the petals. Those of *H. orientalis* subsp. *guttatus* are some of my favourites and are usually an attractive mixture of **wine red**, **rose** and **white**. The Ashwood Garden hybrids are also spectacular and, although many of these intensely spotted plants can be quite variable, you can be sure that even the profuse seedlings will be well worth having.

Hellebores do well in shade or part shade, but for them to thrive it is essential that the soil is kept moist at all stages, so incorporating plenty of leaf mould and well-rotted compost is a good idea and then, after flowering is over, mulching again with leaf mould or garden compost will pay dividends.

Iris

SPRING	SUMMER	AUTUMN	WINTER
flowers			
seed heads			

I. foetidissima (gladdon iris), **H** 45–50cm (18–20in). During the summer months, the gladdon iris produces rather uninspiring **greyish** flowers, brown- and pink-flushed, with anything up to eight or nine of them on each stem. These are not very exciting, but the seedpods that follow are fantastic. From autumn and right through the winter the **bright-scarlet** rounded seeds remain in the ruptured pods and provide an eyecatching bead-like decoration in any slightly moist and preferably shaded spot. There is only one disadvantage to this plant: as its Latin species name suggests, it can have a very unpleasant smell, particularly if you crush or cut into the evergreen foliage.

I. reticulata (Reticulata group) produces flowers that reach a height of about 15cm (6in), so needs to be planted in a position where it will not be masked by anything else whilst it blooms during winter and early spring. However, once the flowering is over, extraordinarily narrow, almost whip-like leaves, measuring anything up to 45cm (18in) in length, are produced; so make sure that when these develop they in turn do not mask anything else, because it is necessary to keep them in place for the bulbs to continue flowering well from year to year. *I. reticulata* has really rich, **blueish-violet** or **near-purple** flowers, with a bright-yellow crest on them. There are also plenty of other Reticulata irises which are well worth looking at, including 'Joyce' (sky **blue** with a flash of orange), 'Katharine Hodgkin' (peculiar **greeny-blue** flowers with **yellowy-green** lower petals) and 'George' (relatively large **purply** flowers with a yellow crest). I have a real weakness for these irises, partly because they are so easy to grow. Whether you cram plenty in towards the front or around the edge of a border, or

ABOVE RIGHT The blooms of all the winter-flowering irises have intricately marked and patterned flowers, seemingly too good to be left out in the cold, but that is where they need to be.

whether you incorporate them into the compost around existing long-term container plantings, you can be sure that they will put on a wonderful performance during winter and often into early spring. Get close to them and you will also find that many have a delicate perfume, which you can enjoy if you plant up a container with them close to your front door or perhaps a windowbox near a window that is opened occasionally during the cooler weather.

I. unguicularis (Algerian iris), **H** 23–25cm (9–10in), is one of those plants that never ceases to amaze me and something which, once my own garden has a bit more space to it, I am determined to include. The specimen I know that grows best is in my mother's

London garden, where from the autumn through much of winter and often into early spring it produces good quantities of truly beautiful and very delicate **mauvish-lilac** flowers with a bright yellow blaze on them. Each flower measures up to 7cm (3in) across and is somehow made all the more beautiful because of their flowering season – generally we associate other larger irises with late spring and summer, when conditions are less harsh. The evergreen foliage is quite rampant and to some extent almost oversized for the plant so, if it gets out of hand, it may be best to give it a haircut in the autumn, so that it does not mask the display of the flowers too much. A sunny spot with a really dry soil is essential if this plant is to flower well, and despite the fact that the flowers are relatively tough, you should also choose somewhere that is protected from cold wintery winds. I have fallen for the basic Algerian iris, but there are several really good forms available, including 'Walter Butt' (delicately perfumed **lavender** flowers), 'Mary Barnard' (rich **violet**) and 'Alba' (**white**).

Leucojum vernum SPRING SNOWFLAKE

SPRING	SUMMER	AUTUMN	WINTER
flowers			

H 20cm (8in). Despite its name, this wonderful little plant actually begins to flower in winter and then carries through until the beginning of spring. The cup-shaped flowers (which always remind me of overdecorated and out-of-date lampshades) are quite sturdy, and bright white with green points to each of the petals. A soil with plenty of humus seems to suit this snowflake best. It is definitely worth growing, but something that I would not plant too close to snowdrops, as somehow, although they are quite different, one detracts from the other.

Scilla mischtschenkoana

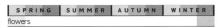

SPRING	SUMMER	AUTUMN	WINTER
flowers			

H 10cm (4in). Towards the end of winter and often at a similar time to that of the arrival of the first of the snowdrops, this plant produces delicate **pale-blue** bell-like flowers, each with a dark blue stripe. There are up to six flowers on each stem and they look particularly fantastic planted together with snowdrops. A well-drained soil in partial shade suits them best, but they also look good in containers.

Senecio cineraria 'Silver Dust'

(ALSO KNOWN AS CINERARIA MARITIMA 'SILVER DUST') AND OTHER VARIETIES

SPRING	SUMMER	AUTUMN	WINTER
foliage			

H 30–40cm (12–16in), **S** 15cm (6in). These are usually regarded as annual summer bedding plants, but in reality

this particular foliage cineraria is amazingly tough and I often plant it up in autumn containers and have invariably kept it looking good throughout the winter. The finely divided foliage is covered in a dense mat of felty hairs, which gives it a **silvery-white** appearance that looks particularly dramatic during the winter months and acts as a marvellous foil for the brighter colours of other winter-flowering plants, such as pansies, miniature iris and cyclamen. Cinerarias can, of course, be grown in beds and borders too, but generally they seem to do better in containers, and this also allows you to ensure that they are not in the most exposed position in the garden.

Viola x wittrockiana PANSY

SPRING	SUMMER	AUTUMN	WINTER
flowers			

H 15cm (6in), **S** 20cm (8in). At this time of year the winter-flowering pansies are a real bonus. They come in a wide range of bright colours, including the normal selection provided by their summer-flowering relatives (see p. 133), and yet are amazingly tough. Quite often you see them held rigid by a hard frost, looking as if they could not possibly survive, but then lo and behold, once the frost moves off, the flowers perk up again and continue

to perform. It is always worthwhile looking for the Universal Series, as I find that these particular winter-flowering pansies, which have been available for years, seem to be some of the toughest, and you can get them in pretty well any colour you like. There are, however, plenty of other winter-flowering pansies that are well worth including, either as a way of brightening up your flowerbeds or to add colour to containers. It is important to remember that although the flowering may be good from the end of autumn and right through into spring, it is the latter part of the display that is often the most flamboyant, so try to plan it so that you can leave these plants in position for as long as possible – I often find it quite difficult to dismantle winter-flowering containers because the pansies are looking so fantastic, and I simply let them continue flowering for as long as possible.

OTHER FLOWERS WITH GOOD WINTER INTEREST

Ajuga p. 98

Armeria p. 99

Bellis perennis p. 112

Some *Narcissus* p. 110

Pulmonaria p. 105

Scilla trifolia p. 110

containers

Growing flowering and foliage plants in containers can bring a whole new angle to your gardening, and in particular can play an important part in the creation of a garden for all seasons. Plant up pots, troughs, baskets, tubs, windowboxes or other containers with good-looking plants and you can use them for a multitude of purposes throughout the garden. Whether planted for a successional flowering or for a instant effect, whether displaying bulbs for seasonal colour or a shrub for a permanent focal point, containers of different kinds have a role to play in your garden throughout the year.

OPPOSITE Go for bold! A container that shouts out loud is something every garden deserves, and if the main seasonal display — here bright red tulips — is underplanted with seasonal bedding, such as pompom bellis, the container looks good for even longer.

Movable feast

One of the advantages of containers over open ground is that they are movable. A tub that looks great during, say, spring can be put in a prominent position for that season and then moved to an out-of-the-way spot once it is past its best. This gives you the opportunity to replace it with another container, perhaps one that looks especially good in another season. Believe me, pot rotation is all the rage, or at least it should be!

You can introduce potted colour into an area of the garden even at short notice. So if your terrace is looking rather dull, some steps appear miserable or a flower border is suddenly flowerless, pop in a few pots of seasonal plants to bring it back to life. In flowerbeds and borders the plants need not even be in particularly attractive pots – you can use anything. Simply ease the pots into gaps between existing plants and nestle them in so that each pot is masked by the nearby foliage.

ABOVE Use containers like ornaments: here a pot of miniature narcissus framed with ivy and variegated holly foliage draws your eye to an unexpected corner of the garden.

RIGHT Flanked by a pair of pink hydrangeas this stately and elegant tall pot of geraniums shows just how stunning a simply planted container can look.

If you plant up a selection of different containers they can be used to brighten up and add a flowery face to your house, garage or shed too. If you have a very attractive or rather flamboyant climber on the house wall, once its main season of interest is over the wall may look gloomy by comparison. Install or plant up a few windowboxes, wall baskets or hanging baskets and you bring in a whole new season of colour to that place.

A range of plants

Planting in containers also allows you to grow plants that would not thrive in your own soil, perhaps because it is too heavy or too alkaline. So those pots of colour will not only help to extend the seasons of interest, but also bring in an element of surprise when, say, a fabulously healthy rhododendron appears in full flower apparently in a flowerbed surrounded by chalk-loving plants.

Containers that provide a dramatic display, albeit for a relatively short period, may be useful, but remember too that they can be even better value if planted up to provide colour, shape or texture for more than one season. An attractive evergreen shrub in a good-sized container planted up with bulbs and seasonal bedding has something to offer throughout the year and may have a period of heightened interest; a pieris, for instance, peaks in the spring when the bright-red new foliage and the delicate creamy-white flowers are on show. Underplant the shrub with seasonal bedding plants such as winter-flowering pansies for the colder months, and then petunias, lobelia or other summer flowers, and the entire container takes on a new, year-round lease of life.

When planting a shrub into a container I always try to include some small bulbs. Create the container in the autumn and this will be particularly easy as you will have the full range of spring-flowering bulbs at your disposal. You can of course add seasonal bedding on top of bulbs. Come the spring the pot becomes a riot of colour as the bulbs appear. Although it is essential to take care not to damage too many plant roots, you can also add bulbs to an existing container.

TOP PLANTS FOR SPRING CONTAINERS

Bellis p. 112

Camellia p. 37

Chionodoxa p. 106

Crocus p. 107

Euphorbia, e.g. *E. dulcis* 'Chameleon' p. 104

Narcissus, especially dwarf forms such as 'Tête-à-tête' p. 110, 'Minnow' and 'Peeping Tom'

Pieris p. 38

Polyanthus p. 113

Primula p. 113

Tulipa, especially shorter forms such as 'Red Riding Hood'

OPPOSITE Combine a bold and architectural container with strong colours and dramatic foliage for real impact. Agave and nasturtiums, an unusual combination, score top points for style.

What kind of container?

So you know you want containers, but what do you choose? A visit to any good garden centre will reveal just how many different shapes, styles and sizes of container are now readily available, and at a reasonable price. Select a pot that itself has impact and you automatically produce a year-round effect.

Less than attractive containers or those that have started to look rather tired after a few years in the garden can often be painted or decorated to make them more interesting. Consider painting the metal bands on a half-barrel, or even painting alternating upright wooden slats on a barrel different colours. You certainly won't be able to miss one of these, at any time of year. You could even go for seasonal colour changes to reflect the changing face of the garden itself. Having said this, I should also say that I often find that too colourful or exciting a pot detracts from the plants.

If you plan to use a container over the winter months, you will need to take this into consideration when making your selection. If you want to be able to use any container for several years and throughout the seasons, choosing the right one is not as easy as you might think.

Thin, flimsy pots or tubs will not provide protection against low temperatures in the same way that a sturdier, thicker one will. Wood provides particularly good insulation (both against winter cold and extreme heat in summer), whereas thin, single-walled plastic or the trendy galvanised metal containers will not be so good in this way. I have a definite weakness for terracotta but, if you go for this, it is vital to pay that bit more and buy only frost-proof terracotta, not that sold as frost-resistant, or worse still not labelled at all. Many of the very beautifully decorated and often fascinatingly inexpensive glazed and terracotta pots that are made in exotic and certainly much warmer locations have a nasty tendency to crumble when subjected to a typical temperate-climate winter.

A larger container that will hold more compost will be less likely to freeze solid than a small one. Buying as big as you can get is especially important for containers like hanging baskets, which tend to be used in particularly exposed positions.

Wise preparation

Whichever type of container you choose, you should still be able to improve the chances of the plants' roots surviving a tough winter without too much damage. Try lining the interior walls of a favourite container with a layer or two of bubblewrap polythene. To make life easier for yourself, you will need to do this when you first plant up the container. The bubblewrap will really help to keep the roots and the compost snug. Provided that you ensure that the base is left completely clear, drainage will not be impeded. An insulating lining like this will not cause problems during the rest of the year – in fact it may help to keep the plants' roots relatively cool in the hottest weather. A good, deep (5–7cm/2–3in) mulch on the compost surface will also help to protect the plants over winter. It is essential that whatever you use is completely permeable, as moisture and air must still be allowed to get through.

Drainage may be a problem for plants in containers, especially those on display during the wetter months. So if you are planting a container for year-round interest make sure that it has adequate drainage holes, that you use a deep layer of crocks or other suitable material in the bottom of the pot, and that any container whose base is in contact with a hard surface is stood on pot feet or a few well-concealed bricks, to prevent the drainage holes from becoming blocked.

When choosing a hanging basket which you want to look good throughout the year you will also need to consider insulation. Again big is better, so go for a basket with a minimum diameter of 30cm (12in), and use a liner which is thick – coco-fibre or recycled wool should do the trick. Provided that drainage is not obstructed it may also be worthwhile using two liners, one inside the other, perhaps keeping the one you find more attractive on the outside.

If you cannot guarantee that you will always be on hand with your watering can, any container planted up and on display during the summer will benefit from some sort of irrigation system. Simple trickle systems are surprisingly inexpensive and can often make the difference between flourishing and failure, or even between devastating good looks and death. They seem even better value when you consider all the time

TOP PLANTS FOR AUTUMN CONTAINERS

Acer palmatum p. 48

Amaryllis belladonna p. 140

Arbutus unedo (strawberry tree) p. 49

Argyranthemum p. 135

Calluna vulgaris – autumn-flowering varieties, e.g. 'White Lawn'

Cosmos p. 144

Gazania p. 144

Lilium later-flowering types p. 142

Nerine bowdenii p. 143

Rudbeckia dwarf forms, e.g. 'Toto'

OPPOSITE Trailing stems are combined with white flowered pelargoniums and cosmos to create a living waterfall in this multi-tiered container. Using foliage as well as flowers helps to give containers more depth and interest for a greater part of the year.

TOP PLANTS FOR WINTER CONTAINERS

Buxus sempervirens (especially when clipped) p. 27

Erica – winter-flowering
e.g. *Erica* x *darleyensis* p. 147

Galanthus nivalis p. 148

Hedera helix – variegated forms p. 83

Ilex, especially variegated ones p. 58

Iris reticulata p. 80

Senecio cineraria (also known as Cineraria maritima) p. 151

Skimmia

Viola x *wittrockiana* – winter-flowering varieties p. 151

OPPOSITE A container for every season – every garden needs them.
For spring **TOP LEFT**, try violas and *Tulipa* 'Angelique', 'Fantasy' and 'Esther' in front of a contrasting purple trellis; for summer **TOP RIGHT**, annuals in a terracotta pot, *Lobelia erinus* and *Verbena digitalis*; for autumn **BOTTOM LEFT**, group chrysanthemum, kale, origanum, viola, aster and berberis and for winter **BOTTOM RIGHT**, a window box made from wood and bamboo, planted with variegated hedera, calluna, *Gaultheria procumbens* in berry against red brick wall.

you save and of course the cost of replacing your container plants, especially larger things like shrubs. Adding moisture-retaining granules to the compost or using a compost especially formulated for containers will also help to ensure that the plants are less likely to suffer water stress.

Planting up

Once you have prepared your containers, the fun really starts and you can choose the plants for them. Many smaller shrubs will do well in a large container such as a half-barrel, or perhaps even something smaller in the short term. Similarly most bulbs and many annual, perennial herbaceous or climbing plants can take to life in a suitably sized pot.

For a permanent or at least longer-term container, an evergreen shrub or small tree such as an acer makes a perfect and permanent centrepiece. Surround it and underplant it with smaller seasonal plants such as annuals and bulbs (see the lists in Chapter 3 for suggestions) and change these on a regular basis and it could be one of the high spots of your garden for all seasons. Many evergreens, including hollies and box, respond well to routine clipping, so whatever their potential ultimate heights may be they can still spend a good few years in a container (for topiary shapes, see p. 27). Other plants such as the patio roses and smaller forms of pieris have been bred with life in a pot in mind. If you want to add a special effect over winter, train a few small, white fairy lights through the branches of a well-shaped shrub in a container and plug them into a suitable electricity supply with a circuit breaker.

Sometimes great impact can be achieved with a simple planting consisting of just one variety of just one type of plant – a pot crammed full of lilies or narcissus, or summer annuals such as petunias or nicotiana, or winter-flowering pansies, for instance. Although these do not produce a year-long effect, they are so striking whilst at their best that they are well worth including, and you can grow a selection of different flowers or foliage plants in this way to provide a succession of containers full of interest throughout the year.

structures AND features

Plants may be the key ingredient to any garden for all seasons, but if you want to ensure that your plot has as much as possible to offer, you need to look at non-living elements too – structures such as arches and pergolas, and ornamental features, which all play a part in making a garden a pleasing place to be in, whatever the season. If like me, you garden on a site that has its fair share of extremes of weather, it is also very important to look at ways in which you can try to have a garden usable throughout the year.

OPPOSITE An arbour planted with *Clematis montana* 'Freda' and a delightfully scented honesuckle provides a perfect place for me to sit and relax and soak up the view.

Sitting places

You may have a fantastic selection of plants that will put on a good display throughout the year and put up with every type of weather but, if there is nowhere for you or your friends and family to sit, your garden will become purely something to look at, not somewhere you can enjoy being during any of the twelve months of the year. I love to have somewhere I can sit out in a garden – and even a postage stamp-sized plot is useful and attractive with somewhere to perch and relax, enjoy the view or perhaps even have a meal.

In cooler or windier weather a sheltered spot is essential. Choosing somewhere sheltered from prevailing winds to position a seat or arbour, or perhaps even a table and chairs, should help to extend the season over which you can happily sit outside; it may even make the garden usable during the winter, albeit for shorter periods of time. Anywhere close to a south- or west-facing wall tends to work well, and if there is a natural windbreak of trees or large shrubs near by, so much the better. If there is nothing suitable there already, try to arrange your planting to take this into account – a fence or trellis covered with attractive climbers will do a great deal to filter wind and provide a perfect spot to sit. Trees, shrubs or even bamboos will help to provide shelter too. The view you enjoy when sitting is important too, so take any old chair out into the garden and try sitting on it in various different locations until you find a spot that fits the bill.

I take every opportunity to eat meals outside, but the climate in this country is such that the opportunities are very limited. One way around this is to use heating appliances. There are now very effective (and not too ugly) free-standing heaters, which have been designed specifically for use outside and, although running them too often would no doubt prove very expensive, as a means to prolong a warm evening or to allow you to eat outside at either end of the main period of warm weather, they are definitely worth considering. Similarly the pottery barbecues, which resemble a cross between a large clay vase and a chimney pot, not only provide a useful place for outdoor cooking but also give off a great deal of heat.

OPPOSITE A place to sit or lie, to read, snooze or eat is something most of us want in a garden, but all-weather access is essential if it is to be used to its potential and adjacent planting must not be too invasive.

ABOVE I never leave a space in paving or any other hard surface unfilled. Many alpines thrive in relatively small gaps, provided they have some fresh soil, good drainage beneath and an adequate supply of moisture.

OPPOSITE Yorkstone steps and stepping stones look at ease with a dry stone wall and a nearby circle edged with brick. The whole area is brought to life further by crevice plantings, and a family of Swaziland guinea fowl.

Conversely, even if you are a sun-worshipper, the middle of a hot day in the height of summer can become uncomfortable, and may put you off enjoying lunch on your sunny terrace or patio. So it is essential that you also consider the need to provide shelter from excessive heat as well as from the cold. Large parasols are perfect for use over an outdoor eating space and can of course be folded down if not needed. Planting up a living arbour, perhaps using willow, can also produce a shelter from the sun – and it will also be gorgeous to look at. Erecting a wooden or metal arbour that includes a seat with a solid roof will mean that the sheltered spot can be used throughout the year, providing shelter not only from excessive heat but also from drizzling rain. An arbour that relies purely on climbing plants for its roof may not be so useful in this respect, but it will still provide a good focal point and, if well planted, can make a perfect, pretty and well-ventilated place to sit from late spring through until the autumn. Plant it up with perfumed climbers such as honeysuckle, roses or even sweet peas and it will prove even more enticing. It is also worth considering what you plant in the vicinity of the seating area – aromatic or perfumed plants such as lavenders and thymes not only look good and thrive in warm sunny spots but also produce a delicious fragrance.

Suitable surfaces

When planning your garden for all seasons you will need to consider how you are going to gain access to various parts of the garden when the weather is less than perfect; some sort of all-weather access is essential if you are to be able to make full use of the garden. A lawn may be what you are attracted to, but it often becomes unsuitable in the wetter or more wintery months: tramping across it when it is wet or frosted will not only prove slippery and muddy, but will also damage the lawn. A tougher surface is in order for at least some areas or paths in your garden.

I am a great fan of stone paving and brick pavers, but beware: some of these surfaces are also liable to become very slippery in winter – Yorkstone paving in particular can prove lethal unless regularly dusted with sand. Other popular harder and non-living surfaces such as paving slabs and wooden decking can be useful too but, even if you choose rough-surfaced paving slabs, you may still find that both these surfaces are unusable in winter when they are wetted repeatedly.

A permeable path or terrace, which will allow rain to drain straight through it, is another option: gravel, shingle, slate chippings or similar materials should allow you to get where you want without damaging the garden or yourself in the process.

In some instances it may be possible to reduce the risk of excessive slipperiness. Creating a slight camber means that less water will accumulate on the surfaces of hardstanding, so minimising the problems with algae – a common cause of a slippery surface. If you are using decking squares to create a pathway or deck, lay these so that the parallel lines of timber on each square run at right angles to the lines on the neighbouring squares, so as to reduce the risk of a serious slip. You could also consider using special non-slip deck paints. In extreme cases, such as a very damp area of the garden where the pathway is not easily visible, stapling chicken mesh to the surface of wooden decking should help to provide a good non-slip surface.

If you are looking to create a lawn close to an arbour or other seating area, why not consider planting up with camomile 'Treneague' or one of the numerous forms of creeping thyme? Admittedly this will not make a good winter surface, but provided that the area is traversed by something tougher (perhaps a couple of stepping stones), winter access need not be a problem, and in the summer months these deliciously aromatic plants will be worth their weight in gold. In my garden I have interspersed a sizable paved and gravelled area with small planting holes in which I have planted a few favourite crevice-loving alpines and several thymes. It looks good all year round and is fantastic on a hot summer's day.

Arches, pergolas and garden furniture

An arch or pergola may be something you consider to be simply a sturdy plant support, an excellent way of growing a climbing or rambling plant. But if you choose one that, whether metal, brick or timber, looks attractive even when unclothed, you will find that even in the early days, or if planted up with a fairly short-season plant, it will still bring height and style to the garden for twelve months of the year. If you have the ability to design and erect a suitable structure yourself, you can obviously have precisely what you desire, but if carpentry is not your strongest point, there is a plentiful supply of good-looking pergolas and arches in a wide range of styles, and at various prices, available in kit form. Whatever you choose, try to consider how it will look when erected in the garden and make sure that it will be sturdy enough to carry the weight of the plants you plan to use. The ultimate size and possible weight of the climber is important as some, such as wisteria and laburnum, have the potential to be extremely heavy and so need a very strong structure, whilst others such as most clematis are much lighter.

If you decide to use a kit, make sure you look closely at what is available before you take the plunge, as the quality varies quite considerably. Most timber products of this type are made from softwood and it is essential to select one which has been tannalised or pressure-treated with wood preservative. All screws or other fittings should be steel, brass or galvanised to minimise rusting.

The choice of plants is obviously a very personal decision, but if you want the structure to look as attractive as possible throughout the year it makes sense to plant more than one type of plant and to look for a combination that will provide interest for much of the year. Although most climbers are fairly vigorous and require a reasonable amount of space for their roots, it is usually possible to grow at least one plant up each side of even quite a small arch. By adding annual climbers (see pp. 66–68) you can bring near-instant colour even to an arch or pergola that has only just been planted up and, if you continue to use these short-lived but pretty annuals each year, you can also provide extra colour, either to extend the main season of interest, or to combine with it.

Any wooden structure in the garden, whether an arch, arbour, pergola, trellis, decking or garden furniture, can be painted with a

coloured wood preservative or stain, which will then bring year-round colour to the garden and at the same time provide an attractive backdrop for the plants themselves.

The range of garden furniture seems to be ever-expanding but whether you opt for something low-budget or more expensive – wood, plastic, resin, metal, stone or concrete – positioning your furniture so that it can be used to best effect is essential.

Although very inexpensive furniture may catch your eye, it may not actually be such good value if it has a much shorter lifespan than a product that costs a bit more. Hinges, fixtures and fittings are often a

ABOVE Here the fairly formal, straight-edged rectangular beds, backed by geometric wooden trellis, seem totally at home with the square stone setts – and year-round access to all the beds and the house is guaranteed to be trouble-free.

give-away: check to see if they are made from rust-proof materials and that they look really strong, as well as being very firmly attached to the main body of the furniture.

Like most timber garden structures, the less expensive types of timber furniture are usually constructed from softwoods, whilst hardwoods generally fetch a higher price. I always try to ensure that any hardwood products I buy are taken from a sustainable forest too. There is no doubt that hardwood furniture lasts longer, and it also needs somewhat less maintenance than softwood.

Wrought iron, powder-coated aluminium, steel, resin and plastic are all also widely used. To be honest, each has its own set of advantages and disadvantages. Wrought iron has a traditional look but is very heavy; aluminium is much lighter in weight; steel may look very smart but it is relatively difficult to find it in a range of styles; resin and plastic are often available in many colours, tend to be fairly lightweight and less expensive, but for some gardens they can look too obtrusive. Again the best choice is largely down to personal preference, but getting it right is important, so do not rush into a decision until you have looked at a lot of different types.

Whichever furniture you opt for, make sure that you know how to look after it, how to maintain it, whether it needs to be stored under protection during the winter, how to clean it and, if it is made of wood, whether it needs to be treated and, if so, how frequently and with what. If you are uncertain, check the manufacturer's instructions or ask the supplier before you buy.

Look after your furniture properly and it will not only last longer but also look better throughout the year. I find that a good-looking set of chairs and a table, or a bench, can add to the way a garden looks, even in mid-winter.

Statues, urns, water features and other ornaments

Increasing the off-season interest in a garden can also be achieved by using other non-living features such as urns, statues, mirrors and water features. Again it is well worth spending plenty of time deciding what

you are going to choose and where to put it, so that it has the greatest effect and for as much of the year as possible.

Urns and statues need not be terribly expensive and yet can bring substance and glamour to a garden in rain, sun or snow. Go for large or small, for traditional or modern, but make sure that it – or even they – fit in with the style of your garden and are positioned so that they can be enjoyed as much as possible, or so that they come as unexpected surprise when, say, you go around a corner or enter another part of the garden.

Another surprise element in a garden could be a mirror. Skilfully erected and positioned, a mirror can be used to reflect beautiful views, so doubling their value, and to provide that extra bit of light on a gloomy day; and of course they can give you an almighty surprise when you come around a corner and see yourself.

A water feature, such as a spitting gargoyle, a millstone or mound of

ABOVE I have not got enough time to keep real pigs but this pair are completely trouble-free as they rootle through the grass under the shade of a large tree in my own garden.

OPPOSITE Arches and pergolas help to bring height to a garden of any size and look delightful when draped in a selection of plants chosen to give a good display for several seasons.

pebbles with water cascading over it, or a tiny fountain, can usually be squeezed in to even a small garden. While these are all more likely to be admired frequently in the hotter summer months, there is nothing to stop them from being used during all but the coldest of weather. They bring a refreshing element to a garden and provide that relaxing sound of water on the move that I, for one, find delightful and immensely calming. Provided that the water is kept moving during the summer months there should not be many problems with the water turning green because of the build-up of algae but, whatever type of water feature you install, it is easiest to maintain if you avoid placing it too close to a deciduous tree or large shrub: regular removal of fallen leaves in autumn can be a tedious job, and if you do not keep up with the task, the leaves may clog up the feature.

Most water features are powered by an electric pump. Unless you are unusually capable when it comes to electrical installation, I would always advise leaving this to a properly qualified and experience electrician. Water and electricity can be a lethal combination and there is no room for errors! You will also need to make it clear to whoever installs it that you intend to use the water feature for much or all of the year and that you want the installation to be completely safe.

ABOVE The sound of water on the move adds yet another dimension to a garden. Introducing this water-feature surrounded by informal foliage-based planting creates a really relaxing spot.

OPPOSITE In a more formal part of my garden this lovely lead water-feature looks at home, and is fondly known as the 'spitting gremlin'; the great thing is it was easy to install and came complete with its own pump.

keepingUPappearances

If you want your garden always to be good-looking and interesting, and an enjoyable place to be in, apart from planning and choosing plants and features with care, you will need to spend some time and effort looking after the plants. By giving a plant a good start, paying attention to its needs and then properly maintaining it, you will not only make it look better but also be likely to extend the periods over which it performs to its peak – and prolonging, say, the flowering of an herbaceous perennial increases the contribution it makes to your garden for all seasons.

OPPOSITE A beautiful border like this will reward you every time you look at it from close or afar, but to keep it at its best for as much of the year as possible a regular programme of feeding, watering, deadheading and staking is needed.

Getting the soil into shape

Very few of us have the perfect 'light crumbly loam' often referred to in gardening books. All too often I have found myself faced with either an extremely light substance that strongly resembles pure sand or, as in my current garden, a very heavy clay. You can of course grow plants on either of these soils, but to increase the range of plants that you can grow - and hence the amount of plants that contribute to year-round interest - and the chances of their thriving, you will need to do something to improve the soil's texture.

Digging in large quantities of horticultural grit, well-rotted manure, garden compost or leaf mould should help to provide aeration in a heavy soil, and may also add to its fertility. On a heavy soil it is always best to 'dig' with a fork rather than a spade, as a spade may effectively seal off the edges of a trench, making the situation worse. Bulky organic matter will also reduce the tendency of the soil to crack during hot, dry summer weather.

A soil that is excessively light or sandy drains very rapidly and tends to have a low organic matter and also relatively low fertility. Grit will do nothing to improve this type of soil, but bulky organic materials such as compost, manure or leaf mould have the potential to transform it. Digging these in may seem an interminable task, as a very sandy soil appears to have an unending appetite for them, but just keep on and on adding. You can also help to ameliorate the adverse effects of either a very heavy or very sandy soil when planting. Planting on a slight mound in heavy soil will help to reduce the risk of a plant's roots becoming excessively wet, as drainage will be slightly better in an elevated section; planting in a slight depression in a sandy soil will help to reduce the risk of a plant suffering from drought. When planting trees, climbers or shrubs on a dry soil you could also consider inserting a short length of pipe that runs from the soil surface down into the root-ball. This will allow you to water directly where the plant needs it.

Merits of mulch

Mulching is best carried out in spring, but it can be done at any time of the year, provided that the soil is moist. The simple application of a 5-7.5cm

(2-3in) deep layer of mulch on to the soil around the root of the plant will have several benefits. It will help to keep the soil somewhat cooler in very hot weather; it will help to cut moisture loss from the soil surface, so reducing the risk of the plant becoming too dry; and it will go some way to limiting weed competition around the base of the plant. Keeping the soil at relatively constant temperatures and fairly moist during summer, and minimising the competition from weeds, will help to persuade your plants to grow well and perform to perfection for as long a period as possible.

A mulch is only likely to do harm to the plant and reduce its performance if it is applied right up to the stems or trunk - the above-ground parts of the plant are not adapted to the relatively damp conditions the mulch produces and may deteriorate. It is therefore always wise to leave a small area in the immediate vicinity of the stems completely clear of mulch. For a mulch to be most effective you should remove weeds from the area and ensure that the soil is thoroughly moist before applying it.

Watering

Regular watering is essential for all plants. If a plant is dry at the roots, one of the first things to suffer is its ability to produce viable flower buds and then to sustain flowering. In extreme cases the whole plant's appearance may be spoiled by lack of water, perhaps with its foliage wilting or dropping, and its usefulness in the garden will be a lot more limited than it would be otherwise. For most plants it is the time shortly after planting that is most important when it comes to watering - this time is when the plant is getting established, and may mean anything from a few weeks for bedding plants to the first eighteen months to two years for a tree or shrub.

Feeding

There is currently a good deal of debate about the merits of feeding. I would say that it is difficult to generalise, as the amount of food a plant needs will depend on many factors, including the time of year, the soil type, the plant's size, the amount of competition it is subjected to and, of course, which plants you are dealing with. This may mean an autumn and/or spring application of sulphate of potash on a shrub, or regular applications

ABOVE Watering is essential to maintain the health and vitality of your plants. I use a watering can to direct water to the base of the plants.

OPPOSITE Garden centres are packed with a mind-blowing selection of tools, but avoid the gadgets and gizmos and choose good-quality, basic tools. Auctions and junk shops often yield some of my real favourites.

of a liquid high-potash fertiliser to summer bedding plants, to encourage a good and prolonged show of flowers. On plants like bedding, which are invariably grown for their flowers and a relatively short-term but high-impact display, feeding in this way will completely alter the plant's performance, especially when it is grown in a container. Many other types of fertiliser are available, including controlled-release granules, which can be incorporated into the compost or into the additional compost when a larger plant is potted on. Foliar feeds are useful too, as, being applied through the leaves, they are absorbed relatively rapidly. Granular and other general liquid feeds can be used on most things, but these are generally slow in action.

Supplying support

Many herbaceous plants and some annuals benefit from some subtle support. Supports have a range of purposes and benefits: to help to

ensure that the plant's shape is appealing, that the flowers are kept away from the ground and many potential pests such as slugs, and that the flower spike does not get broken or flop to the ground. Support may take the form of a few canes and some twine, a single more sturdy cane perhaps for the flower spike of a hollyhock, some carefully positioned twiggy sticks or a proprietary plant support. To a good extent it may be best to make the decision whether to stake or not to stake once you have seen the plant in full growth. Generally speaking the taller and thinnner-stemmed plants are more likely to need a bit of support, as are those with particularly tall flower spikes. To get the best possible results from staking you should put supports in position early in the year - this will reduce the likelihood of any damage being done to the plant by, for instance, wind or heavy rain and increase the chances of the support (often not the most attractive item) being completely hidden by foliage later in the year.

Encouraging more and longer flowering

For some plants, climbers and shrubs in particular, the correct pruning regime is also essential if they are to look their best. All too often an over-enthusiastic, secateur-wielding gardener succeeds in pruning out the plant's potential to flower; on the other hand some plants never put on the desired display because they have not been pruned. Pruning is not necessarily very complicated, but each plant has its own requirements, and indeed some prefer never to be pruned at all, so you should always check before you bring out your secateurs or saw.

Deadheading or removing flowers as they fade is a sure way to increase the quantity of flowers and the length of time for which they are produced. It prevents the plant from setting seed, which not only uses up a lot of energy but also reduces the flowering period because the plant has, to its mind, achieved its aim of producing seed and so the flowering starts to slow down and stop. Annuals seem to benefit from deadheading most noticeably, but I have often seen significant increases in performance with many other plants too, including shrubs, and certainly many herbaceous perennials.

Some herbaceous perennials benefit from being cut back or given

ABOVE Dead-heading or removing faded blooms from tulips may not be the norm in a border, but as soon as they are past their best I snip them off cleanly to make room for the next crop – creamy coloured tulips. **OPPOSITE** Annuals are a great way to increase the time over which a container or border looks good and with this type of flower regular deadheading is essential if the plants are to continue producing buds for as long as possible.

quite a severe haircut once their main period of flowering is over. Geraniums are the classic example of this: many can be persuaded to put on a very respectable second flush of flowers at the end of summer or in early autumn if they are clipped in this way. Some other plants, such as aubrieta and most heathers, simply look more attractive if cut back - even if flowering is not boosted, cutting back creates a good-looking, compact plant that can have great appeal, even when not in bloom.

Keeping pests and diseases to a minimum

It may well be impossible to have a garden that is completely free from pests and diseases, but there is no doubt that pretty well every one of us strives to keep these uninvited bugs, beasties and blights to a minimum. A healthy plant that is not diseased or playing host to a pest will invariably look better and is more likely to flower profusely or keep its beautifully coloured foliage in place for as long as possible.

Try to check your plants as regularly and frequently as you can, as any problem spotted early on is invariably easier to control and less likely to do too much damage to the plant in the long term. Acting promptly is equally important. Once you have worked out what is wrong, it is essential to select an appropriate treatment - without chemicals, if you are gardening organically - and then get to work as soon as possible. Whether you pick off aphids, for instance, by hand, spray them with a soap-based insecticide or grab the nearest suitable pot of pesticide, early action will prevent their numbers from getting out of hand and ensure that little if any leaf distortion or discoloration occurs.

If you notice a plant looking peculiar, you may need to check it all over, not just on the obviously affected parts, as quite often the real cause of a problem lies elsewhere. Trees suffering from an attack of honey fungus are the classic example of this. If the leaves or flowers die off, examination of these will give no direct indication of what is responsible. In fact, the fungus attacks the roots, causing them to fail to function properly - hence the symptoms of wilting and die back. It is only when you inspect the roots that you will see the culprit.

Weather

The weather conditions likely to hit your garden on a regular basis are something you will need to consider when first choosing which plants to grow. These conditions will vary from garden to garden, but for most of us in the temperate climate there are bound to be some sizeable variations in temperature and wind levels, and these can have a huge impact on a plant's appearance and the amount of colour, texture, shape or other interest it contributes to your garden at any time of year.

Protection against cold is a common need. Frosts or simply a sudden, albeit not particularly big, change in temperature can do a lot of damage - even to a perfectly hardy plant. In many cases protecting the plant with a layer or two of horticultural fleece will do the trick. For frost-prone blooms, such as those on camellias, you can drape the fleece over the plant when frosts are forecast, anchor it firmly and then remove it the following day. When the entire plant is at risk, a covering of fleece may be adequate, but you may need to create an even greater level of protection from cold. This can be done by forming a 'cage' out of chicken wire, popping it over the plant and then filling it with dry straw, bracken or similar material. Such a cage can also be used on plants that need constant protection over a longer period of time. Provided that you remove it before the plant becomes too mollycoddled or produces excessively soft new growth, it should ensure that the plant looks good throughout the cooler season.

With plants in containers it is usually the roots that are most at risk from low winter temperatures, as the rootball may be prone to freezing. This may cause the plant to perform poorly, or perhaps even kill it. In very cold conditions, if possible plunge the container into the open ground, or move it in to a much more sheltered position if you are sure that will suffice. If you cannot do either of these, insulating the container with bubblewrap polythene or some old hessian will help. Admittedly it may not look too attractive but, unless the plant is peaking during the winter months, this does not matter too much and it is worth it so as not to lose the plant.

ABOVE Extra winter protection is easily supplied using horticultural fleece, or here bubble wrap polythene – perfect for slightly tender shrubs or those which are newly planted. It is essential that air is still able to move around the plant, or else moulds may thrive.

choosingTHErightPLANTS

So you have fallen in love with a fabulous array of plants and you are sure that between them they can go a long way towards producing your personal Garden for All Seasons.

Great, but you will also need to give consideration to how many of each you will need, how to combine those individuals in to a cohesive and exciting tapestry and which are the most important attributes of each plant.

How will they grow?

Start by checking the characteristics, dimensions and main attributes of the plants you like. How tall will they grow, and how rapidly. How broad will be their spread; and of course what are their main seasons of interest? It is no earthly use completely obscuring a choice plant because you have grown something much taller or broader too close by. Think, too, about whether one plant is likely to upstage another, if so it is perhaps worth trying to keep them relatively far apart, thus giving each a chance to show you what it is really worth without being compromised.

Shape and feature

The overall shape and the texture of each plant is important. You may want to grow several plants with similar shapes in close proximity. You may want something more dramatic allowing, say, a shrub or larger perennial with a bolder, and sharply defined outline, to stand really proud among companions which have a calmer, perhaps more rounded shape and so provide contrast, creating a foil for their more ostentatious neighbour.

The colour of flowers...

Flower colour – and indeed in some cases foliage colour – is an important consideration. I have no intention of telling you what you must plant with what, because that would be purely my choice, and not necessarily what you personally would want to see when you look out of the window. But, having said that there are a few ground rules, which I do feel are worth bearing in mind, whether you want bright, contrast, subtle or downright subdued. Think of leaves – leaf green is a wonderful linking point in a garden, often helping to separate colours which jar when too close, and to prevent what I call the, 'Help, where are my sunglasses?' syndrome! Similarly creamy, white or silvery foliage or flowers have much the same effect. Many gardeners use a 'colour wheel' to help them to decide which shades are most likely to work well together. If you want a border (or indeed a whole garden) which shrieks loudly and is packed with full-colour drama, then this is not

a technique for you; but if you are after a striking effect but with a degree of control and harmony, a colour wheel is useful as it advocates planting, say, purples close to pinks, but avoiding purples and reds, or orange next to red but at a distance from blue.

...and foliage

The textures and colours of leaves are important too, as in few cases is a plant producing a good show of flowers for more than just a fraction of the year. Evergreen shrubs and groundcover plants, and herbaceous perennials such as *heucheras*, *hostas* and *Alchemilla mollis*, ferns, *Eryngium* are exciting even when not in flower, and provide a definite texture too.

Remember the basics

Before you get carried away with plans for creating a fantastic combination of all those plants you have fallen for, it is essential that you pause, remember the gardening basics, and then ensure that you put them in to practice. Remember to check what each of the living ingredients requires in terms of growing conditions – a well-drained soil, a damp or boggy site, a heavy soil, and does that soil need to be alkaline, acidic or neutral in pH? Does it need full sunshine, partial shade, or is it one of the relatively few plants which tolerate full shade? If the plant is not put in to the right spot it is unlikely to perform to its full potential, and may even fail miserably. Put it where it should be and the results will be dramatically different. Put these suggestions, and your favourite, suitable plants together – always bearing that year-long effect in mind – and enjoy your personalised Garden for All Seasons for many years to come.

ABOVE Alchemilla mollis ; This is a flower which seeds itself readily, cramming its new plants into cracks and crevices and putting on a fabulous display of delicate green, slightly fury foliage, later topped with clouds of tiny bright-yellow flowers.

year PLANNER

If you want a garden

for all seasons, you

will need to maintain

a level of input and

get jobs done at the

appropriate time – and

what better way to

start than a checklist

of what to do when?

early spring

Maintenance

• Provided that the soil is not too wet, dig in manure or other organic matter on new flower beds.

• Apply a general fertiliser around the base of clumps of spring-flowering bulbs.

• Prepare the soil for direct sowing of annual flowers – fork it over and incorporate some general fertiliser.

• Lift, divide and replant congested clumps of snowdrops and winter aconites as soon as they have finished flowering.

• Lift and divide large, established or congested clumps of herbaceous perennials, discarding the less vigorous sections and replanting the best bits.

• Take cuttings of pelargoniums and fuchsias and they should make good-quality plants for flowering later this year.

• Start getting plant supports in place in flower borders.

• Remove faded flowers from spring-flowering plants including bulbs to help to conserve their energy.

• Prune bush and climbing roses, using sharp secateurs.

• Remove old, dead or diseased foliage from herbaceous perennials left on over winter.

Sowing and planting

• Start direct sowing of hardy annual flowers, such as China aster, cornflower, clarkia, tobacco plant, poppies, night-scented stock, phlox and *Convolvulus tricolor*. As soon as seedlings are large enough to handle, prick them out into slightly larger pots of fresh compost.

• Sow sunflower seeds to create a seasonal screen with a difference.

• Last chance to sow sweet peas in pots for brightening up trellis or an obelisk or other support.

• Most garden centres now have a good selection of small herbaceous perennials in stock at a very reasonable price. Choose yours early whilst the range and quality is still good.

• Plant gladioli and lily bulbs.

• Plant dahlia tubers.

• Last chance to plant bare-root trees, shrubs or hedging. Try to do this before the foliage breaks.

• Continue to plant pot-grown trees, shrubs and climbers.

• Sow seeds of perennials such as arabis, snapdragon and columbine in a cold greenhouse or on a window sill.

• Plant newly purchased trees, shrubs and herbaceous perennials as soon as you can.

Planning ahead

• If you want to obtain less widely available summer- or autumn-flowering bulbs, it would be as well to order them from a specialist bulb nursery now.

mid-spring

Maintenance

• Make sure that all herbaceous plant supports are firmly in position.

• As soon as possible, harden off sweet peas ready for planting out.

• Start to harden off summer-flowering annuals which have been raised in the greenhouse.

• If you want to sow a new lawn, prepare the ground, then, after a week or two, sow lawn seed.

• Prune forsythia as soon as it finishes flowering.

• Start to mow the lawn when dry enough.

• Weed regularly.

• Apply a general fertiliser around the base of plants, watering in well if necessary.

• Apply a bulky organic mulch around the base of trees, shrubs, herbaceous perennials and climbers.

Sowing and planting

• Continue to sow seeds of annual flowers, such as cornflower, campanula, clarkia, cosmos, Californian poppy, sunflower, busy lizzie, morning glory, mallow, nigella and poppies.

• Plant out chrysanthemums (overwintered in a greenhouse) after a few weeks of gradual hardening off.

• Continue to plant trees, shrubs and climbers.

late spring

Maintenance

• Regularly hoe off or carefully hand-weed annual weeds.

• Ease out deeper-rooted perennial weeds, using a hand fork.

• Remove any winter- and spring-flowering bedding plants such as winter-flowering pansies and bellis, wallflowers and forget-me-nots.

• Thin out direct-sown annuals as necessary.

• During dry weather make sure all plants are adequately watered, especially those that are young or recently planted.

• Tie in new growths of rambler or climbing roses, making sure that they are secure on their supports.

• At least six weeks after the flowers on bulbs have faded, cut back or tie up the foliage, but delay this as long as possible.

Sowing and planting

• Plant up containers such as hanging baskets, window boxes and terrace tubs. If you are using summer bedding, keep these containers in a frost-free spot until the last of the frosts is over.

• Plant up containers for filling gaps in beds and borders later in the season.

• Continue to sow annual flowers directly where you want them to flower later in the year.

• Continue to plant pot-grown trees, shrubs, climbers and herbaceous perennials.

• Plant out tougher annuals such as sweet peas, watering them in well.

early summer

Maintenance

• Clip topiary.

• Continue to weed and water as necessary.

• Top up mulch to help to keep the soil moist.

• Make sure that all herbaceous plants are well supported, including the flower stems of delphiniums and hollyhocks.

• Lift and divide congested clumps of primulas.

• Lift and divide congested clumps of iris.

• Mow the lawn regularly.

• Prune shrubs that flowered earlier in the year such as weigela, philadelphus and deutzia.

Sowing and planting

• Plant out the rest of your summer bedding and other tender plants as soon as the last frost is past.

• Sow seeds such as forget-me-not, pansy, wallflower, foxglove, sweet William, poppy, bellis, aubrieta, hollyhock and honesty.

• Position hanging baskets and other containers of summer bedding outside.

Planning ahead

• Buy or order autumn-flowering bulbs such as autumn crocus, colchicum and sternbergia and, when available, winter-flowering bulbs such as snowdrop and aconite too.

mid-summer

Maintenance

• Continue to weed and water, and feed as necessary.

• Summer-flowering plants of all types would benefit from feeding with a high-potash fertiliser.

• Regularly remove faded blooms. Clip over early-flowering herbaceous perennials, such as many geraniums, to encourage a later flush of flowers.

Sowing and planting

• Continue to sow poppies, delphinium, forget-me-not, geum and pansy.

• If planting container-grown plants now, keep them really well watered.

• Pot on seedlings of winter- and spring-flowering plants sown earlier in the year.

• Check plant supports.

• Plant autumn-flowering bulbs.

• Transplant sweet William, campanula and wallflowers into a nursery bed.

Planning ahead

• Find someone to look after your plants and garden when you go on holiday!

late summer

Maintenance

• Regularly remove faded blooms.

• Regularly weed and water as necessary.

• Feed hanging baskets and other containers frequently to encourage plenty more flowers.

• Prune rambler roses as they cease flowering.

• Give herbs such as thymes a haircut to keep them compact and flowering well.

• Clip topiary.

Sowing and planting

• Avoid planting if possible, because moisture stress is more likely.

• Plant belladonna lily and fritillaria bulbs.

Planning ahead

• Order spring-flowering bulbs, particularly those that are not so easy to find in a garden centre.

early autumn

Maintenance

• Continue to weed, water and feed as necessary.

• Tie in later-flowering herbaceous perennials as necessary.

• Regularly remove faded blooms.

• Clip off foliage from herbaceous plants heavily attacked by mildew or other diseases.

• Remove bedding plants that are past their best.

• Lift gladioli and store in a frost-free shed.

• Cut flower spikes of plants like red-hot poker as soon as they fade.

• Pinch off flowers on winter-flowering pansies to encourage sturdier plants and more flowers when you really need them.

• Regularly rake up leaves as they fall.

Sowing and planting

• Buy lots of spring-flowering bulbs and get planting – in beds, grass or containers.

• Plant winter-flowering bulbs as soon as possible.

• Repair damaged areas on lawns.

• Sow lawn seed or lay turf on to prepared soil to create a new lawn.

Planning ahead

• Rake over recently cleared areas and fork in a fertiliser so that the soil is ready for new plants.

• Move garden furniture into the shed or protect it from winter wet if you do not intend to continue using it.

mid-autumn

Maintenance

• Weed regularly and once the soil is clear, consider applying more mulch around all plants.

• Rake up fallen leaves.

• Remove supports from herbaceous perennials as they fade, clearing any obviously diseased or deteriorating foliage too.

• Lift dahlias as soon as the tops of dahlias have been damaged by frost.

Sowing and planting

• Continue to plant spring-flowering bulbs. This is the best time to plant tulips.

• Plant winter and spring bedding flowers such as polyanthus, forget-me-not and wallflowers.

• Plant trees, shrubs and perennials. It is a great time for planting anything – except perhaps plants that are particularly intolerant of winter wet. Water the plant in well unless the soil is moist and then apply a mulch.

• Try to buy plants grown for autumn colour – by doing so now you can see precisely how good the colour is and make sure you get the pick of the bunch.

Planning ahead

• Order trees, shrubs and hedging plants from specialist nurseries. Bare-root plants should definitely be ordered now ready for planting when completely dormant.

late autumn

Maintenance

• Continue to clear the top growth of plants in herbaceous borders, but try to leave some foliage on the plants to provide protection over winter.

• Lift less hardy agapanthus.

• Regularly rake up fallen leaves from the lawn and flower bed.

Sowing and planting

• Continue planting trees, shrubs, climbers and herbaceous plants. Water in and then apply a mulch.

Planning ahead

• Send off for lots of seed catalogues so that you can choose precisely what you want for the year ahead.

winter

Maintenance

• Remove the last of the year's weeds.

• Make sure that tender plants are properly protected against cold.

• Regularly check stakes and ties and refix or replace as necessary.

• Dig soil over and get it ready for any spring planting by digging or forking the soil over thoroughly, removing debris and weeds and then forking in plenty of well-rotted manure or garden compost.

• Disconnect pumps from water features and insulate as necessary.

• Take the opportunity to carry out any repairs necessary on garden machinery and furniture.

• Check overwintered plants.

Sowing and planting

• Continue planting, provided that the soil is neither too wet nor too cold. Now is a good time for planting bare-root hedging, trees and shrubs.

Planning ahead

• Get your seed orders in early for annuals, biennials and perennials so that nothing runs out before you get what you want.

• Visit gardens renowned for their winter plants and see what you could include to make yours even better-looking.

INDEX

ACKNOWLEDGEMENTS

I would like to thank everyone at Headline who has had input in to this book, you have been great to work with. Particular thanks to Heather Holden-Brown and Celia Kent, Bryone Picton, Rachel Geere and indeed their entire team, all of whom have tackled everything with such great enthusiasm and flair. Thanks, too, to Anne Askwith, my ever-patient editor, to Colin Walton for his arty bits and Mel Watson for sourcing so many of the pictures (and successfully avoiding all my pet hates). This book has been a great introduction to Headline and a pleasure to produce, not least because of you all.

Finally thanks to Sarah Heneghan and Peter Anderson for their photographic contribution and last, but definitely not least, to my wonderful literary agent, Luigi Bonomi, for getting us all together.

The publishers wish to thank Peter Anderson for his special photography and the following picture sources:

2 GPL/ John Glover; **5** Peter Anderson; **7** GPL/ Eric Crichton; **9** GPL/ Mayer/Le Scanff; **11** GPL/ Howard Rice; **13** GPL/ John Glover; **14** GPL/ Mark Bolton; **17** GPL/ John Glover; **21** GPL/ Clive Nichols; **22** GPL/ Howard Rice; **24** GPL/ Mayer/Le Scanff; **25** Peter Anderson; **26** GPL/ Howard Rice; **27** GPL/ Eric Crichton; **28** Peter Anderson; **30** GPL/ John Glover, The Dillon's garden, Dublin; **31** GPL/ Howard Rice; **32** GPL/ John Ferro Sims; **34** GPL/ Jerry Pavia; **35** bl GPL/ Howard Rice; **35** tr GPL/ Howard Rice; **36** GPL/ John Glover; **37** GPL/ JS Sira; **38** GPL/ JS Sira; **39** GPL/ JS Sira; **40** GPL/ Christii Carter; **41** GPL/ JS Sira; **42** GPL/ Neil Holmes; **43** GPL/ Neil Holmes; **44** GPL/ Clive Nichols; **45** GPL/ Neil Holmes; **46** GPL/ Eric Crichton; **47** GPL/ Neil Holmes; **48** GPL/ Clive Nichols; **49** GPL/ Howard Rice; **50** GPL/ JS Sira; **51** GPL/ Clive Nichols; **53** b GPL/ Neil Holmes; **53** t GPL/ Clive Nichols; **54** GPL/ John Glover; **55** GPL/ Howard Rice; **56** GPL/ Howard Rice; **57** GPL/ Howard Rice; **58** GPL/ Neil Holmes; **59** GPL/ Clive Nichols, Cornwell Manor Garden, Oxfordshire; **60** GPL/ Howard Rice; **61** br GPL/ Howard Rice; **61** tl GPL/ Howard Rice; **62** GPL/ Neil Holmes; **63** GPL/ JS Sira; **65** GPL/ Howard Rice; **67** GPL/ JS Sira; **69** GPL/ Mark Bolton; **71** Peter Anderson; **73** b GPL/ Mark Bolton; **73** t GPL/ Howard Rice; **74** GPL/ JS Sira; **75** GPL/ Neil Holmes; **77** GPL/ Howard Rice, Woodland garden, Cambridge Botanic Garden; **78** GPL/ John Glover, Mannington Hall, Norfolk; **79** GPL/ Clive Nichols; **80** GPL/ Howard Rice; **81** GPL/ Neil Holmes; **82** GPL/ John Glover; **83** GPL/ John Glover; **85** GPL/ JS Sira; **86** GPL/ Mayer/Le Scanff; **88** GPL/ Clive Nichols, Lambeth Horticultural Society courtyard garden; **89** GPL/ JS Sira; **91** GPL/ Mark Bolton; **93** Peter Anderson; **95** GPL/ Howard Rice; **96** GPL/ Clive Nichols, The garden of Wolfson College, Oxford; **98** GPL/ Clive Nichols; **99** GPL/ JS Sira; **100** GPL/ Howard Rice; **102** GPL/ Ron Evans; **103** GPL/ Howard Rice; **104** GPL/ John Glover; **105** GPL/ Ron Evans; **107** GPL/ Mayer/Le Scanff; **108** GPL/ JS Sira; **110** GPL/ John Glover; **111** GPL/ Howard Rice; **112** GPL/ JS Sira; **113** GPL/ John Glover; **114** GPL/ Steve Wooster, Dolph Sweerts' garden, designer Anthony Paul; **115** GPL/ John Glover; **117** GPL/ Juliette Wade; **118** GPL/ Chris Burrows; **119** GPL/ John Glover; **121** bl GPL/ Mark Bolton; **121** tr GPL/ John Glover; **122** GPL/ Neil Holmes; **123** GPL/ John Glover; **124** GPL/ JS Sira; **125** GPL/ Clive Nichols; **126** GPL/ Eric Crichton; **128** GPL/ Marie O'Hara; **129** GPL/ John Glover; **131** GPL/ Chris Burrows; **132** GPL/ JS Sira; **133** GPL/ David Cavagnaro; **134** GPL/ John Glover; **135** GPL/ Clive Nichols, designer Nigel Colborn; **136** GPL/ Howard Rice; **138** GPL/ John Neubauer; **140** GPL/ John Glover; **141** GPL/ Christopher Fairweather; **142** GPL/ Howard Rice; **143** GPL/ Mayer/Le Scanff; **145** GPL/ John Glover; **147** GPL/ John Glover; **148** GPL/ Howard Rice; **149** GPL/ Howard Rice; **149** GPL/ JS Sira; **150** GPL/ Sunniva Harte; **153** Peter Anderson; **154** br GPL/ JS Sira; **154** tl GPL/ Juliette Wade; **157** GPL/ JS Sira; **158** GPL/ Steven Wooster, designer Sheila Jackson; **161** bl GPL/ Graham Stong; **161** br GPL/ John Glover; **161** tl GPL/ Clive Nichols; **161** tr GPL/ Henk Dijkman; **163** Peter Anderson; **164** GPL/ Juliet Greene, designer Pamela Woods; **166** Peter Anderson; **167** Peter Anderson; **169** GPL/ Clive Nichols; **170** GPL/ JS Sira; **171** GPL/ Clive Nichols; **172** Peter Anderson; **173** GPL/ Clive Nichols, designer Roger Platts; **175** GPL/ Howard Rice; **176** GPL/ Steven Wooster, designer Jacquie Gordon; **177** Peter Anderson; **178** Peter Anderson; **179** Peter Anderson; **181** GPL/ Brian Carter; **183** GPL/ Mayer/Le Scanff; **Endpapers** GPL/ Mark Bolton